Windows Network Administration

Project Manual

L. WARD ULMER

ACQUISITIONS EDITOR	Lois Freier
MARKETING MANAGER	Jennifer Slomack
PRODUCTION MANAGER	Kelly Tavares

To order books or for customer service please, call 1-800-CALL WILEY (225-5945).

ISBN 978-0-470-11413-1

Printed by R. R. Donnelley

10 9 8 7 6 5 4 3 2 1

PREFACE

Windows Network Administration Project Manual is a learning tool for individuals who are new to Windows network administration, as well as those who seek to expand their skills in the field. It is an ideal companion to Suehring et al.'s *Windows Network Administration (Copyright 2008, John Wiley & Sons, 9-780-470-10191-9).*

Easy-to-read, practical, and up-to-date, this Project Manual includes activities that reinforce the fundamental concepts of Windows network administration while helping students develop core competencies and real-world skills. The sheer variety and span of activities let students learn at their own pace.

Each chapter contains five to seven projects. Projects range from easy to more advanced, and many include multiple parts. Each project contains the following elements:
- **Overview:** Introduces the topic of the project, and reviews relevant concepts.
- **Outcomes:** Lists what students will know how to do after completing the project.
- **What You'll Need:** Lists specific requirements for the project.
- **Completion Time:** Provides an estimated completion time as a guide. (Actual completion times may vary depending on experience levels.)
- **Precautions:** Notes on issues that should be taken into account prior to undertaking the project.
- **Projects:** A variety of project types are included. The majority of projects involve hands-on activities in which students are guided through the steps required to accomplish a task. Some projects involve case-based scenarios, while others assess student familiarity with basic concepts through matching and other paper-and-pen exercises. Many of the projects include multiple parts related to the project topic.
- **Assessment questions:** Embedded within each project, these questions help students assess their understanding as they go.
- **Graphic Elements:** Each project contains screenshots, conceptual graphics and/or tables that help inform and guide students as they proceed through the project.

After completing the activities in this Project Manual, users will be able to:
- Install Windows Server 2003
- Install and configure the TCP/IP protocol
- Configure a DNS Client
- Administer DHCP Servers
- Use special permissions
- Configure a remote access server
- Troubleshoot RRAS Connectivity
- Configure IPSec Authentication
- Manage IP filter lists and filter actions

CONTENTS

1 Understanding Networks

2 Introduction to Network Protocols

3 Implementing and Administering WINS

7 Troubleshooting DHCP

8 Managing Security

Important Note about Completing the Activities in this Manual:
For all activities that require documents and other content not included in this printed Project Manual, please visit the Book Companion Site indicated on the back of this manual. Once there, click on Student Companion Site at the upper right of the page, then Project Manual, then the chapter in which the activity appears.

1
UNDERSTANDING NETWORKS

PROJECTS

Project 1.1	Basic OSI Knowledge
Overview	The increased diversity of networks creates a higher level of complexity. The key to making networks work is ensuring that they use and comply with communication standards. For these communication standards to be successful at exchanging information, they have to be built around a communication model.
	Computers use a set of rules that allow them to communicate, even when the computers are running different operating systems or are located on different types of networks. The model used for communication between devices on a network is the Open Systems Interconnection (OSI) model. This model is considered the fundamental framework for the way all devices on a network should communicate; once you understand how the OSI model works, you can use it to compare network implementations on different systems.
	The OSI model doesn't do anything in the communication process; appropriate software and hardware do the actual work. The OSI model simply defines which tasks need to be done and which protocols will handle those tasks at each of the seven *layers* of the model. The seven layers are:
	• Application (layer 7)
	• Presentation
	• Session
	• Transport
	• Network
	• Data link
	• Physical (layer 1)
Outcomes	After completing this project, you will know how to:
	▲ identify some of the functions that take place at different layers of the OSI model
What you'll need	To complete this project, you will need:
	▲ the worksheet below
Completion time	10 minutes
Precautions	None

■ Part A: Use the OSI model

Using Figure 1-1, answer the following questions.

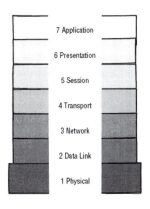

Figure 1-1: The OSI model

1. Multitasking by a user is facilitated by the ability for the computer to have multiple protocols operating at the same time. This is often referred to as multiplexing. The _____ layer makes this possible.
2. MAC addresses appear at the _____ layer.
3. Services that support high-level applications such as e-mail and FTP operate at the _____ layer.
4. The _____ layer has three functions: establish, maintain, and terminate the connection on separate computers.
5. The network redirector is found at the _____ layer.
6. The actual connection between the computer and the network medium takes place at the _____ layer.
7. Sequencing and flow control are functions of the _____ layer.

■ Part B: Match functions with the appropriate OSI models layers

Match with the items on the left with the appropriate OSI models layers on the right.

Application	_____	_____	UTP	10BaseT
Presentation	_____	_____	NetBIOS	Data synchronization
Session	_____	_____	IP	SAPs
Transport	_____	_____	Bridge	Router

Network	_____	_____	TCP	UDP
Data Link	_____	_____	Graphic formats	SMTP
Physical	_____	_____	HTTP	Encryption

Project 1.2	Determining a MAC Address
Overview	The Data-Link layer of the OSI model is split into two sublayers: the Logical Link Control (LLC) layer and the Media Access Control (MAC) layer. The MAC sublayer communicates directly with a computer's network interface card (NIC). Each NIC has a unique 48-bit address represented in the form of a 12-digit hexadecimal number, assigned to it by its manufacturer and referred to as its MAC address. The LLC sublayer uses MAC addresses to establish logical links between devices on the same LAN. In this project, you will learn how to determine the MAC address for a computer's NIC.
Outcomes	After completing this project, you will know how to: ▲ determine the MAC address for a network adapter
What you'll need	To complete this project, you will need: ▲ a Windows XP computer with a NIC installed ▲ Internet access
Completion time	10 minutes
Precautions	None

1. Turn on the computer, click **Start** and then select **Run** to open the **Run** dialog box. Enter **cmd** in the **Open** text box to open a **Command** window.
2. At the command prompt, enter **ipconfig /all**.
3. You should see a heading titled "Ethernet adapter Local Area Connection". The MAC address of your NIC is displayed in the Physical Address line (see Figure 1-2).

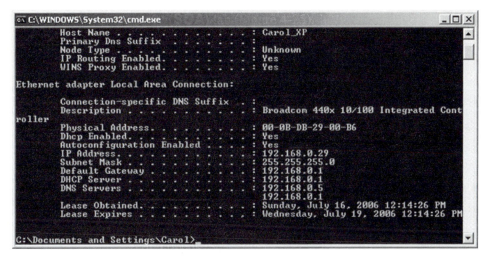

```
C:\WINDOWS\System32\cmd.exe                                          _ □ x
        Host Name . . . . . . . . . . . . : Carol_XP                    ▲
        Primary Dns Suffix . . . . . . . :
        Node Type . . . . . . . . . . . . : Unknown
        IP Routing Enabled. . . . . . . . : Yes
        WINS Proxy Enabled. . . . . . . . : Yes

Ethernet adapter Local Area Connection:

        Connection-specific DNS Suffix  . :
        Description . . . . . . . . . . . : Broadcom 440x 10/100 Integrated Cont
roller
        Physical Address. . . . . . . . . : 00-0B-DB-29-00-B6
        Dhcp Enabled. . . . . . . . . . . : Yes
        Autoconfiguration Enabled . . . . : Yes
        IP Address. . . . . . . . . . . . : 192.168.0.29
        Subnet Mask . . . . . . . . . . . : 255.255.255.0
        Default Gateway . . . . . . . . . : 192.168.0.1
        DHCP Server . . . . . . . . . . . : 192.168.0.1
        DNS Servers . . . . . . . . . . . : 192.168.0.5
                                            192.168.0.1
        Lease Obtained. . . . . . . . . . : Sunday, July 16, 2006 12:14:26 PM
        Lease Expires . . . . . . . . . . : Wednesday, July 19, 2006 12:14:26 PM

C:\Documents and Settings\Carol>_                                        ▼
```

Figure 1-2: Displaying the MAC address of your network adapter

4. Record the MAC address.

    _____ _____

5. The manufacturer of the NIC should be listed in the Description line. Record what you see there.

    _____

6. You can also use the first six digits of the MAC address to identify the manufacturer of the NIC. Open a Web browser and go to the following Web page: **http://standards.ieee.org/regauth/oui/oui.txt**. The first six digits are an Organizationally Unique Identifier assigned to each NIC manufacturer by the Institute of Electrical and Electronics Engineers (IEEE), a standards-setting organization. The final six digits of the MAC address are then assigned by the manufacturer to give the NIC an unique address. For example, in the MAC address 00-0B-DB-29-00-B6, 00-0B-DB identifies the manufacturer of the NIC.

7. Using your Web browser's **Find** command, locate the entry that corresponds to the first six digits of you MAC address.

    _____

8. Is the manufacturer of the NIC as listed with the IEEE the same as you identified above? If not, record the manufacturer listed by the IEEE.

    _____

9. The reason they may be different is that some companies that manufacture NICs allow them to be sold under another company's name. For example, the manufacturer of the NIC in Figure 1-2 is Broadcom, but the MAC address is registered by the IEEE to Dell, which is the manufacturer of the computer that contains the NIC.

10. You can also use the command line utility **getmac** to return the MAC address and to list network protocols associated with each address on the local computer or on other network

computers. At the command prompt, enter **getmac**. Figure 1-3 the shows the hexadecimal address. You can also use various parameters to obtain addresses of network computers.

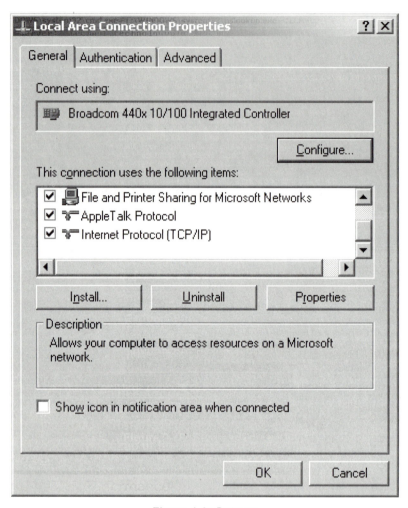

Figure 1-3: Getmac

Project 1.3	Viewing the Protocol Stacks Installed on a Computer
Overview	There are a number of protocol stacks used in the world's networks today. Among the most common are TCP/IP, NWLink IPX/SPX, AppleTalk, and NetBEUI. In this project, you will examine the various protocols that are installed on a computer in a network.
Outcomes	After completing this project, you will know how to: ▲ examine the various protocols that are installed on a computer in a network
What you'll need	To complete this project, you will need: ▲ a Windows XP/2000 client computer or a Windows Server 2003/2000 Server computer connected to a network
Completion time	10 minutes
Precautions	None

1. Turn on the computer and log on.
2. Click **Start** and then open the **Control Panel**. Click **Network Connections** to open the **Network Connections** window.
3. Double-click **Local Area Connection** and click the **Properties** button to open the **Local Area Connection Properties** dialog box (Figure 1-4).

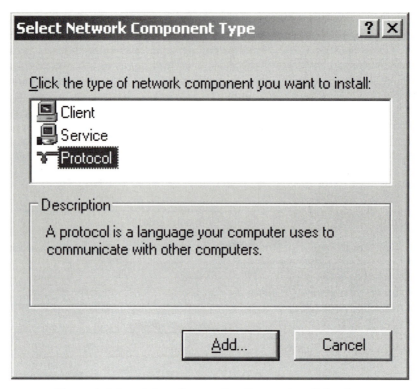

Figure 1-4: Local Area Connection Properties dialog box

4. Record the information about the network protocols installed (indicated by a check in the check box next to the name of the protocol).

_____

5. Click each network protocol installed (e.g, Internet Protocol [TCP/IP]) and then click the **Properties** button to display the **Properties** dialog box for the protocol. Record the information you see there for each protocol and then close the **Properties** dialog box for the protocol.

_____

_____

_____

_____

6. Now, click the **Install** button in **Local Area Connection Properties** dialog box to open the **Select Network Component Type** dialog box (Figure 1-5).

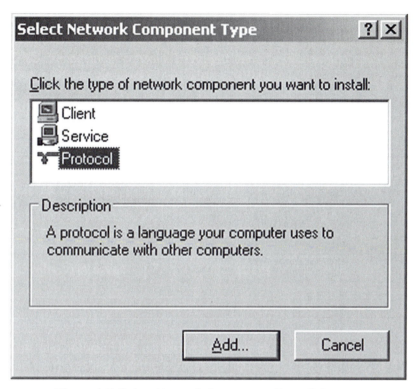

Figure 1-5: Select Network Component Type dialog box

7. Select **Protocol** and click the **Add** button to open the **Select Network Protocol** dialog box. Record the protocols you see listed there.

_____

_____

_____

Note: Any protocol that is already installed will not be listed here.

8. When you have finished, close the **Select Network Protocol** dialog box and any other open dialog boxes and windows and turn off the computer.

Project 1.4	Using the OSI Model to Troubleshoot
Overview	Although the OSI model is fairly abstract, when it is applied appropriately, breaking down your troubleshooting tactics into general OSI layers and attempting to identify at which layer in the OSI model symptoms appear can give you an idea of where problems lie and which services to look at. Doing so gives you a structure for thinking about the overall network and provides a framework for following methodical troubleshooting tactics.
Outcomes	After completing this project, you will know how to: ▲ use the OSI model to troubleshoot network issues
What you'll need	To complete this project, you will need: ▲ the worksheet below
Completion time	10 minutes
Precautions	None

■ Part A: Use the OSI layers to create a systematic approach to solving problems

1. A user calls the Help Desk and you answer. The user states she has just arrived at her desk and she cannot open her e-mail. After asking a few simple questions, she also realizes she cannot open any Web pages. The user is using a standard desktop computer that is hard-wired to a network. There is no wireless connection involved.

    Using the first three layers of the OSI model, what steps would you take to diagnose her problems?

    Layer 1 :

    _____

    _____

    Layer 2:

    _____

    _____

    Layer 3:

    _____

    _____

2. You are an administrator for a Windows 2000 network that has been used primarily for just basic file and print services. You have been asked to upgrade the network to Windows Server 2003 and also allow the users of the network to access the Internet. Currently, the network is running NWLink. You need to change the network protocol to TCP/IP to support Internet connectivity. What layers of the OSI model do you need to consider to allow the workstations to access the Internet? Explain your answer.

_____

_____

_____

_____

_____

3. You have been asked to troubleshoot intermittent communication problems on an old network for a company that builds and repairs high-voltage motors. You have determined that the network is a straightforward thin-coax Ethernet Windows NT LAN running TCP/IP. The company wants to upgrade to Windows Server 2003, hoping to resolve the intermittent problems. You perform the upgrade, all goes smoothly, and initially everything seems to function properly. However, the intermittent problems show up again. What layer in the OSI model is the likely place for the problems to be occurring? Explain your answer.

_____

_____

_____

_____

_____

Project 1.5	Topology Recognition and Selection
Overview	A topology is basically a map of a network. The physical topology of a network describes the layout of the cables and workstations and the location of all network components. The ability to recognize the different types of physical topologies is a basic skill for a network administrator. Selecting the correct topology for a network is also critical. An incorrect decision about the physical topology can be costly and disruptive to fix. Each topology has its advantages and drawbacks. Generally speaking, you should balance the following considerations when choosing a physical topology for a network: • cost • ease of installation • ease of maintenance • cable fault tolerance
Outcomes	After completing this project, you will know how to: ▲ differentiate between network topologies ▲ select the appropriate topology for a network
What you'll need	To complete this project, you will need: ▲ the worksheet below
Completion time	10 minutes
Precautions	None

■ **Part A: Identify topologies**

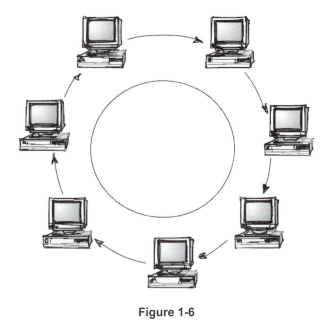

Figure 1-6

1. Topology represented by Figure 1-6 _____

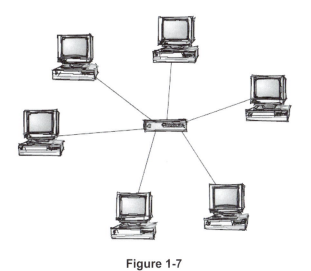

Figure 1-7

2. Topology represented by Figure 1-7_____

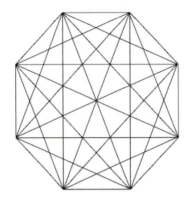

Figure 1-8

3. Topology represented by Figure 1-8 _____

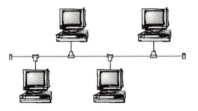

Figure 1-9

4. Topology represented by Figure 1-9 _____

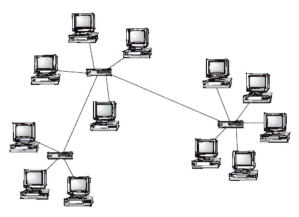

Figure 1-10

5. Topology represented by Figure 1-10 _____

■ Part B: Select the best topology

1. A company is rebuilding its network infrastructure. It is looking at different types of physical topologies, trying to find the one that would suit it best. The most important thing it is looking for is fault tolerance. Neither cost nor the future addition of workstations is a factor. What type of topology would you recommend? Explain your answer.

_____

_____

_____

_____

_____

2. A company is rebuilding its network infrastructure and wants your advice about which type of physical topology would best suit its needs. The most important thing that the company is looking for is flexibility, and the ability to easily move or add workstations and make changes to the network. What type of topology would you recommend? Explain your answer.

_____

_____

_____

_____

_____

Project 1.6	Choosing Network Media
Overview	An important part of any network administrator's job is to know when and where to use certain devices and network media. A network's transmission media is a long-term investment. Unlike computer equipment, which is often replaced every 2 to 5 years, a company may use the same networking media for 10 years. Thus, choosing the correct media is crucial to a functioning network. There are many types of network media that can be used to carry transmission across a network to allow end devices to communicate. Common types include coaxial cable (thinnet), unshielded twisted-pair cable (UTP), and fiber-optic cable. In this project, you will practice your ability to recognize the various advantages and disadvantages of different types of network media and research the functionality provided by different types of Ethernet cable.
Outcomes	After completing this project, you will know how to: ▲ recognize the advantages and disadvantages of different types of network media ▲ identify the cabling used, maximum speed, and maximum transmission distance for different Ethernet cable types
What you'll need	To complete this project, you will need: ▲ a computer with Internet access
Completion time	30 minutes
Precautions	None

■ **Part A: Identify the advantages and disadvantages of different types of network media**

Match one item from the top section to one item from the bottom section. Items are not used more than once.

1. Thinnet

    a. The advantages of thinnet

    b. The disadvantages of thinnet

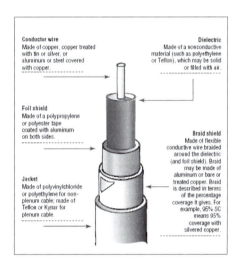

Figure 1-11: Thinnet

2. Unshielded Twisted Pair
   a. The advantages of Category 5 unshielded twisted pair
   b. The disadvantages of Category 5 unshielded twisted pair

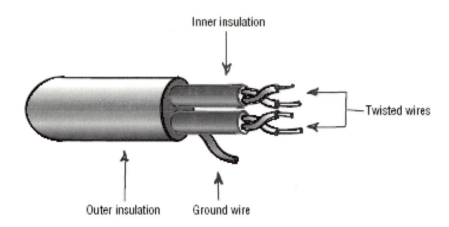

Figure 1-12: Unshielded twisted pair

3. Fiber-Optic Cable
   a. The advantages of fiber-optic cable
   b. The disadvantages of fiber-optic cable

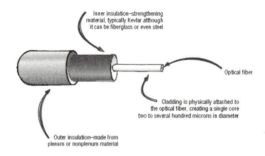

Figure 1-13: Fiber-optic cable

Item # _____	If a cable breaks, the entire network goes down.
	The cable must be grounded to prevent interference.
	It's more expensive than unshielded twisted pair.
	The connectors can be expensive.
	It does not support high-speed transmissions.
Item # _____	It is susceptible to interference.
	It is prone to damage during installation.
	Distance limitations are often misunderstood or not followed.
Item # _____	It is the most expensive media to purchase and install.
	Strict installation guidelines must be met for the cabling to be certified.
Item # _____	It can be installed over long distances.
	It provides large amounts of bandwidth.
	It is not susceptible to electromagnetic interference (EMI) or radio frequency interference (RFI).
	It cannot be tapped easily, so security is better.
Item # _____	It is inexpensive to install.
	It is easy to terminate.
	It is widely used and tested.
	It supports many network types.
Item # _____	It is easy to install.
	It is small in diameter.
	Its shielding, when grounded, reduces EMI and RFI.

■ Part B: Use the Internet to research the capabilities of Ethernet cable types

Fill in the cable type, maximum speed, and maximum transmission distance for each type.

Ethernet Name	Cable Type	Maximum Speed	Maximum Transmission Distance
10Base2			
10Base5			
10Base-T			
100Base-TX (Fast Ethernet)			
100Base-FL			
1000Base-TX (Gigabit Ethernet)			

Project 1.7	Using Network Devices
Overview	Many devices can be used in different situations within a network. Some of the more common network connectivity devices include repeaters, hubs, bridges, switches, routers, and Layer 2 switches. The ability to recognize the various types of functionality that different network devices provide is a basic skill for a network administrator. In this project, you will practice this skill.
Outcomes	After completing this project, you will know how to: ▲ recognize the various types of functionality that different network devices provide
What you'll need	To complete this project, you will need: ▲ the worksheet below
Completion time	10 minutes
Precautions	None

■ Part A: Recognize the functionality provided by different network devices

Match one item from the top section to one of the figures in the bottom section. Items are not used more than once.

Item #:

1. This figure shows several networks connected with routers. Even though there are several paths that the data could take to travel from network 1 to network 6, the router will determine the best path, based on the cost (number of hops) associated with getting there.

2. This figure shows a simple four-port hub connected to networking devices and creating a physical star topology.

3. This figure shows how a bridge receives data, filters it based on the MAC address, and forwards it if necessary.

4. This figure shows how a switch connecting segments of a network filters traffic that would otherwise be passed along to all devices by a hub.

5. This figure shows how a repeater can extend the distance a network can reach, beyond the limits of a single cable segment.

Item # _____	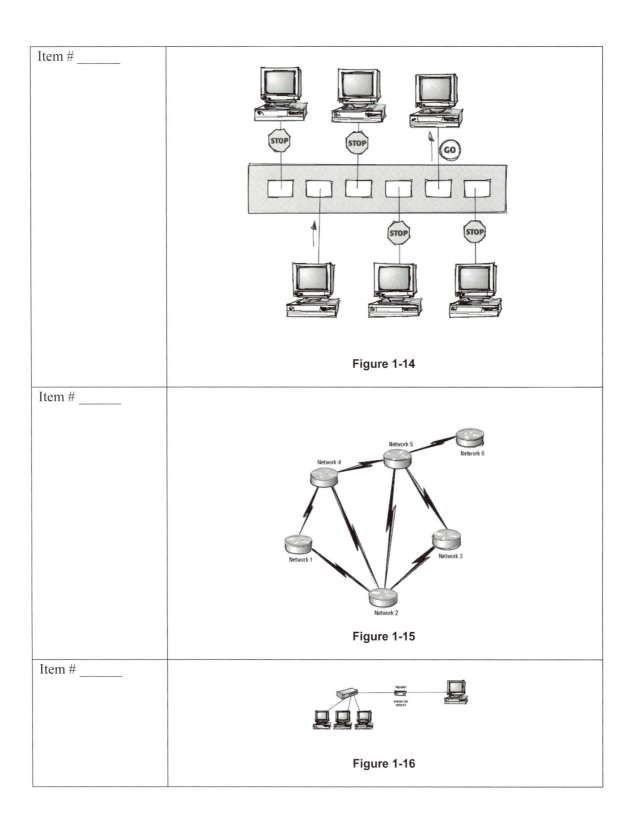

Item # _____

Figure 1-14

Item # _____

Figure 1-15

Item # _____

Figure 1-16

Item # _____	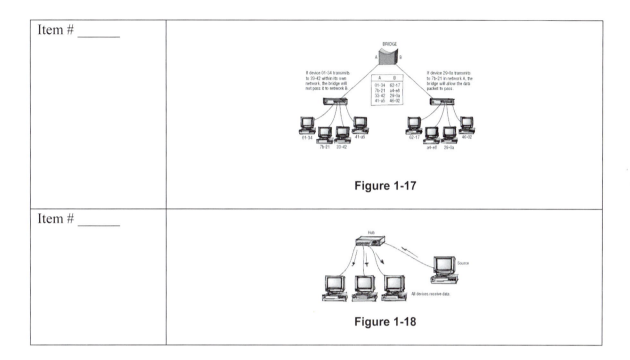
	Figure 1-17
Item # _____	**Figure 1-18**

■ Part B: Answer the following questions

1. In Figure 1-19, what kind of device must Device A be?

_____

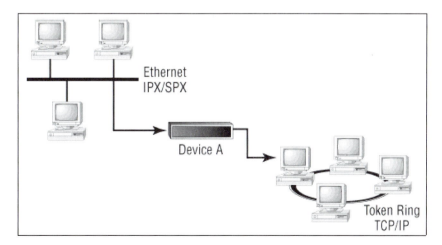

Figure 1-19

2. What kind of device should be used to connect an Ethernet and Token ring network?

    _____

3. A network has two segments with large amounts of traffic originating from one of the segments. What type of device could be placed between the two segments to restrict the heavy traffic to only one of the segments?

    _____

Project 1.8	Preparing to Install Windows Server 2003
Overview	As a network administrator, you are expected to have a wide range of knowledge and skills. One of the most basic skills is the ability to install and maintain the different operating systems the network uses. You need to be able to install client operating systems, such as Windows XP, and server operating systems, such as Windows Server 2003.

When you install any operating system, the preinstallation tasks are similar. You must always check to make sure that the computer meets a minimum set of hardware requirements. Attempting to install an operating system on a computer that does not meet the minimum requirements is not possible and the installation will stop automatically. In fact, you will notice that one of the automatic processes that takes place early in the installation of the operating system is verifying system requirements against the computer specifications. Although this is again automatic, it is a good practice and a time-saving activity.

The minimum hardware requirements for Windows Server 2003 are as follows:

- Pentium 133 MHz or faster processor
- VGA monitor
- 128 MB RAM for five or fewer clients and 256 MB for larger networks
- 1.5 GB hard disk space is required for setup; however, at least 2.5 GB hard disk space is recommended
- High-density, 3.5-inch floppy disk drive OR a 12x CD-ROM drive, if the installation is performed from a CD
- A NIC, if network connectivity is required
- Mouse and keyboard |
| Outcomes | After completing this project, you will know how to:

▲ prepare for Windows Server 2003 installation
▲ verify system components for installation |
| What you'll need | To complete this project, you will need:

▲ the computer on which you plan to install Windows Server 2003 |
| Completion time | 15 minutes |
| Precautions | Installing Windows Server 2003 on the C: drive will override any operating system currently installed and delete anything on the hard disk. |

1. Click **Start**, point to **Settings**, and click **Control Panel** to open the **Control Panel** window.
2. Double-click the **System** icon to open the **System Properties** dialog box.
3. At the bottom of the **General** tab, the processor, processor speed, and amount of RAM are listed. Enter the information you find.
   a. Processor (e.g., Intel Pentium 4):

   _____

   b. Processor speed (e.g., 2.66 GHz):

   _____

   c. Amount of RAM:

   _____

4. Does the computer meet the minimum hardware requirements for the processor and memory?

   _____

5. Click the **Hardware** tab.
6. Click the **Device Manager** button to open the **Device Manager** window.
7. Double-click the **Network adapters** node to expand it. Record the name and specifications for the NIC.

   _____

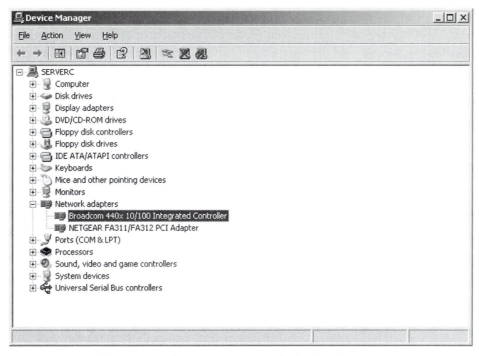

Figure 1-20: Checking hardware in Device Manager

8. Double-click the **Display adapters** node. Record the specifications for the video adapter.

    _____

9. Double-click the video adapter name to open the **Properties** dialog box for the display adapter. You may have to visit the manufacturer's Web site to determine if the resolution meets the minimum requirements. Click **OK** to close the **Properties** dialog box.

10. Double-click the **Keyboards** and **Mice and other pointing devices** nodes to make sure that the drivers for the necessary peripheral devices are installed. Record the specifications for the keyboard and mouse.

    a. Peripherals present and drivers installed?

    _____

    b. Keyboard:

    _____

    c. Mouse:

    _____

11. Double-click the **DVD/CD-ROM drives** node to make sure that the drivers for the removable storage devices are installed. If a DVD/CD-ROM drive is present, are its drivers installed?.

    _____

12. Double-click the DVD/CD-ROM drive name to open the **Properties** dialog box for the device. You may have to visit the manufacturer's Web site to determine if the CD or DVD drive is 12x or faster. Record the specifications for the DVD/CD-ROM drive and drivers.

_____

13. Click **OK** to close the **Properties** dialog box for the DVD/C-ROM drive.

14. Close the **Device Manager** and the **System Properties** dialog box.

15. Right-click **Start**, and click **Explore** to open the **Windows Explorer** window.

16. In the **Folders** list, right-click **Local Disk (C:)** and click **Properties** to open the **Properties** dialog box for the hard disk.

17. Record the **Used space** and **Free space** on the disk below. Is there adequate free disk space on the disk?

    a. Used space:

    _____

    b. Free space:

    _____

18. Is there adequate disk space for Windows Server 2003?

_____

19. If necessary, check any other hard disk drives on the computer to determine if there is adequate free disk space on an alternate hard drive.

20. Close the **Properties** dialog box for the disk and **Windows Explorer**.

Project 1.9	Installing Windows Server 2003
Overview	Once you have verified your system will run Windows Server 2003, you can begin the installation. Proper installation of the operating system is actually the first "hands-on" computer activity in setting up a network. It is imperative that this foundation of the network operate correctly before moving further in the process. Although many setup configurations can be corrected after the installation, you could compare it to building a house. It is much easier to build the house with six rooms than to build it with four rooms and have to add two more later. Spend a little extra time with the installation and save a great deal of time later.
Outcomes	After completing this project, you will know how to: ▲ install Windows Server 2003 ▲ select various configuration settings during installation
What you'll need	To complete this project, you will need: ▲ a Windows Server 2003 installation CD-ROM ▲ a computer that meets, and preferably exceeds, the minimum requirements for installing Windows Server 2003 If you want to keep the current operating system (e.g., Windows XP) and have enough RAM and hard disk space on your systems, you can use Microsoft Virtual PC to install Windows Server 2003. Microsoft provides Virtual PC free of charge at **www.microsoft.com/virtualpc**.
Completion time	60 minutes
Precautions	Installing Windows Server 2003 on the C: drive will override any operating system currently installed and delete any files on the hard disk. Deleting partitions on the hard disk will remove all data. Be sure you have a working backup of any data you want to save.

1. Reboot the computer with the **Windows Server 2003 installation CD-ROM** in the CD-ROM or DVD drive. When you are prompted to **Press any key to boot from CD**, press the spacebar to boot the computer with the Windows Server 2003 installation CD. If you are not prompted to boot from the CD, your computer's boot options may not be set correctly. In most cases, the boot order is set to Floppy, CD, Hard Disk. If this is not the case, you may need to edit your BIOS/CMOS (Complementary Metal Oxide Semiconductor) configuration settings.

2. When the **Windows Server 2003 Setup** screen opens, the edition you are installing (Standard, Enterprise, Web, etc.) is shown. Depending on the licensing arrangement, you may also see a message telling you that you have only a certain period of time in which to activate the installation. Press **Enter**. The Setup program then begins loading the necessary files for the GUI portion of the installation.

3. After the files have loaded, the **Welcome to Setup** screen presents the following three choices:

- To set up Windows now, press **Enter**.
- To repair a Windows installation using Recovery Console, press **R**.
- To quit Setup without installing Windows, press **F3**.

Press **Enter** to continue.

4. The **Windows Licensing Agreement** screen opens (see Figure 1-21). Press the **F8** key to agree to the license. Setup searches for previous installations of Windows and if a previous version is found, the following choices display:

- If one of the following Windows installations is damaged, Setup can try to repair it.
- To repair the selected Windows installation, press **R**
- To continue installing a fresh copy of Windows without repairing, press **ESC**.

Press **ESC** to continue with the installation.

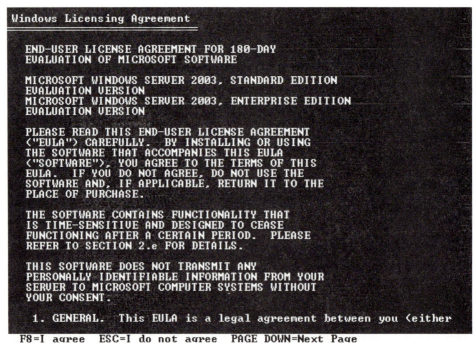

Figure 1-21: Windows Licensing Agreement

5. Next, Setup displays a list of the existing partitions and unpartitioned space on the computer and the following three choices:

- To set up Windows on the selected item, press **Enter**.
- To create a partition in the unpartitioned space, press **C**.
- To delete the selected partition, press **D**.

To delete a partition, use the arrow key to select it and press **D**. To confirm the deletion, you will be prompted to press **L**. Do not delete a partition with data stored on it unless you are sure you have a working backup of the disk.

6. To select an area of free disk space or an existing partition, use the **Up** and **Down** arrow keys to select the partition and press **Enter**. Press the **C** key to create a partition on the unpartitioned space on the first available drive.

7. The **Create a New Partition** screen opens. To create a partition equal to the maximum size of the drive, press **Enter**, or enter the size you want to make the partition and press **Enter** to create a partition of the desired size.

8. The **Existing Partitions** screen opens with the newly created partition selected. Press **Enter** to continue with the installation.

9. The next screen informs you that the newly created partition is not formatted. You must select the file system and either a Quick or Normal formatting process (see Figure 1-22). Select **Format the partition using the NTFS file system (Quick)** and press **Enter**.

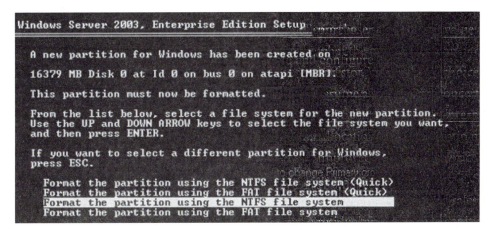

Figure 1-22: Formatting the partition

10. After the partition is formatted, Setup examines the disks, copies files to the installation folders, and initializes the Windows Server 2003 configuration. This can take several minutes.

11. Next, the computer reboots and the **Windows Server 2003** splash screen opens, followed by the **Windows Server 2003 Setup** screen.

12. Next, Setup detects and installs the devices on your computer while an **Installing Devices** progress bar lets you know how much of the process has been completed. The computer screen may flicker during this process.

13. Next, the **Regional and Language Options** screen opens (see Figure 1-23). To modify the regional and language settings, click the **Customize** button. To change the keyboard layout, click the **Details** button, or simply click **Next** to accept the default settings.

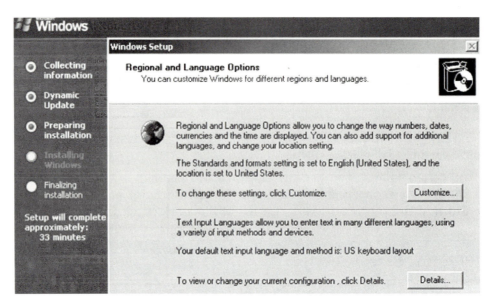

Figure 1-23: Regional and Language Options screen

14. The **Personalize Your Software** screen opens. Enter your name in the **Name** text box and your organization name in the **Organization** text box.

15. Click **Next** to open the **Your Product Key** screen (see Figure 1-24). Enter the product key in the spaces provided.

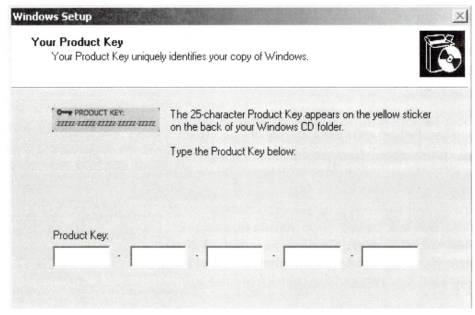

Figure 1-24: Your Product Key screen

16. Click **Next** to open the **Licensing Modes** screen. Here you must choose either **Per Server** or **Per Device or Per User**. If you choose Per Server, enter the number of Per Server concurrent connections based on the number of licenses you or your organization have purchased and use the **Number of concurrent connections** spin box to enter the correct number. Note that in most situations, Per Device or Per User is the most economical licensing option. However, if you are unsure which licensing mode to use, choose Per Server because you can change to Per User or Per Device at no additional cost, but you cannot convert from Per Device or Per User to Per Server.

17. Click **Next** to open the **Computer Name and Administrator Password** screen (see Figure 1-25). Enter a computer name, for example, **Server1**, in the **Computer name** text box, and an administrator password in the **Administrator password** text box. If you do not select a password that meets Microsoft's criteria for strong passwords, a message box prompts you to change the password. Then, enter the administrator password again in the **Confirm password** text box.

    Record the password used here: _____

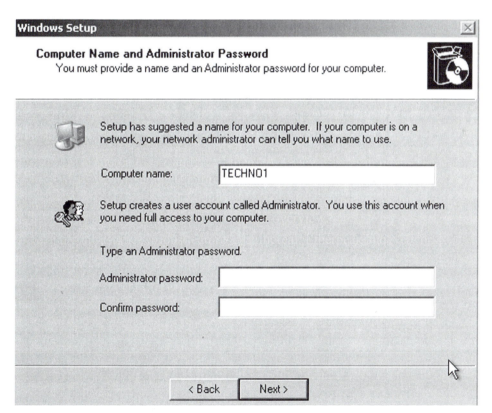

Figure 1-25: Computer Name and Administrator Password screen

18. Click **Next**. If a modem is detected, the **Modem Dialing Information** screen opens. Enter the necessary information including the area code or city code, if necessary. This screen is omitted if the computer does not have a modem.

19. Click **Next** to open the **Date and Time Settings** screen. Set the correct date and time, if necessary.

20. Click **Next** to reopen the **Windows Server 2003 Setup** screen. Networking software is now installed while the Installing Network progress bar lets you know how much of the process has been completed.

21. When the process is complete, the **Networking Settings** screen opens. Select the **Typical Settings** option button. This includes the installation of Client for Microsoft Networks (the redirector), File and Printer Sharing for Microsoft Networks (the server service), and the TCP/IP protocol stack.

22. Click **Next** to open the **Workgroup or Computer Domain** screen. Here, you must specify whether you want your computer to join a workgroup or a domain. If there is no domain present, the computer will default to Workgroup. If there is a domain present, click the **Yes, make this computer a member of the following domain** option button and enter your domain name in the text box, for example, **mydomain.com**. As a convention, your domain will be referred to as <*mydomain.com*> throughout the remainder of this book whenever the domain name is referred to.

23. Click **Next**. The **Join Computer to <*mydomain.com*> Domain** dialog box prompts you to enter the user name and password for a user who is authorized to join the computer to the domain. Enter the name and password for the domain administrator (or your own if you are the administrator on the target domain) and click **OK**.

24. Next, the **Windows Server 2003 Setup** screen returns and Setup copies files and completes the installation, including installing **Start** menu items, registering components, saving settings, and removing any temporary files. Progress bars will keep you apprised of the time remaining until these tasks are complete, which may be a total of 20 to 30 minutes.

25. When all tasks have been completed, if the system notices that the screen resolution is not optimally configured, you will be prompted to modify it and then to confirm that the new settings are correct.

26. Next, the computer reboots to the **Welcome to Windows Microsoft Windows Server 2003** initial logon screen.

27. Press **Ctrl** + **Alt** + **Delete** to open the **Log on to Windows** dialog box. Enter the password for the administrator account and click **OK**.

28. Most copies of Windows Server 2003 must be activated within a certain time period; however, if your organization licenses Windows Server 2003 through one of the Microsoft volume licensing agreement programs, such as Open License, Select License, or Enterprise Agreement, you will not have to follow this procedure. When you activate the operating system, the activation program verifies that the product key has not been used on more computers than intended by the software license. After you enter the product key during the installation, it is transformed into an installation ID number, which is provided to Microsoft through the Activation Wizard and transmitted either over a secure Internet transfer or by telephone. If you make a substantial number of hardware components changes, you may be required to reactivate Windows Server 2003 within 3 days to continue to log on.

2

INTRODUCTION TO NETWORK PROTOCOLS

PROJECTS

Project 2.1	Understanding Binary Numbering, Conversion to Decimal Numbering, and Logical Operations

Overview	Understanding IP addressing is an important skill that network administrators must possess. To do so, you must first understand how binary numbering works, and how to convert from binary to decimal. This is key to being able to convert binary IP addresses into their decimal equivalents. You also need to be able to understand the basic logical operations AND, OR, and XOR. It is also nearly impossible to understand subnetting (a method of splitting an IP network address into smaller groups of IP addresses that can be used on different networks) without fully understanding these concepts.

Binary is a counting system that uses only two numerals: 0 and 1. The positions in a binary number (called bits rather than digits) represent powers of 2 rather than powers of 10: 1, 2, 4, 8, 16, 32, and so on. To figure the decimal value of a binary number, you multiply each bit by its corresponding power of 2 and then add the results. The decimal value of binary 11111, for example, which is 31, is calculated as follows:

$$
\begin{aligned}
& 1 * 2^0 = 1 * \ 1 = \ \ 1 \\
+ \ & 1 * 2^1 = 1 * \ 2 = \ \ 2 \\
+ \ & 1 * 2^2 = 1 * \ 4 = \ \ 4 \\
+ \ & 1 * 2^3 = 0 * 8 = \ \ 8 \\
+ \ & 1 * 2^4 = 1 * 16 = 16
\end{aligned}
$$

The table below summarizes how AND, OR, and XOR work. The first two columns of the table indicate the two values used in the process. The result of the process (AND, OR, or XOR) is indicated under their column headings.

Logical Operations for Binary Values

First Value	Second Value		AND
0	0	0	0
0	1	0	1
1	0	0	1
1	1	1	1

The following example shows how you would calculate 10010101 AND 11011101:

```
        10010101
AND     11011101
Result: 10010101
```

Project 2.1	Understanding Binary Numbering, Conversion to Decimal Numbering, and Logical Operations
Outcomes	After completing this project, you will know how to: ▲ convert binary numbers into their decimal equivalents ▲ use basic logical operations such as AND ▲ convert binary IP addresses into their decimal equivalents
What you'll need	To complete this project, you will need: ▲ the worksheet below
Completion time	30 minutes
Precautions	None

■ Part A: Convert binary numbers to their decimal equivalents

1. 11000000:

_____

2. 10101000:

_____

3. 11111111:

_____

4. 00000101:

_____

5. 00010100:

_____

■ Part B: Perform the AND operation

1. 11000000
   11111111
   Result:

_____

2. 10101000
    11111111
    Result:

    _____

3. 00000101
    00000000
    Result:

    _____

■ **Part C: Convert binary numbers to an IP address using dotted decimal notation**

1. 01111111.00000000.00000000.00000001

    _____

2. 01111111.00000000.00000000.00000001

    _____

3. 11111111.11111111.11111111.11111111

    _____

Project 2.2	Subnetting
Overview	There are two parts of an IP address: the network ID and the host ID. When data are transferred from one network to another, the router reads the header information to determine the path to the next router or to the other network. You can use the AND operation (known as ANDing) to determine the network ID of an IP address if you know the subnet mask. For instance, for the IP address 144.28.16.17, with a subnet mask of 255.255.240.0, you can find the network ID as follows:

	144 .	28 .	16 .	17
IP address:	10010000	00011100	00010000	00010001
Subnet mask:	11111111	11111111	11110000	00000000
Network ID:	10010000	00011100	00010000	00000000
	144 .	28 .	16 .	0

	Subnetting is a method of splitting an IP network address into smaller groups of IP addresses that can be used on different networks. A smaller segment of a larger network that is created by a network administrator through the use of a subnet mask is referred to as a subnetwork. Subnetting can make network traffic management more efficient. Network administrators use subnetting to create these subnetworks to avoid having to lease an extraordinary amount of IP addresses. Without subnetting, each node on every network would have to have its own public IP address. There are simply not enough public IP addresses to make this happen.
Outcomes	After completing this project, you will know how to:

▲ use ANDing to determine the network ID of an IP address

▲ create a basic subnet scheme that segments a network into 12 networks |
| What you'll need | To complete this project, you will need:

▲ the worksheet below |
| Completion time | 30 minutes |
| Precautions | None |

■ Part A: Use ANDing to find the network ID of an IP address

1. IP address: 192.168.5.20
   Subnet mask: 255.255.255.0
   Network ID:

2. IP address: 172.20.0.0
    Subnet mask: 255.255.0.0
    Network ID:

    _____

■ Part B: Subnet a Class C IP Address

Subnet the Class C IP address, 192.168.1.0, into 12 subnets. There are a limited number of host
  IDs because the first three octets are part of the network ID.

1. What will your subnet mask be?

    _____

2. What is the first and second network IDs? What is the last network ID?

    _____

3. What is the first host ID? What is the last host ID?

    _____

    _____

Project 2.3	Examining Routing
Overview	It is important for a network administrator to understand the process of routing. To reduce broadcast traffic, networks are split into broadcast domains using a router. A routing table is a table maintained by all IP hosts that contains a list of routes for all networks of which the client is aware. You can also manually add a route to the routing table. In this project, you will use the route print command to view the routing table maintained by your computer and add a static route specified by your instructor.
Outcomes	After completing this project, you will know how to: ▲ use the route print command to view a routing table ▲ add a route to a routing table manually
What you'll need	To complete this project, you will need: ▲ a Windows XP/2000 or Windows Server 2003/2000 Server computer ▲ the IP address, subnet mask, and gateway for the new route
Completion time	10 minutes
Precautions	None

1. Turn on the computer and log on as an administrator
2. Click **Start**, and then click **Run** to open the **Run** dialog box. Enter **cmd** in the **Open** text box to open a **Command** window.
3. At the command prompt, enter **route print** and press **Enter** (see Figure 2-1).

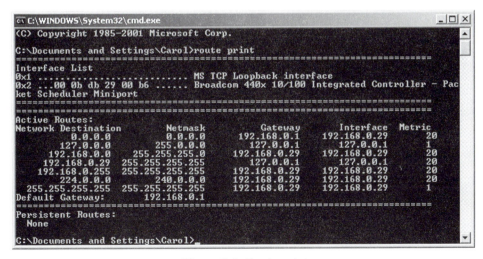

Figure 2-1: Route print

4. What is the default route?

    _____

5. What is the default gateway?

    _____

6. What other routes exist in the table?

    _____

    _____

7. At the command prompt, enter **route add [IP address] mask [subnet mask gateway]** and press **Enter** to update the routing table manually with the new route.

8. At the command prompt, enter **route print** and press **Enter** to view the new route added to the routing table. Capture a screenshot of the routing table and print a copy to hand in to your instructor.

9. Close the **Command** window when you have finished.

Project 2.4	Installing and Configuring the TCP/IP Protocol
Overview	Transmission Control Protocol/Internet Protocol (TCP/IP) is a suite of protocols that enables communications among resources across a network. TCP/IP is the main networking protocol in use today and is the core protocol for the Internet. TCP/IP is automatically installed when Windows Server 2003 is installed, but you should verify that it has not been uninstalled. It is important for a network administrator to understand the process of routing. To reduce broadcast traffic, networks are split into broadcast domains using a router. A routing table is a table maintained by all IP hosts that contains a list of routes for all networks of which the client is aware. You can also manually add a route to the routing table. In this project, you will use the route print command to view the routing table maintained by your computer and add a static route specified by your instructor.
Outcomes	After completing this project, you will know how to: ▲ check to see if TCP/IP is installed ▲ install TCP/IP if it is not installed ▲ manually configure TCP/IP
What you'll need	To complete this project, you will need: ▲ a Windows XP/2000 computer connected in a network. Your instructor should provide you with the following information: • IP address • default gateway • IP address of preferred DNS server
Completion time	10 minutes
Precautions	Be sure to check with your system administrator before altering settings on a school networked client computer.

1. If necessary, start your computer and log on as an administrator
2. To confirm that TCP/IP is installed, click **Start**, and then open the **Control Panel**.
3. Click **Network Connections**, and then right-click **Local Area Connection**. A shortcut menu will appear.
4. Click **Properties** to open the **Local Area Connection Properties** dialog box (Figure 2-2). If **Internet Protocol (TCP/IP)** is listed, it is already installed.

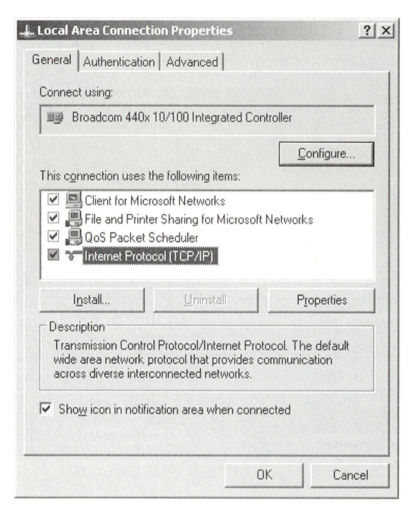

Figure 2-2: Local Area Connection Properties dialog box

5. If TCP/IP is not installed, install it. To do so, click **Install** to open the **Select Network Component Type** dialog box.

6. Click **Protocol**, then click **Add** to open the **Select Network Protocol** dialog box.

7. Select the **Internet Protocol (TCP/IP)** option and click **OK**. Close the **Select Network Component Type** dialog box.

8. On the **General** tab of the **Local Area Connection Properties** dialog box, select **Internet Protocol (TCP/IP**) and then click the **Properties** button to open the **Internet Protocol (TCP/IP Properties)** dialog box.

9. If the **Obtain an IP address automatically** option button is selected, this means the computer is configured to obtain an IP address automatically from a DHCP server, whose role is automatically assign addresses to LAN members and also automatically configure the other TCP/IP parameters for network hosts as they boot. However, some of the computers on a network must have what is known as a "static" IP address. In a static IP addressing system, the IP addresses and other TCP/IP parameters for the hosts are manually configured and do not change. Record what you see in the **Internet Protocol (TCP/IP) Properties** dialog box.

_____

_____

10. To manually configure TCP/IP, select the **Use the following IP address** option button and enter the IP address provided to you by your instructor. The default subnet mask for that class of IP address is automatically assigned. Next enter the default gateway provided to you by your instructor. This is the IP address for the router that will link this computer with other networks (e.g., the Internet).

11. The **Use the following DNS server addresses** option button is automatically selected. Enter the IP address of the preferred DNS server, and if applicable, the IP address of an alternate DNS server.

12. Click the **Advanced** button. Record the name of the dialog box that appears and the data that are visible within the dialog box.

_____

_____

_____

_____

13. Click the **DNS** tab. List the three settings that are applied to all connections with TCP/IP enabled:

_____

_____

_____

14. Click the **WINS** tab. Are any WINS addresses listed? Is LMHosts lookup enabled? What is the NetBIOS setting?

_____

_____

_____

15. Click the **Options** tab. Then click the **Properties** button. Record the default IP security settings.

_____

_____

_____

16. Click **Cancel** to return to the **Advanced TCP/IP Settings** dialog box.
17. Click the **TCP/IP filtering** option. Then click the **Properties** button. Record the three types of packet filtering that you can apply.

_____

_____

_____

18. Click **Cancel** to return to the **Advanced TCP/IP Settings** dialog box.
19. Click **OK** to save the settings and return to the **Internet Protocol (TCP/IP) Properties** dialog box.
20. Click **OK** to return to the **Local Area Connection Properties** dialog box.

Project 2.5	Configuring Bindings
Overview	Binding is the process by which a protocol is linked to a network adapter and certain network services. Windows operating systems enable you to adjust the order in which protocols are used so the protocols used most often are accessed first when a connection is established, which will enhance network performance.
Outcomes	After completing this project, you will know how to: ▲ adjust the order in which protocols are used by various services by adjusting the bindings for your adapter
What you'll need	To complete this project, you will need: ▲ a Windows XP/2000 or Windows Server 2003/2000 Server computer
Completion time	10 minutes
Precautions	Be sure to check with your system administrator before altering settings on a school networked client computer.

1. Turn on the computer and log on as an administrator.
2. Click **Start**, and then open the **Control Panel**. Select **Network Connections** to open the **Network Connections** window. Open the **Advanced** menu and select **Advanced Settings**.
3. The **Advanced Setting** dialog box opens. **Examine the Bindings for <Local Area Connections>** list box on the **Adapters and Bindings** tab (see Figure 2-3). What protocols are listed there and to what network services are they bound?

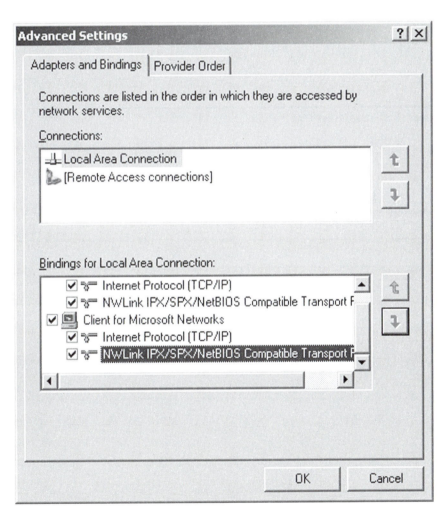

Figure 2-3: Advanced Settings dialog box

4. You can change the order in which the protocols are used by various services with the Up and Down arrow buttons on the side of the box. You can also remove a particular protocol from a particular service by unchecking its check box.

Project 2.6	Using TCP/IP Troubleshooting Tools
Overview	There are a number of tools that you can use to troubleshoot TCP/IP. Among them are ipconfig, ping, tracert and pathping. The ipconfig command is used to check TCP/IP configuration on a local computer. The ping command allows you to check the computer's network connectivity. The tracert command maps the path that packets take as they flow to a remote system. The pathping command combines the functionality of both ping and tracert. In this project, you will practice using all of these tools.
Outcomes	After completing this project, you will know how to: ▲ use the ipconfig command ▲ use the ping command ▲ use the tracert command ▲ use the pathping command
What you'll need	To complete this project, you will need: ▲ a Windows XP/Windows 2000 computer or a Windows Server 2003/2000 Server computer configured with TCP/IP and connected to a network ▲ the IP address of a remote host
Completion time	30 minutes
Precautions	None

1. Turn on the computer and log on as an administrator.
2. Click **Start**, and then click **Run** to open the **Run** dialog box. Enter **cmd** in the **Open** text box to open a **Command** window.
3. At the command prompt, enter **ipconfig** and press **Enter** to view the computer's IP configuration (see Figure 2-4).

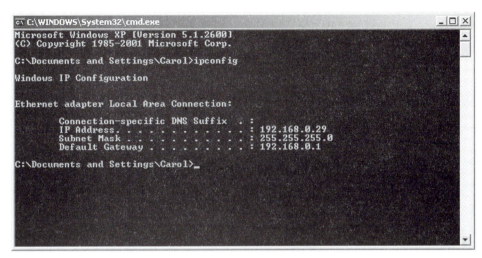

Figure 2-4: Using Ipconfig

4. Record the configuration settings for your computer including the IP address, subnet mask, default gateway, and DNS servers.

   _____

   _____

   _____

5. At the command prompt, enter **ipconfig /all** and press **Enter**. How does what you see differ from what you viewed using just the ipconfig command?

   _____

   _____

   _____

6. At the command prompt, enter **ipconfig /release** and press **Enter.** This command releases the IP address from the computer causing the computer to lose connectivity to any node outside the computer.

7. At the command prompt, enter **ipconfig /renew** and press **Enter**. This command restores an IP address from the computer, causing the computer to reestablish its identity and restore connectivity that was established prior to the execution of the ipconfig /release command. It is quite common that during the ipconfig /release and ipconfig /renew process, the IP address will be the same as assigned before. However, this is not always the case. If it is not, record the newly established configuration settings for your computer including the IP address, subnet mask, default gateway, and DNS servers.

   _____

   _____

   _____

8. At the command prompt, enter **ping 127.0.0.1** and press **Enter**. This address, known as the loopback address, verifies your network interface card is functioning (see Figure 2-5).

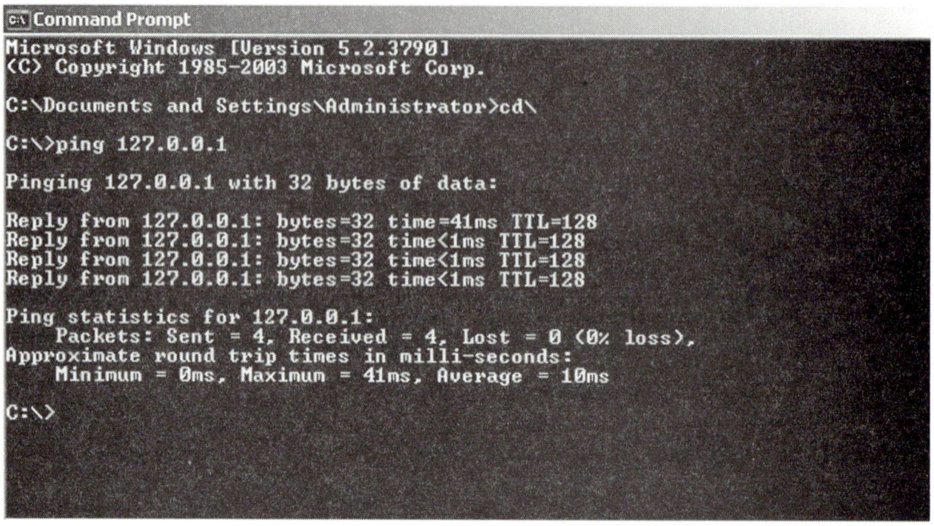
Command Prompt
Microsoft Windows [Version 5.2.3790]
(C) Copyright 1985-2003 Microsoft Corp.
C:\Documents and Settings\Administrator>cd\
C:\>ping 127.0.0.1
Pinging 127.0.0.1 with 32 bytes of data:
Reply from 127.0.0.1: bytes=32 time=41ms TTL=128
Reply from 127.0.0.1: bytes=32 time<1ms TTL=128
Reply from 127.0.0.1: bytes=32 time<1ms TTL=128
Reply from 127.0.0.1: bytes=32 time<1ms TTL=128
Ping statistics for 127.0.0.1:
Packets: Sent = 4, Received = 4, Lost = 0 (0% loss),
Approximate round trip times in milli-seconds:
Minimum = 0ms, Maximum = 41ms, Average = 10ms
C:\>

Figure 2-5: Pinging the loopback address

9. At the command prompt, enter **ping [IP address of a remote host]** and press **Enter**. Record the Ping statistics for the ping, including the packets sent, packets received, packets lost, and the minimum, maximum, and average approximate round trip times in milliseconds below.

10. At the command prompt, enter **tracert [IP address of remote host]** and press **Enter**. Examine the results. Did the tracert complete successfully? If yes, how many hops did it take? If not, how do you know?

11. At the command prompt, enter **pathping [IP address of a remote host]** and press **Enter**. How does what you see differ from what you viewed using the tracert command?

Project 2.7 Monitoring Network Traffic

Overview	Once you get your network up and running, it is imperative that you be able to quickly diagnose potential problem areas. One of the biggest concerns for network users is bandwidth. Bandwidth is the most important factor in the speed and effectiveness of a network. Monitoring your network allows you to be proactive, rather than reactive in your network management processes. Furthermore, once you realize you, indeed, have a problem in your network, the ability to monitor network traffic is crucial to the successful remedy for these problems. Windows Server 2003 comes with a monitoring tool that allows you to capture frames sent to and from the server. This built-in function of the operating system is used daily in today's networking world and it is an effective tool.
Outcomes	After completing this project, you will know how to: ▲ install Network Monitor ▲ use Network Monitor
What you'll need	To complete this project, you will need: ▲ a Windows Server 2003 computer with the Network Monitor driver installed and connected to a Windows client
Completion time	30 minutes
Precautions	Attempting to monitor network traffic on a production system is normally prohibited in most organizations.

1. Turn on the computer and log on as an administrator.
2. Click **Start**, open the **Control Panel**, and then click **Add or Remove Programs**. Then, click **Add/Remove Windows Components**.
3. Scroll down the Components list and select the check box in front of **Management and Monitoring Tools** (see Figure 2-6). You do not need to select the other tools at this time. Click **OK**.
4. Click the **Next** button. After the configuration changes are complete, click **Finish** and close any open windows.

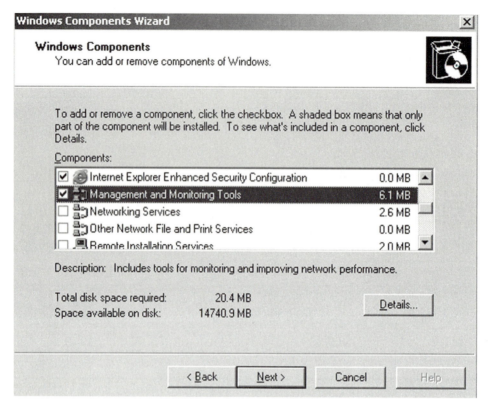

Figure 2-6: Windows Components

5. You can now capture traffic on your network. If you have a second computer, you can capture data traffic between the two systems.

6. Click **Start**, point to **Administrative Tools**, and click **Network Monitor**. The **Microsoft Network Monitor** window opens. You will be prompted to select a network on which you want to capture data. If you do not select a network, Network Monitor will select the local area network by default.

7. Click **OK** to open the **Select a Network** dialog box. Select the connection you want to monitor and click **OK**.

8. The **Capture Window (Station Stats)** for the connection selected opens in the **Microsoft Network Monitor** window. Click the **Start Capture** button. Allow some time to pass (see Figure 2-7).

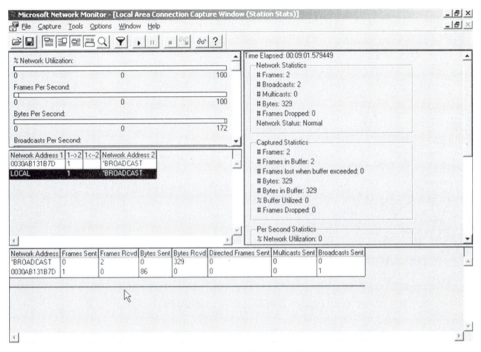

Figure 2-7: Viewing Network Statistics

9. How many frames have been captured? How many bytes were sent? How many bytes were received? What kind of traffic was sent?

_____

_____

_____

_____

_____

10. Then, click the **Stop Capture** button. A message box asks if you want to save the captured summary data to a file. Click **Yes** and enter a file name, and then click **Save** to save the file (see Figure 2-8).

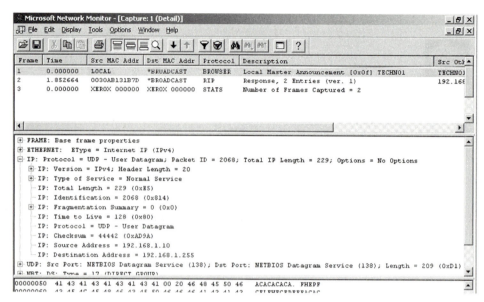

Figure 2-8: Capture summary

11. Examine the file. What are the protocols used? What are the source and destination addresses? Notice if there are any the broadcast messages. How large are the frames? Record what you observe.

_____

_____

_____

_____

_____

3

IMPLEMENTING AND ADMINISTERING WINS

PROJECTS

Project 3.1	Understanding Browsing
Overview	In this project, you will investigate the browser service. The browser service displays the workgroup or domain name for each computer. The master browser keeps a list of the browser announcements from other computers. If your Windows 2003 system is connected to a local area network, it will display other computers or devices on the network in the My Network Places folder. Older versions of Windows use the Network Neighborhood folder. You can also use the net view utility to see computers which are sharing resources. Network Monitor enables you to view browser traffic.
Outcomes	After completing this project, you will know how to: ▲ view devices that are displayed by the browser service ▲ use the net view utility to see systems on the network ▲ use Network Monitor to view browser traffic
What you'll need	To complete this project, you will need: ▲ a Windows Server 2003 computer connected to a local network
Completion time	15 minutes
Precautions	None

■ Part A: Understand the browser service

1. Turn on the computer and log on as an administrator.
2. Click **Start**, then click **My Network Places**. Select **Entire Network**, and then **Microsoft Windows Network**. Record what you see.

   _____

   _____

   _____

3. Another way to view a browse list is via the **Command** window. Click **Start**, select **Run** to open the **Run** dialog box, and enter **cmd** in the **Open** text box. At the command prompt, enter **net view** and press **Enter** (see Figure 3-1).

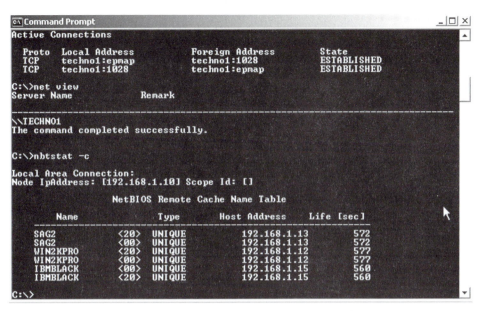

Figure 3-1: Using the net view command

4. To view the resources offered by a specific computer, enter **net view \\computername** at the command prompt. Record what you see.

_____

_____

_____

■ Part B: View browser traffic

1. To view browser traffic in Network Monitor, you can capture startup frames. Follow the instructions in Project 2.7 to do so.

2. What kind of message is a browser announcement? What is the IP protocol? What source port is used for the browser service?

_____

_____

_____

Project 3.2	Name Resolution
Overview	Computers identify each other using numbers such as the MAC address or the IP address. Address Resolution Protocol (ARP) resolves IP addresses to hardware MAC addresses, both of which are numbers.
	To make things easier for humans, Windows networks use the computer name or NetBIOS name to display resources to users on the network. However, there must be a pairing of the computer name and the IP address so computers must either keep a list of all the name-to-number relationships or be able to ask another computer for the information. This process is called name resolution.
	NetBIOS name resolution matches a computer name with an IP address. There are three methods used to do this:
	• Broadcast: The system broadcasts for the name.
	• LMHOSTS: The system examines a static text file for resolution.
	• WINS: The system queries a Windows Internet Naming Service server for resolution.
	The exact mechanism by which NetBIOS names are resolved to IP addresses depends on the NetBIOS node type that is configured for the node. There are four NetBIOS node, B-node (Broadcast node), P-node (Peer-to-Peer node), M-node (Mixed node), and H-node (Hybrid node). B-nodes first check the LMHosts file and then broadcast. These nodes will never use WINS. This is the default node type if a client is not configured to use WINS. P-nodes first check the LMHosts file and then contact a WINS server. These nodes will never broadcast. M-nodes first check the LMHosts file, then broadcast, and then contact a WINS server. H-nodes first check the LMHosts file, then contact a WINS server, and then broadcast. This is the default node type if the client is configured to use WINS.
Outcomes	After completing this project, you will know how to:
	▲ troubleshoot name resolution
	▲ determine the current method of NetBIOS name resolution
What you'll need	To complete this project, you will need:
	▲ a Windows Server 2003 computer connected to a local network
Completion time	30 minutes
Precautions	Creating a LMHosts file that contains errors can cause network resolution problems.

■ **Part A: View the LMHosts.sam file**

1. Turn on the computer and log on as an administrator
2. Select **Start**. Click **Search**, and select **All files and folders**.
3. Enter **lmhosts.sam** in the **All of part of the file name** text box. Select the drop-down menu and select the drive where the operating system is installed (normally, C: drive). Click **Search** (see Figure 3-2).

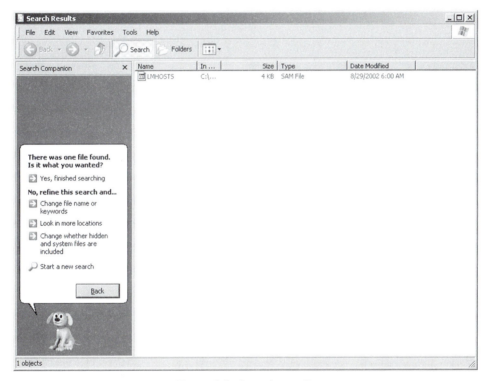

Figure 3-2: Search results

4. Where is the **Lmhosts.sam** file located? Why does this file have a .sam extension?

_____

_____

_____

5. Open the file in **Notepad** (see Figure 3-3). List the various extensions that can be used and explain the effect of using each type.

_____

_____

_____

_____

_____

```
#·Copyright· (c)·1993-1999·Microsoft·Corp.¶
#¶
#·This·is·a·sample·LMHOSTS·file·used·by·the·Microsoft·TCP/IP·for·Windows.¶
#¶
#·This·file·contains·the·mappings·of·IP·addresses·to·computernames¶
#·(NetBIOS)·names.··Each·entry·should·be·kept·on·an·individual·line.¶
#·The·IP·address·should·be·placed·in·the·first·column·followed·by·the¶
#·corresponding·computername.·The·address·and·the·computername¶
#·should·be·separated·by·at·least·one·space·or·tab.··The·"#"·character¶
#·is·generally·used·to·denote·the·start·of·a·comment·(see·the·exceptions¶
#·below).¶
#¶
#·This·file·is·compatible·with·Microsoft·LAN·Manager·2.x·TCP/IP·lmhosts¶
#·files·and·offers·the·following·extensions:¶
#¶
#······#PRE¶
#······#DOM:<domain>¶
#······#INCLUDE·<filename>¶
#······#BEGIN_ALTERNATE¶
#······#END_ALTERNATE¶
#······\0xnn·(non-printing·character·support)¶
#¶
#·Following·any·entry·in·the·file·with·the·characters·"#PRE"·will·cause¶
#·the·entry·to·be·preloaded·into·the·name·cache.·By·default,·entries·are¶
#·not·preloaded,·but·are·parsed·only·after·dynamic·name·resolution·fails.¶
#¶
#·Following·an·entry·with·the·"#DOM:<domain>"·tag·will·associate·the¶
#·entry·with·the·domain·specified·by·<domain>.·This·affects·how·the¶
#·browser·and·logon·services·behave·in·TCP/IP·environments.·To·preload¶
#·the·host·name·associated·with·#DOM·entry,·it·is·necessary·to·also·add·a¶
#·#PRE·to·the·line.·The·<domain>·is·always·preloaded·although·it·will·not¶
#·be·shown·when·the·name·cache·is·viewed.¶
#¶
#·Specifying·"#INCLUDE·<filename>"·will·force·the·RFC·NetBIOS·(NBT)¶
#·software·to·seek·the·specified·<filename>·and·parse·it·as·if·it·were¶
#·local.·<filename>·is·generally·a·UNC-based·name,·allowing·a¶
#·centralized·lmhosts·file·to·be·maintained·on·a·server.¶
#·It·is·ALWAYS·necessary·to·provide·a·mapping·for·the·IP·address·of·the¶
#·server·prior·to·the·#INCLUDE.·This·mapping·must·use·the·#PRE·directive.¶
#·In·addtion·the·share·"public"·in·the·example·below·must·be·in·the¶
#·LanManServer·list·of·"NullSessionShares"·in·order·for·client·machines·to¶
#·be·able·to·read·the·lmhosts·file·successfully.··This·key·is·under¶
```

Figure 3-3: LMHosts.sam

■ **Part B: Determine current NetBIOS name resolution method using the ipconfig /all command to determine the node type**

1. Open a **Command** window and at the command prompt, enter **ipconfig /all** and press **Enter**. What is the Node type? What is the sequence of the NetBIOS name resolution for this node type?

_____

_____

_____

_____

Project 3.3	Viewing the NetBIOS Name Cache
Overview	Each Windows computer saves recent name resolutions in memory to find them more quickly if data are being sent to the same computer. This cache is checked first before any other form of resolution is applied. The NetBIOS name cache or name table can be viewed by using the nbtstat command.
Outcomes	After completing this project, you will know how to: ▲ use the nbtstat command to view and troubleshoot NetBIOS resolution
What you'll need	To complete this project, you will need: ▲ a Windows Server 2003 computer connected to a local network
Completion time	30 minutes
Precautions	None

1. Open a **Command** window and at the command prompt enter **nbtstat** and press **Enter** (see Figure 3-4).

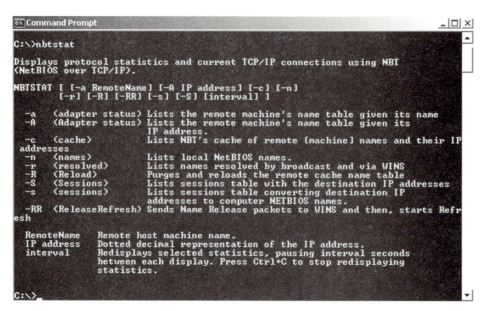

Figure 3-4: Using the nbstat command

2. What parameter would you use to view the NetBIOS name cache? What parameter would you use to view NetBIOS names resolved by broadcast? What parameter would you use to purge the NetBIOS name cache?

_____

_____

_____

_____

3. At the command prompt, enter **nbstat –n** and press **Enter**. What is the function of the –n parameter.

_____

_____

_____

Project 3.4	Understanding WINS
Overview	NetBIOS works by broadcasting network resource information, such as which shares a server offers and where the domain master browser is, so any client can hear what its peers have to offer. Broadcasts work for smaller networks but generate unnecessary and undesirable clutter in larger networks. Because NetBIOS packets aren't routable, not only do all those broadcasts clutter the network, they don't even do any good because only computers on the local subnet can hear them.

Microsoft solved the routability problem by offering NetBIOS over TCP/IP or NBT. However, NBT still sends out broadcasts. Although NBT broadcasts do allow NetBIOS-style name resolution on TCP/IP networks, Microsoft's designers realized that it was possible to come up with a better solution, and the Windows Internet Name Service (WINS) was born.

When a WINS client starts, the client exchanges WINS messages with its designated WINS server. Each client can actually hold addresses for a primary and a secondary WINS server; the secondary will be used if the primary doesn't answer. The intent of these messages is to allow the client to register its address with the server, without allowing name or address duplication. This message exchange occurs in four phases: name registration, name renewal, name release, and name resolution.

WINS listens to NBT broadcasts and collates them in a central source. In this role, it effectively serves as a clearinghouse for NetBIOS naming information. |
| Outcomes | After completing this project, you will know how to:

▲ recognize the function and purpose of WINS |
| What you'll need | To complete this project, you will need:

▲ the worksheet below |
| Completion time | 10 minutes |
| Precautions | None |

1. What type of broadcast does WINS listens to?

   _____

2. Why are duplicate names a problem for WINS?

   _____

3. WINS client sends a name renewal message to the primary WINS server when the TTL has reached what percent of its original value?

   _____

4. What is the name of the service that allows WINS data stored on your servers to be made available to other WINS servers?

_____

5. What are the two different types of replication partners used in WINS?

_____

Project 3.5	Installing and Configuring WINS
Overview	To operate, WINS must be installed on both a server and client computer. The WINS server maintains a database of all these entries, and when a client computer requests another computer's name or IP address, the WINS server provides it.
	Installing the WINS service on a production network should be planned to provide maximum functionality. Try not to install the WINS service on a domain controller or on a system with multiple NIC cards.
	After WINS has been installed on the server, you should examine and become familiar with the default settings for the service. You should also become familiar with the database records that WINS generates.
Outcomes	After completing this project, you will know how to:
	▲ install WINS on a server
	▲ install WINS on a client
	▲ examine the default settings for the service
	▲ view WINS database entries
What you'll need	To complete this project, you will need:
	▲ a Windows Server 2003 computer connected to a local network
	▲ a client computer on the same network (you can also configure the server as a WINS client). Your instructor should provide you with the IP address to use for the WINS server
	You may also need a Windows Server 2003 installation CD-ROM.
Completion time	30 minutes
Precautions	None

■ Part A: Install WINS on a server

1. Turn on the server computer and log on as an administrator.
2. Click **Start**, open the **Control Panel**, and then click **Add or Remove Programs**.

3. Select **Add/Remove Windows Components** in the **Add or Remove Programs** window.

4. Scroll down and select **Networking Services**.

5. Click the **Details** button.

6. Click the checkbox next to **Windows Internet Name Service (WINS)** (Figure 3-5) and click **OK**.

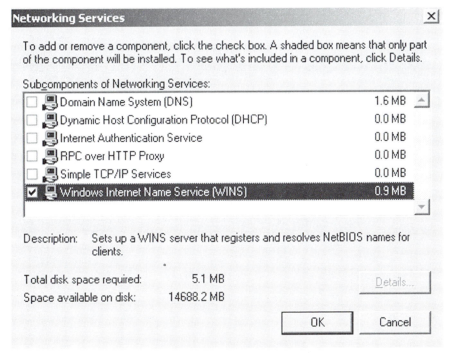

Figure 3-5: Selecting WINS

7. Then click **Next** to install WINS. The system may ask you for the Windows Server 2003 CD. If prompted, insert the CD and follow the instructions to download the files required to finish the installation.

8. When the installation is complete, click **Finish** and close any open windows.

■ Part B: Configure a WINS client

1. Turn on the computer and log on as an administrator.

2. Click **Start**, open the **Control Panel**, select **Network Connections**, click **Local Area Connection**, and then click **Properties**.

3. Click **Internet Protocol (TCP/IP)** and then click the **Properties** button.

4. Click the **Advanced** button in the **Internet Protocol (TCP/IP) Properties** dialog box to open the **Advanced TCP/IP Settings** dialog box, and then open the **WINS** tab (Figure 3-6).

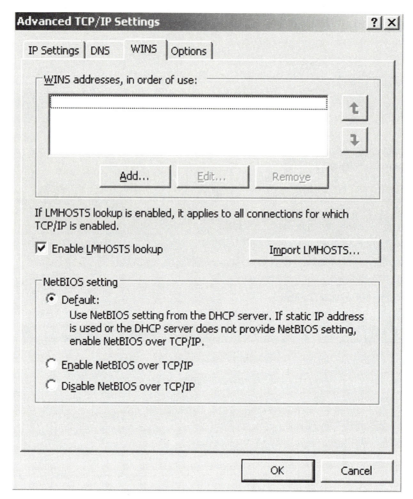

Figure 3-6: WINS tab in Advanced TCP/IP Settings dialog box

5. Are there any WINS addresses already listed?

_____

6. Click the **Add** button. Enter the IP address of the WINS server provided by your instructor in the **TCP/WINS Server** dialog box and click **Add**.

7. Click **OK** in the **Advanced TCP/IP Settings** dialog box and then **OK** in the **Internet Protocol (TCP/IP) Properties** dialog box. Close all other open dialog boxes and windows.

■ **Part C: Configure a WINS server**

(**Note:** This activity requires that none of the default settings for the WINS server have been altered.)

1. To configure the WINS service, click **Start**, select **Administrative Tools**, and then click **WINS**. The WINS console will display (Figure 3-7).

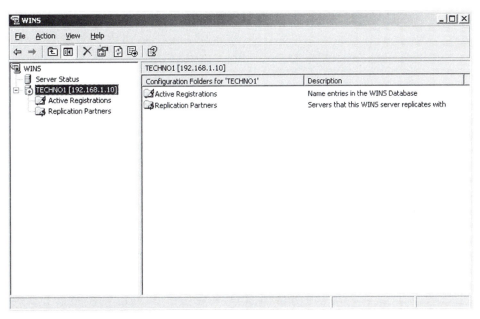

Figure 3-7: WINS console

2. Right-click the server name and then click **Properties** to open the **WINS server Properties** dialog box. What is the default setting for automatic update of WINS statistics?

_____

3. Open the **Intervals** tab. What is the default setting for the rate at which records will be renewed, deleted, and verified by the WINS server?

_____

_____

4. Open the **Database Verifications** tab. What is the default setting for verifying database consistency? What is the default setting for the rate at which records are renewed, deleted, and verified? What is the default setting for the maximum number of records verified for each period?

_____

_____

_____

_____

5. Open the **Advanced** tab. What is the default database path? What is the default setting for burst handling? Explain what burst handling is.

_____

_____

_____

_____

6. Close the **WINS server Properties** dialog box.

■ Part D: View WINS database entries

1. To view WINS database entries, open the **WINS** console if it not already open, select the WINS server in the left pane of the **WINS** console, and open the **Action** menu. Click **Display Server Statistics** to see the WINS queries.

2. Select **Active Registrations**. On the **Action** menu, select **Display Records** and then **Find Now** (see Figure 3-8). Record what you see.

_____

_____

_____

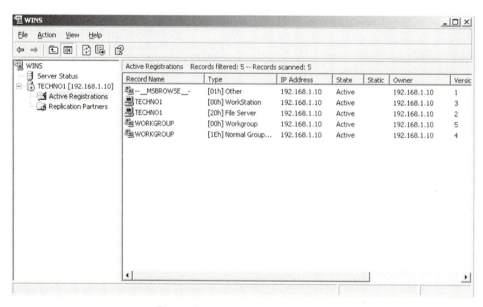

Figure 3-8: Active Registrations

3. Why would an IP address be listed more than once? How do you know if the WINS service is functioning? What are two configuration settings for a replication partner?

_____

_____

_____

_____

_____

Project 3.6	Administering WINS
Overview	One of the most important tasks in administering WINS is controlling replication.
Outcomes	After completing this project, you will know how to: ▲ configure a replication partner
What you'll need	To complete this project, you will need: ▲ a WINS server connected to a local network ▲ an IP address for a second WINS server that acts as a replication partner
Completion time	30 minutes
Precautions	None

1. Turn on the computer and log on as an Administrator.
2. Open the **WINS** console.
3. Right-click the **Replication Partners** node and select **Properties** to open the **Replication Partners Properties** dialog box.
4. Open the **Advanced** tab and select the **Enable automatic partner configuration** check box.
5. For what types of networks is automatic partner configuration appropriate? What is the default multicast time to live (TTL). How are automatic partners configured?

_____

_____

_____

_____

6. Close the **Replication Partners Properties** dialog box.

7. To configure a new replication partner manually, right-click the **Replication Partners** node and select **New Replication Partners**.

8. In the **New Replication Partners** dialog box, enter the IP address of the WINS server that you want to add as a partner, then click **OK**.

9. In the WINS console, select **Replication Partners** to view the partners in the details pane.

10. Right-click a partner name and click **Properties** to set replication properties for that server.

4
IMPLEMENTING AND ADMINISTERING DNS

PROJECTS

Project 4.1	Understanding DNS
Overview	When you install Windows Server 2003, you select one or more server roles. If you are using your server to manage users and resources, you will add the role of domain controller and install Active Directory. Domain controllers store the Active Directory database that contains computer, user and resource information. Active Directory bases its structure on the Domain Name System (DNS). In fact, the hierarchical structure of Active Directory parallels DNS because Active Directory uses DNS for its naming system. The term DNS can be confusing because it describes both the TCP/IP protocol and the service that runs on a server such as a Windows Server 2003 domain controller. To understand DNS, you need to become familiar with a number of DNS technical terms. As you learned previously, the DNS structure is hierarchical, similar to a family tree. An example would be a grandfather and that grandfather's brother who each represent different branches of the family tree. The great-grandfather would be the link between these two branches. DNS works like this with parts of the fully-qualified-domain-name representing each hierarchical level. Domains are segments of the hierarchy indicated by the domain name space. In our example, the great-grandfather's name would be passed on to his sons, his grandsons, and so on. For DNS, a domain name falls under a specific node or branch that indicates a kind of organization or function such as .edu for education or .gov for government. "Com" stands for commercial, so many businesses have .com as their domain name. Top-level domains are registered by Internet Assigned Numbers Authority (IANA); http://www.iana.org/. In order for network traffic to travel across routers all over the world, the domain name needs to be registered with IANA and stored by the root servers, which resolve top-level domain names with the IP addresses of the DNS servers that manage the domain. The DNS server service can run locally on your Windows Server 2003 computer using a local DNS database (also called a zone) to provide registration and client-to-IP address resolution. If you do not want to manage your own DNS zone, DNS information can be stored in a DNS zone managed by your Internet Service Provider.
Outcomes	After completing this project, you will know how to: ▲ identify the RFCs that outline the Domain Name System ▲ explain why DNS was developed ▲ cxamine the hosts file ▲ investigate top-level domain names

What you'll need	To complete this project, you will need:
	▲ a computer connected to the Internet
Completion time	25 minutes
Precautions	None

■ Part A: Locate and examine DNS related RFCs

The Internet Engineering Task Force publishes Request for Comments (RFCs) that outline specific protocols and functions of Internet technology. You can review these RFCs to see how particular technologies have become standards.

1. Go to: http://www.ietf.org/
2. Select the RFC Pages link. Enter **1034** in the **RFC Number** box and select **Go**.
    You will notice this RFC was written in November 1987.

    Network Working Group   P. Mockapetris
    Request for Comments: 1034   ISI
    Obsoletes: RFCs 882, 883, 973   November 1987

           DOMAIN NAMES - CONCEPTS AND FACILITIES

3. A quick review of **RFC 1034** allows you to see how DNS was designed.

    "The domain system assumes that all data originates in master files scattered through the hosts that use the domain system. These master files are updated by local system administrators. Master files are text files that are read by a local name server, and hence become available through the name servers to users of the domain system. The user programs access name servers through standard programs called resolvers."

4. According to **RFC 1034**, what was the impetus for the development of the domain system?

    _____

    _____

    _____

■ Part B: Examine the host file on your computer

1. Turn on the computer and log on as an Administrator
2. Select **Start**. Click **Search** and select **All files and folders**.
3. Enter **hosts** in the **All of part of the file name** text box. Select the drop down menu and select the drive where the operating system is installed (normally C: drive). Click **Search**.
4. If you double-click the hosts file, you can open it with **Notepad** (see Figure 4-1). You should see the same entries as the graphic.

```
#·Copyright·(c)·1993-1999·Microsoft·Corp.¶
#¶
#·This·is·a·sample·HOSTS·file·used·by·Microsoft·TCP/IP·for·Windows.¶
#¶
#·This·file·contains·the·mappings·of·IP·addresses·to·host·names.·Each¶
#·entry·should·be·kept·on·an·individual·line.·The·IP·address·should¶
#·be·placed·in·the·first·column·followed·by·the·corresponding·host·name.¶
#·The·IP·address·and·the·host·name·should·be·separated·by·at·least·one¶
#·space.¶
#¶
#·Additionally,·comments·(such·as·these)·may·be·inserted·on·individual¶
#·lines·or·following·the·machine·name·denoted·by·a·'#'·symbol.¶
#¶
#·For·example:¶
#¶
#······102.54.94.97·····rhino.acme.com··········#·source·server¶
#·······38.25.63.10·····x.acme.com·············#·x·client·host¶
¶
127.0.0.1·······localhost¶
```

Figure 4-1: Sample HOSTS file

5. Where is the **hosts** file located? What mapping does it show? (**Note**: In this type of file, the **#** symbol at the beginning of a line means the line will be ignored or skipped when the system reads the file.)

_____

_____

_____

6. The localhost is your computer. You can use the **127.0.0.1** (also called the loopback address) to test the installation of TCP/IP on your computer by typing **ping 127.0.0.1** at the Command Prompt.

■ Part C: Examine different types of DNS RFCs

1. Visit http://www.dns.net/dnsrd/rfc/. This site reviews the RFCs related to DNS. It shows whether the RFC is a standard, proposed standard, informational or experimental.
2. Select **RFC 1178**, and review document. Notice it is designated at *Informational*. In other words, it is not an approved standard, but offered for subject knowledge.

3. What is one guideline to follow in choosing a computer name?

_____

■ Part D: Understand domain names

1. View the list of top-level domains by going to: http://www.iana.org/domain-names.htm
2. Also view the IANA Whois service Web site: http://whois.iana.org/
3. Enter the country code **tv**
4. What country has registered this top-level domain name?

_____

5. Enter www.tv into the address of your browser. What can you do at this Web site?

_____

Project 4.2	Configuring a DNS Client
Overview	In this project, you configure a client computer to use DNS.
Outcomes	After completing this project, you will know how to: ▲ configure DNS on a network client computer ▲ determine if the client needs static DNS IP addresses ▲ view a client computer's DNS configuration
What you'll need	To complete this project, you will need: ▲ a client computer connected to a local network
Completion time	15 minutes
Precautions	None

1. Turn on the computer and log on as an Administrator
2. Select **Start**. Click **Control Panel**, and select **Network Connections**.

3. Select the **Local Area Connection** and right click to bring up the menu. Select **Properties** and the **Local Area Connection Properties** dialog box will display (see Figure 4-2).

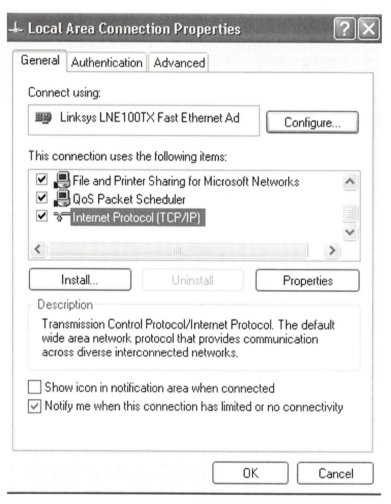

Figure 4-2: Local Area Connection Properties dialog box

4. Highlight **Internet Protocol (TCP/IP)** and select the **Properties** button below the box.

5. The **Internet Protocol (TCP/IP) Properties** dialog box displays showing the DNS settings in the bottom section of the box (see **Figure 4-3**). Your settings may not be the same as those shown in the graphic.

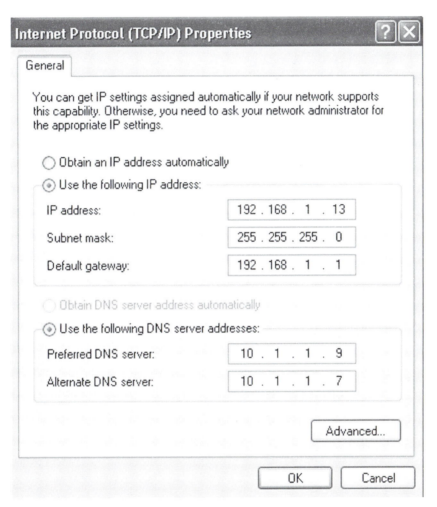

Figure 4-3: Internet Protocol (TCP/IP) Properties dialog box

6. Select the **Advanced** button in the lower right corner of the box. Select the **DNS** tab from the top of the **Advanced TCP/IP Settings** dialog box (see Figure 4-4). You may see different settings than in the graphic.

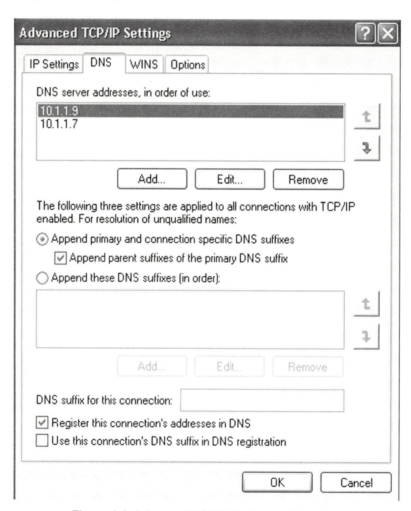

Figure 4-4: Advanced TCP/IP Settings dialog box

7. Notice that there is a question mark **(?)** in the upper right corner. Select this question mark and then click the sentence **DNS server addresses, in order of use.**

8. What does the pop-up dialog box tell you about the DNS entries?

_____

_____

_____

9. Select the question mark (**?**) again and click **Append primary and connection specific DNS suffixes**. Look at the information in the pop-up dialog box. Explain the meaning of this setting.

_____

_____

_____

10. Now that you have examined the default settings, how will you determine if your system should be configured to **Obtain DNS server IP addresses automatically** or if you will manually enter the DNS server IP addresses?

_____

_____

_____

Project 4.3	Installing DNS on a Windows Server 2003 Computer
Overview	In this project you install the DNS service on your Windows Server 2003 system. DNS is required if you are installing Active Directory; however, Active Directory is not required for the DNS service. If you do plan to install Active Directory, then your DNS server can take advantage of the fault tolerance and security features available for Active Directory domain controllers.
	By installing Active Directory on a server, you promote that server to the role of a domain controller. The installation process looks for a DNS server authoritative for the domain you specify and if one cannot be located, you have the option of installing DNS on the server. Once you have installed Active Directory with DNS, you have two options for storing and replicating your zones: standard zone storage, which uses a text-based file and is located in the **<systemroot>\System32\Dns** folder or Active Directory-integrated zone storage, which uses the Active Directory database. These zones are stored in the Active Directory tree under the domain or application directory partition. Each directory-integrated zone is stored in a dnsZone container object.
	You should also be aware that there are also some differences between the way Windows 2000 Server DNS and Windows Server 2003 DNS function. The Active Directory structure on a domain controller contains three directory partitions: configuration, schema, and domain. A partition is a data structure that enables Active Directory to differentiate between types of replication. A directory partition is also called the "_naming context_". Domain controllers in the same forest but in different domains share the same configuration and schema data, but they do not share the same domain data.
	Windows 2000 Server Active Directory-integrated zones store DNS zone data in the _domain naming context_ (DNC) partition of Active Directory.

However, for Windows Server 2003, application directory partitions enable storage and replication of the DNS zones stored in the *non-domain naming context* (NDNC) partition of Active Directory. Every object created in the domain naming context, is replicated to all the global catalog(s) in the domain, but in Windows Server 2003 application directory partitions store the DNS data. This significantly reduces the number of objects normally stored in the global catalog. An application directory partition is replicated to all DNS servers in the forest.

There are a number of advantages to storing DNS zone data in Active Directory. They include the following:

- Multimaster update: For the standard zone storage model, a single DNS server is authoritative a zone, making it a single fixed point of failure. If this one server is not available, update requests from DNS clients fail. With directory-integrated storage, dynamic updates to DNS are conducted based upon a multimaster update model meaning that any authoritative DNS server, such as a domain controller running a DNS server, is designated as a primary source for the zone. Because the master copy of the zone is maintained in the Active Directory database, which is fully replicated to all domain controllers, the zone can be updated by any of the DNS servers.

- Zone replication and synchronization: New domain controllers automatically replicate and synchronize DNS zone data.

- Zone administration: By integrating DNS into Active Directory, you streamline database replication planning. There is no need to plan complex replication structures. By merging the two, you can view them together as a single entity.

- Faster directory replication: Replication in Active Directory is faster and more efficient than standard DNS replication.

Windows Server 2003 includes a DNS auto configuration process, where the dcpromo command-line utility (Active Directory Installation Wizard) enables you to enter specific information for your DNS structure.

This utility will configure DNS if your server has a single network connection; if the same set of preferred and alternate DNS servers are to be used; and if the preferred DNS servers are specified only on one connection. You can configure the local DNS server to forward queries to the DNS server currently specified as the preferred and alternate DNS servers.

Outcomes	After completing this project, you will know how to: ▲ plan a simple DNS structure ▲ install the DNS server service on a Windows 2003 Server computer ▲ plan a simple DNS structure
What you'll need	To complete this project, you will need:

	▲ a Windows XP/2000 client computer or a Windows Server 2003/2000 Server computer connected to a network
Completion time	10 minutes
Precautions	None

■ Part A: Install DNS on a Windows Server 2003 computer and plan a simple DNS structure

There are several ways to install DNS depending on how you intend to use this service.

Option I: You can install DNS on your server <u>without</u> installing Active Directory:

1. Turn on the computer and log on as an Administrator

2. Select **Start**. Click **Control Panel**, and select **Add or Remove Programs**, and **Add/Remove Windows Components**. Highlight **Networking Services** and then select the **Details** button (see Figure 4-5).

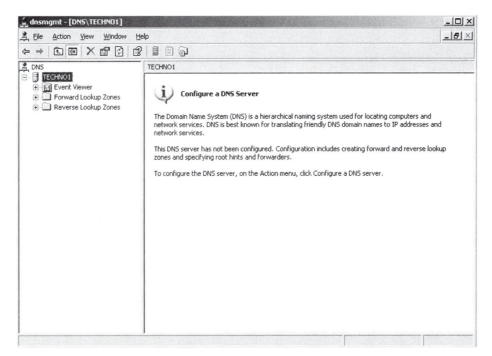

Figure 4-5: Networking Services dialog box

3. Check the box in front of **Domain Name System (DNS)** and select **OK** Once the DNS server is installed you can open **Administrative Tools**, and select **DNS** to manage the service (see Figure 4-6).

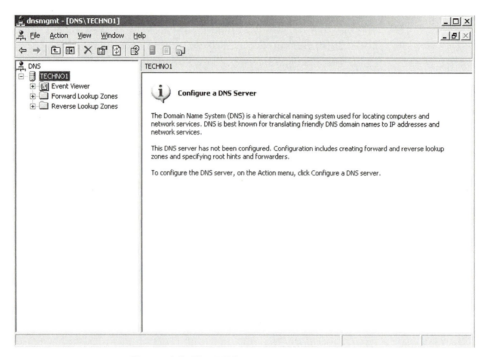

Figure 4-6: The DNS Management console

Option II: Install DNS <u>with</u> Active Directory:

1. Turn on the computer and log on as Administrator.

2. Select **Start,** then **Administrative Tools**. Select **Configure Your Server Wizard** (see Figure 4-7). (You can also use the **Active Directory Installation Wizard** to install or remove Active Directory. If you have already installed Windows Server 2003 without Active Directory by opening the **Start** menu, selecting **Run**, and typing **dcpromo**.)

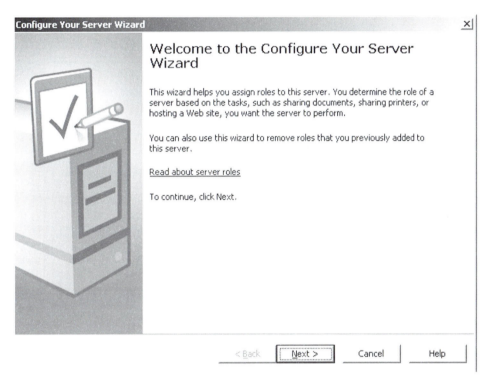

Figure 4-7: The Configure Your Server Wizard welcome screen

3. You will be asked to select either a **Typical configuration for a first server** or a **Custom configuration.** Select **Typical** (see Figure 4-8) and then click **Next**.

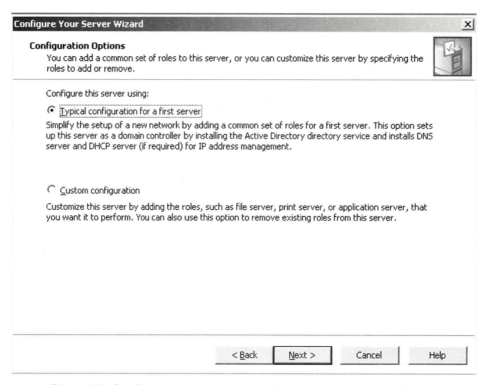

Figure 4-8: Configuration options in the Configure Your Server Wizard

4. Enter the domain name you have chosen (see Figure 4-9). Notice that Figure 4-9 shows **.local**.

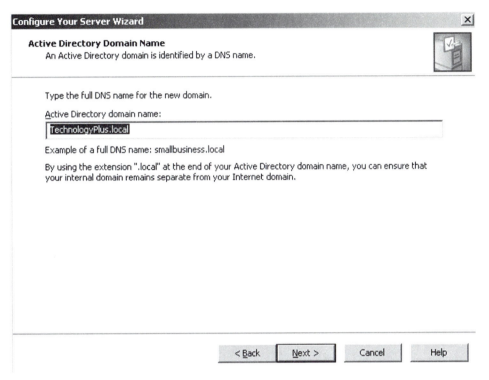

Figure 4-9: Choosing an Active Directory domain name

5. If you were installing DNS in a production environment, you would carefully plan the domain name space. Microsoft recommends that your planning include the following questions:

   • Have you previously chosen and registered a DNS domain name for use on the Internet?

   • Are you going to set up DNS servers on a private network or the Internet?

   • Are you going to use DNS to support your use of Active Directory?

   • What naming requirements do you need to follow when choosing DNS domain names for computers?

For this project you may enter your own name with the **.local** domain.

6. The next screen asks if you want to modify the NetBIOS name, which is derived from the domain name.

7. Next, you are asked to give the IP address of a DNS server that will resolve queries not in this server's local zone called a **forwarder** (see Figure 4-10). Select **Yes** if you know the IP addresses of your ISP's DNS servers or you may want to ask the network administrator on your local network.

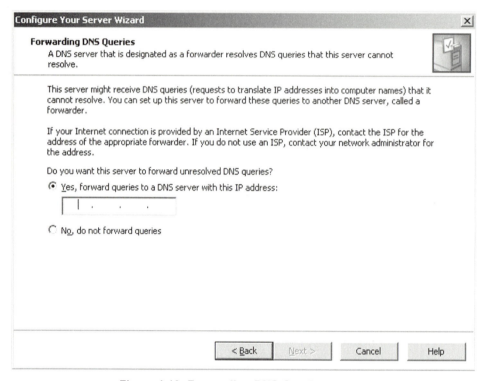

Figure 4-10: Forwarding DNS Queries screen

8. The next screen summarizes the selections you have made (see Figure 4-11). Notice that DHCP, Active Directory and DNS are all on this list of services that will be installed.

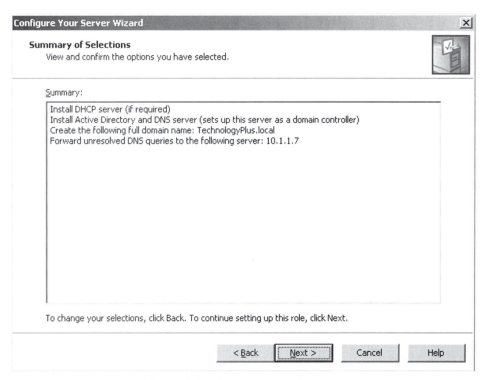

Figure 4-11: Summary of Selections

9. Once the system has installed Active Directory with the DNS service, the system will reboot and you will be asked to log in.

10. Log in as Administrator, select **Start**, then **Administrative Tools**. You should see DNS on the list that displays. Select **DNS**.

■ Part B: View DNS properties

1. The DNS management snap-in displays showing **dnsmgmt** and the server name in the title bar (see Figure 4-12). Select **Action** on the menu bar and then **Properties**.

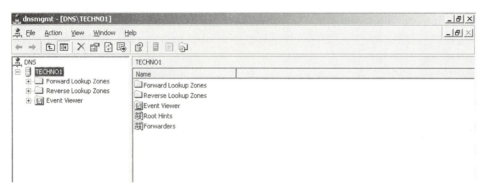

Figure 4-12: The DNS Management console

2. The **Properties** dialog box for the DNS server has a number of tabs at the top. The **Interfaces** tab shows the IP addresses the DNS server will respond to (see Figure 4-13).

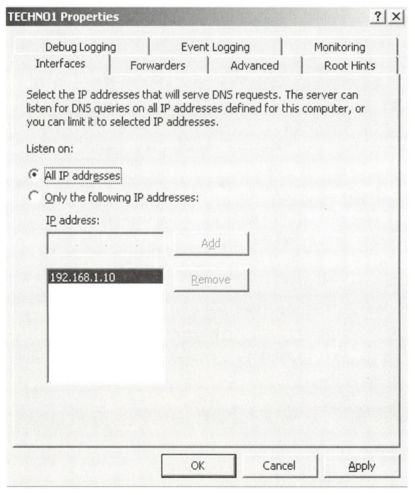

Figure 4-13: The Interfaces tab in the DNS Server Properties dialog box

3. What is the default setting?

_____

4. Select the **Root Hints** tab in the **DNS Server Properties** dialog box (see Figure 4-14).

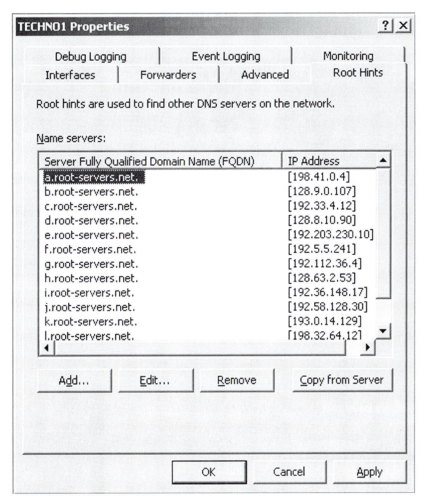

Figure 4-14: The Root Hints tab in the DNS Server Properties dialog box

5. What are the root hints entries used for? How many are there? Why are these called root _hints_?

_____

6. Select the **Forwarders** tab in the **DNS Server Properties** dialog box (see Figure 4-15).

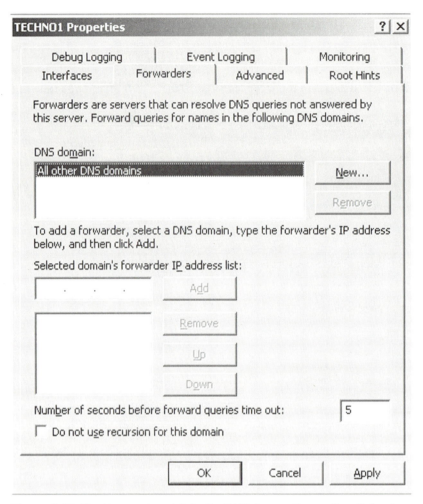

Figure 4-15: The Forwarders tab in the DNS Server Properties dialog box

7. Why would configuring DNS forwarders speed up resolutions?

8. Select the **Event Logging** tab in the **Properties** dialog box (see Figure 4-16).

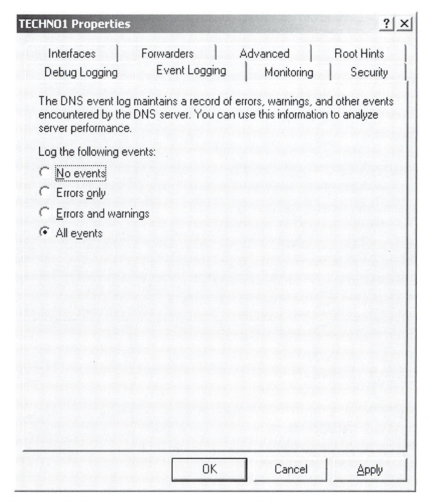

Figure 4-16: The Event Logging tab in the DNS Server Properties dialog box

9. The DNS service can be configured to monitor DNS events such as errors and warnings. The default setting logs all events. Where can you view this log information?

_____

_____

_____

Project 4.4	Configuring and Managing DNS
Overview	Now that DNS is installed, you will use the DNS management console to configure, manage and monitor DNS on your system.
Outcomes	After completing this project, you will know how to: ▲ use the Configure a DNS Server Wizard ▲ create a primary zone ▲ configure dynamic updates ▲ review zone transfers ▲ practice using the nslookup utility
What you'll need	To complete this project, you will need: ▲ a Windows Server 2003 computer connected to a local network
Completion time	30 minutes
Precautions	Using the Configure DNS wizard may create inappropriate settings. For production DNS servers, you will want to do the configurations manually.

■ Part A: Configure DNS

1. To configure DNS, click **Start,** select **Administrative Tools** and then select **DNS**. The **DNS** management console will display. (Note: For this first installation, you can use the wizard, however once you understand how to configure DNS zones, you will want to create them using the New Zone Wizard.)

2. Be sure the DNS server name is highlighted and select **Action** from the menu bar; next select **Configure a DNS Server**. The **Configure a DNS Server Wizard** will display showing the step-by-step creation of a DNS zone (Figure 4-17).

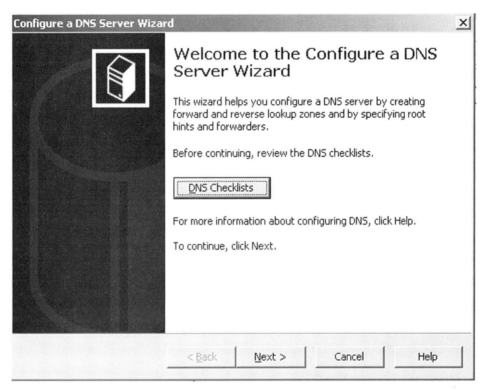

Figure 4-17: The Configure a DNS Server Wizard welcome screen

3. Select **Create a Forward Lookup Zone** (Figure 4-18).

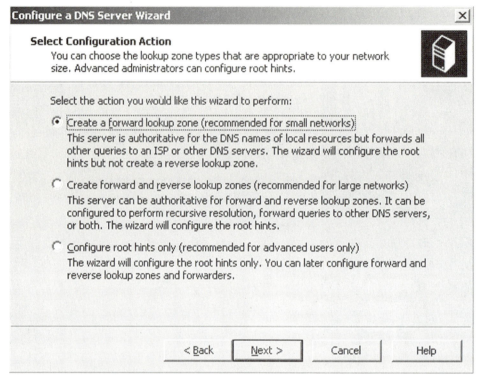

Figure 4-18: Creating a forward lookup zone

4. Select **This server maintains the zone** to create a primary forward lookup zone on your DNS server (Figure 4-19).

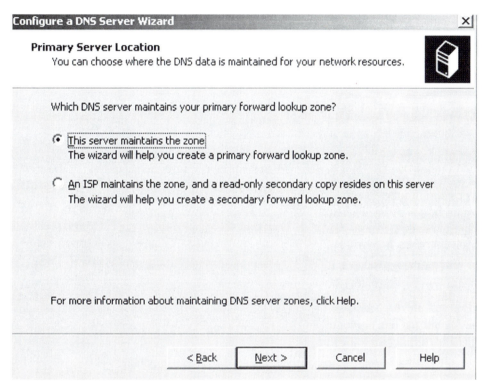

Figure 4-19: Creating a primary forward lookup zone

5. You then give the zone a name (Figure 4-20). Since the DNS service can manage a number of DNS primary and secondary zones on the same server, each zone needs a different name.

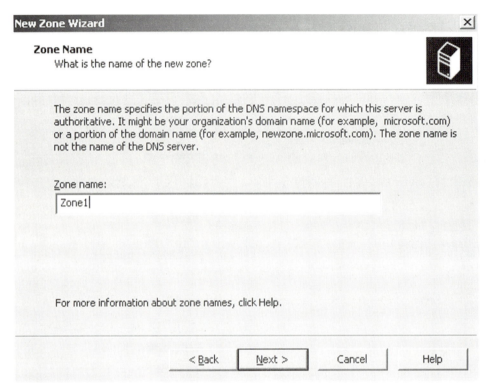

Figure 4-20: Naming the zone

6. What is the difference between a primary and a secondary DNS server?

_____

_____

_____

7. What are the benefits of creating a DNS zone that is Active Directory-Integrated (ADI)?

_____

_____

_____

8. The next configuration is for Dynamic Updates. Because clients obtain IP addresses from DHCP servers their IP addresses may dynamically change. Active Directory can be integrated with DNS to enable clients to register their current IP addresses with the DNS server automatically (Figure 4-21).

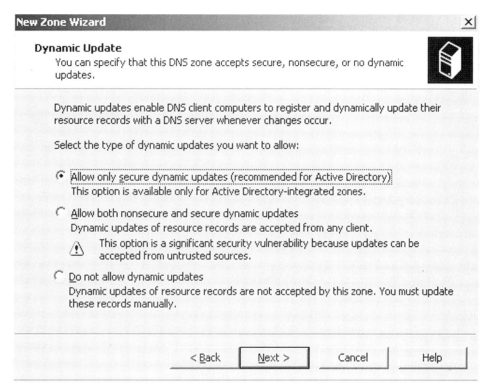

Figure 4-21: Dynamic Update

9. What kind of DNS entries can be made by DHCP clients (or the DHCP server) if the zone is configured for dynamic updates?

_____

_____

_____

10. The last configuration enters the IP addresses for DNS servers that will be forwarded queries that can not be resolved by this zone (Figure 4-22**)**.

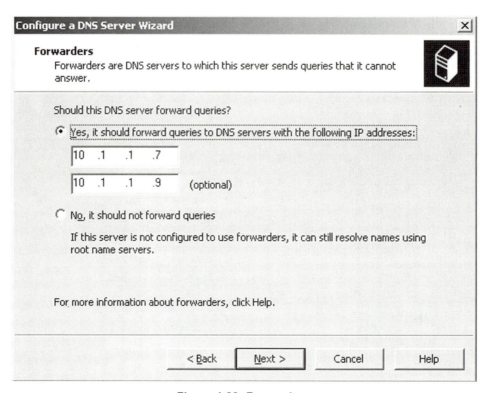

Figure 4-22: Forwarders

11. The final screen displays the summary of the settings you made (Figure 4-23).

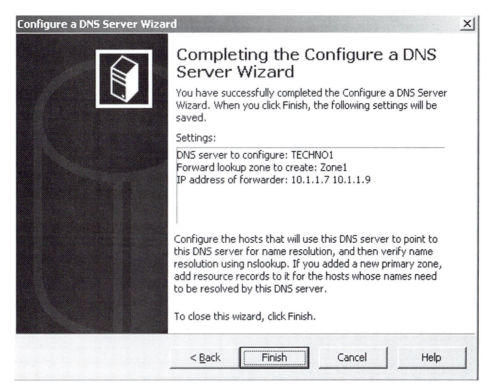

Figure 4-23: Completing the Configure a DNS Server Wizard

12. Why you might want to add specific forwarders to your DNS server?

_____

_____

■ Part B: Zone transfers and replication

The primary DNS server gathers resource records in zones and responds to queries; however the DNS service also includes a process to secure those records by sharing the information with another server. This is called a zone transfer. For Active Directory domains, the zone data is updated between domain controllers and is called replication.

Since the zone's primary DNS server is the only one that can make changes to resource records, adding secondary DNS servers enables those servers to answer requests from their read-only copy of the zone. When the primary DNS server enters a change, it adds or increments the serial number on the zone. Periodically, the secondary DNS servers ask the primary to send the SOA record that contains the serial number. This notifies the secondary servers that a change has been made and they then ask the primary to replicate.

1. Open the **DNS** management console. Highlight the **DNS zone** and select **Action** from the menu (or just use the right-click, or click the Properties icon on the tool bar). Select **Properties**. Choose the **Zone Transfers** tab (Figure 4-24).

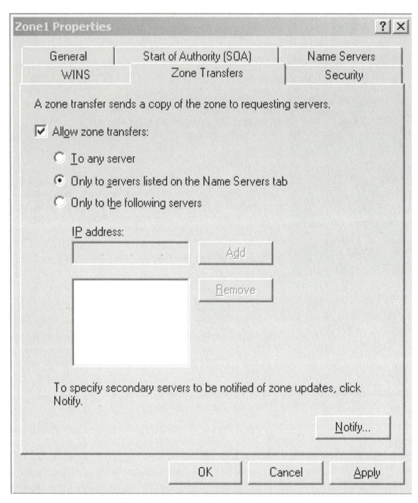

Figure 4-24: The Zone Transfers tab in the Zone Properties dialog box

2. Why would you want to indicate only certain servers for zone transfers?

_____

_____

3. Select the **Start of Authority (SOA)** tab (Figure 4-25).

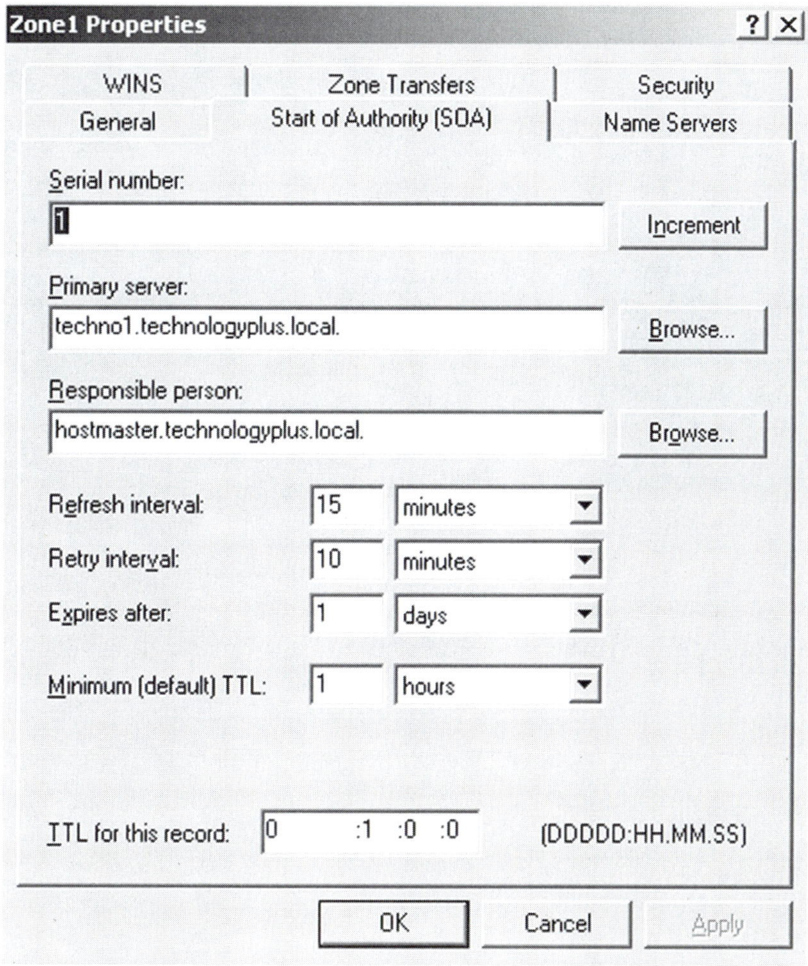

Figure 4-25: The Start of Authority tab in the Zone Properties dialog box

4. What are the default settings for the **Refresh interval**? What happens when the 15 minutes is up?

_____

_____

_____

■ Part C: Using the nslookup utility

1. Open the **DNS** management console. Highlight the DNS server and open the **Action** menu. Select **Launch nslookup**. (You can also use the Command Prompt to start nslookup.)

2. Nslookup displays in the Command Prompt window. Enter a question mark (**?**) next to the greater-than sign (Figure 4-26).

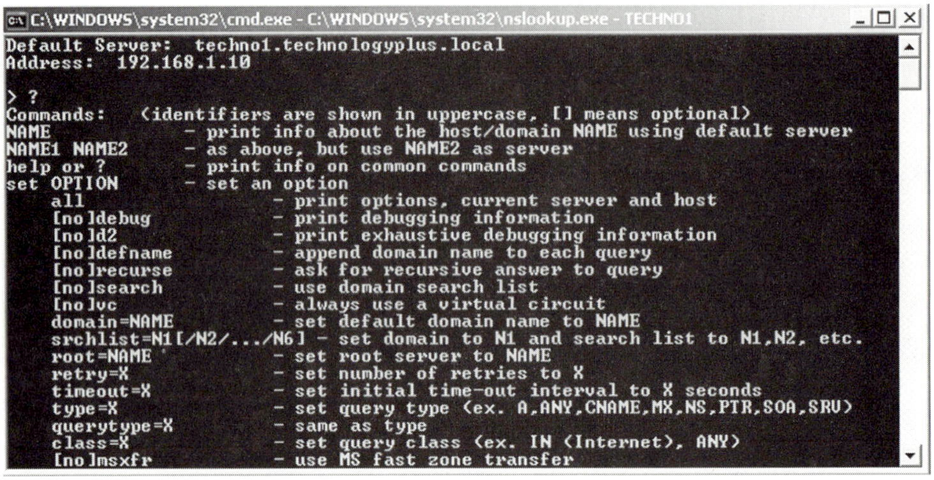

Figure 4-26: The nslookup command

3. Enter **all** at the greater-than sign.

4. What did the utility display when you entered the question mark? What displayed when you entered **all**?

_____

_____

_____

Note: You can use the nslookup utility to transfer a zone using the **ls** command.

Project 4.5	DNS Performance
Overview	Since so many clients depend on the DNS service, keeping it running in tip-top shape is an important administrative function.
Outcomes	After completing this project, you will know how to: ▲ monitor queries ▲ use debug logging ▲ use aging and scavenging
What you'll need	To complete this project, you will need: ▲ a Windows Server 2003 computer connected to a local network ▲ a client computer
Completion time	30 minutes
Precautions	None

■ Part A: Using DNS Monitoring

1. Open the **DNS** management console. Highlight the DNS server and open the **Action** menu. Select **Properties** to open the Properties dialog box, and then open the **Monitoring** tab (Figure 4-27). This tab allows you to manually test the DNS server.

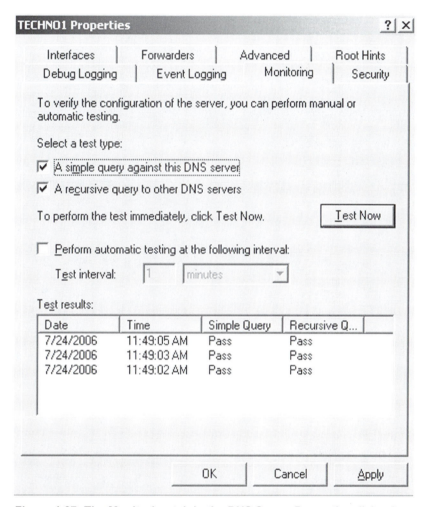

Figure 4-27: The Monitoring tab in the DNS Server Properties dialog box

2. Place a checkmark in the **A simple query against this DNS server**. Select the **Test Now** button. What was the result? Place a checkmark in the **A recursive query to other DNS servers.** Select the **Test Now** button. What was the result?

_____

_____

_____

■ Part B: Configure Debug Logging

1. Open the **DNS** management console. Highlight the DNS server and open the **Action** menu. Select **Properties** and then open the **Debug Logging** tab (Figure 4-28) . This tab enables you to record packets sent and received by the DNS server.

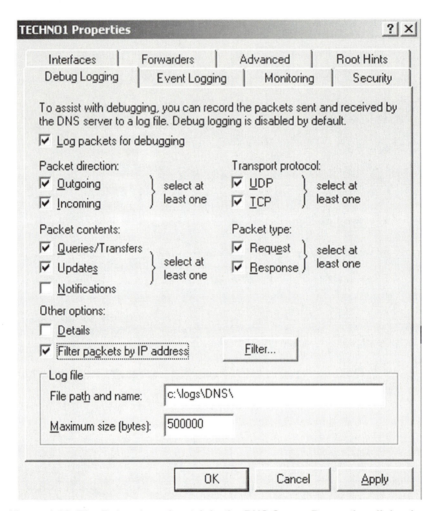

Figure 4-28: The Debug Logging tab in the DNS Server Properties dialog box

2. Select the checkmark for **Log packets for debugging**. You will need to create a folder and text file where the logs will be sent. Under **Log file**, **File path and name**: enter the path to your folder and text file. You can add entries to your log file by connecting to the server from your client and transferring a document. What information did you see in your log?

_____

_____

_____

■ Part C: Aging and Scavenging

1. Open the **DNS** management console. Highlight the DNS server and open the **Action** menu. Select **Set Aging/Scavenging for All Zones** (Figure 4-29).

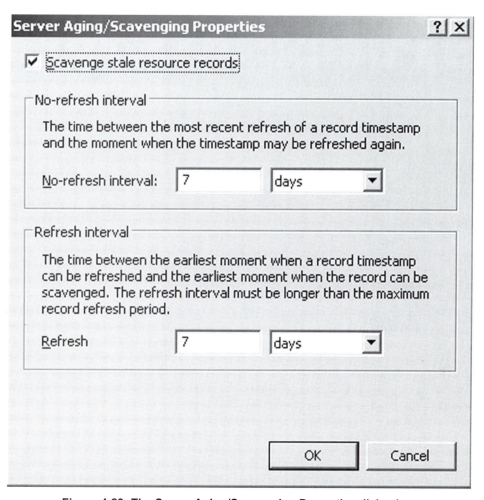

Figure 4-29: The Server Aging/Scavenging Properties dialog box

2. By default, what setting does the DNS server have for removing stale resource records?

_____

_____

_____

5
TROUBLESHOOTING NAME RESOLUTION

PROJECTS

Project 5.1	Examining Troubleshooting Tools and Utilities
Overview	You have installed DNS and WINS on your Windows Server 2003 system and now want to give name resolution a test run. Like most new technology toys, there may be a few parts you haven't figured out. You're going to need some tools.
	To review, both DNS and NetBIOS are name-to IP-address resolution schemes, however they do not use the same protocols or services – therefore each one has different tools or utilities for management and monitoring.
	Programs can use either computer names or host names, depending of the Application Programming Interface (API). An API is a set of routines, protocols, and components used to build a software program. The NetBIOS API allows for communication within the TCP/IP network environment, hence Microsoft's version is NetBIOS over TCP/IP (NBT). Software programs and services such as File and Print Sharing for Microsoft Networks use the NetBIOS API to refer to computer names.
	A network administrator must understand NetBIOS names and how they are resolved to troubleshoot resolution issues. If a NetBIOS name is not resolved using NetBIOS, the system will attempt resolution using DNS.
	With host name or DNS resolution, software programs are built to use the Windows Sockets (WinSock) API. A Web browser would be an example. WinSock enables applications to bind with ports and IP addresses on hosts. When packets are sent, the computer name is referenced.
	Both of these resolution systems have a number of steps. Once you are familiar with the tools and utilities used to view and manage resolution, you'll be able to follow these steps to diagnose problems.
Outcomes	After completing this project, you will know how to:
	▲ use nbtstat to view NetBIOS resolution
	▲ use nslookup and the DNS console to view DNS records
	▲ use ipconfig, ping, net view, net use, tracert and pathping
	▲ view Windows Server name tools, such as Network Monitor
What you'll need	To complete this project, you will need:
	▲ a Windows Server 2003 computer with DNS and Network Monitor installed and connected to a network
	▲ a client computer
Completion time	60 minutes
Precautions	None

■ Part A: View the NetBIOS name for the Windows Server 2003 computer.

Each Windows Server 2003 computer has both a NetBIOS name and a host name. For the following activities, we need to know the NetBIOS name for this computer. (It is also called the computer name.)

1. Open the **Control Panel** and select **System**. The **System Properties** dialog box opens
2. Select the **Computer Name** tab (Figure 5-1). Look at the **Full computer name**. This computer name, **techno1,** has been added to the domain name.

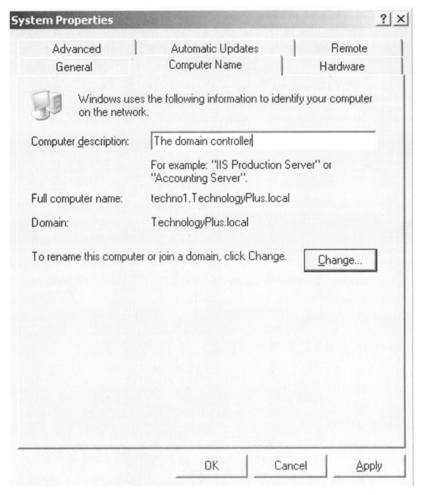

Figure 5-1: The Computer Name tab in the System Properties dialog box

3. Notice the **Change** button. If your system is configured as a domain controller, if you click the Change button you are given a warning when you try to change the computer name (Figure 5-2). This is because the computer name is tied into Active Directory.

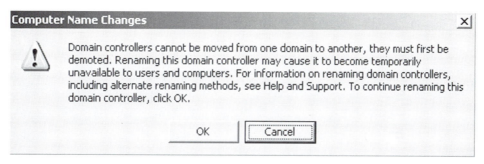

Figure 5-2: Computer Name Change warning

4. Another quick way to view the computer name is to select **Manage Your Server** in the **Control Panel**. The computer name is shown at the top under the title.

■ **Part B: Check the network connection using Repair**

1. Microsoft provides a quick way to check your Windows XP and Windows Server 2003 network connection. Open the **Control Panel** and double-click **Network Connections**, then right-click **Local Area Connection**. Select **Status**. The **Local Area Connection Status** dialog box opens. You will see **Duration** at the top which should be showing seconds incrementing the time the connection has been running. Select the **Support** tab (Figure 5-3) and then click the **Repair** button.

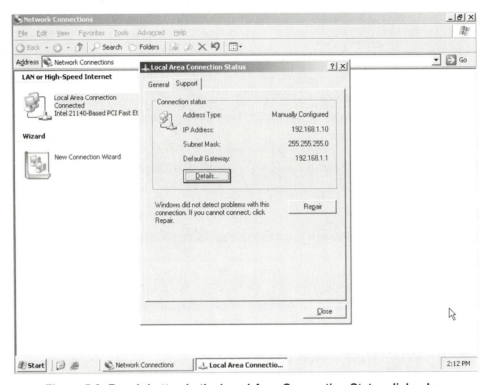

Figure 5-3: Repair button in the Local Area Connection Status dialog box

2. There are a number of tasks this Repair check performs including refreshing the DHCP IPv4 address; flushing the ARP cache; flushing and reloading the DNS client resolver cache with entries from the Hosts file; re-registering DNS names; flushing and reloading the NetBIOS name cache; and releasing and re-registering the NetBIOS names with WINS.

3. What reply did you receive from this Repair check?

_____

_____

4. If you disconnect your network cable from your NIC, what displays when you right-click your network connection?

_____

_____

While this is quick and easy way to check the status of a network connection, you may need to use a few more specialized tools to solve name resolution problems.

■ Part C: View NetBIOS with nbtstat

We have used **nbtstat** before; however, let's take a closer look. You can find the NetBIOS name by using **nbtstat**.

1. Open a **Command Prompt** window, enter **nbtstat** and press **Enter** (Figure 5-4).

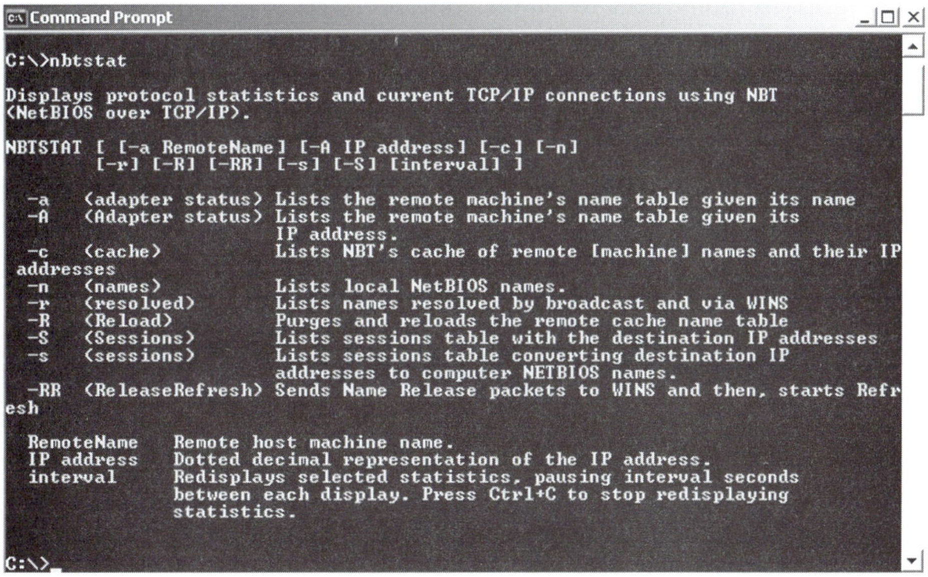

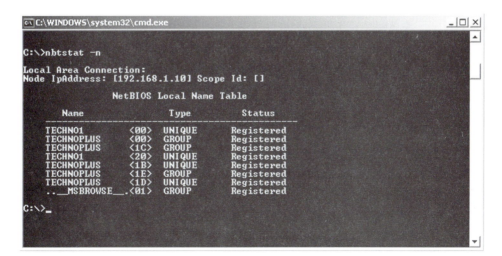

Figure 5-4: Using nbtstat

2. Enter **nbtstat -n** and press **Enter** Figure 5-5). **Note**: By using the function key **F3**, you won't have to retype it.

Figure 5-5: Using nbtstat -n

3. The **-n** option displays the Local Area Connection which lists local NetBIOS names for this computer. This is the **NetBIOS Local Name Table**, or it is sometimes called the NetBIOS name cache. The table has three columns: **Name**, **Type** and **Status**. Looking carefully at the first line in Figure 5-5, the NetBIOS name is shown. NetBIOS names are 16 bytes long, however the actual name can be only 15 bytes because the last byte is reserved for the job or service the computer performs. That's why you will see multiple entries for the same NetBIOS name in the table. The <00> indicates this computer is registered for the Workstation service, sometimes called the redirector. The Type is UNIQUE meaning that there cannot be another computer registered exactly this way on the network. GROUP can have multiple entries. Finally the status is given for each entry indicating whether the name is registered or unregistered with the network. When a computer boots up, it registers its NetBIOS name(s) either by broadcast or by sending a direct message to a WINS server.

4. You can also use **nbtstat** to list the NetBIOS name table of a remote computer; to display the contents of the NetBIOS name cache of this or a remote computer; to manually load the LMHOSTS file with a #PRE option; to list NetBT session statistics; and to release and refresh NetBIOS names in WINS.

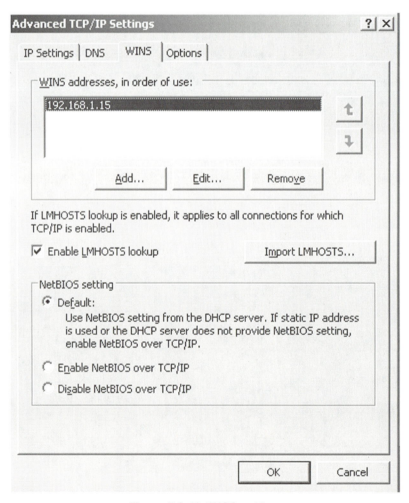

Figure 5-6: NetBIOS setting

5. Where is the NetBIOS Local Name Table stored? Where is the LMHOSTS file stored? What **nbtstat** option lets you register a NetBIOS name change?

_____

_____

_____

_____

_____

6. Name the steps used by default to resolve NetBIOS names by a Windows XP computer on a network using WINS.

_____

_____

_____

_____

_____

7. If you enter **nbtstat –a** and then add the IP address of the local computer, what other information displays with the NetBIOS Name Table?

_____

_____

_____

8. If you enter **nbtstat –r** what does the Resolved by Name Server and Registered by Name Server mean?

_____

_____

_____

9. What might be one cause if a specific XP computer cannot resolve NetBIOS names and it is configured exactly like all the other XP's on the network?

_____

_____

_____

■ Part D: View DNS with nslookup and the DNS management console

A network administrator should have a good understanding of the **nslookup** tool (Figure 5-7) because it can provide valuable DNS information. It can help you view DNS queries from both a client resolver and a server; perform zone transfers; and display resource records on DNS servers. By default, it will display the DNS server information shown in the current computer's TCP/IP configuration, however, you can get information from other DNS servers by providing the name or IP address.

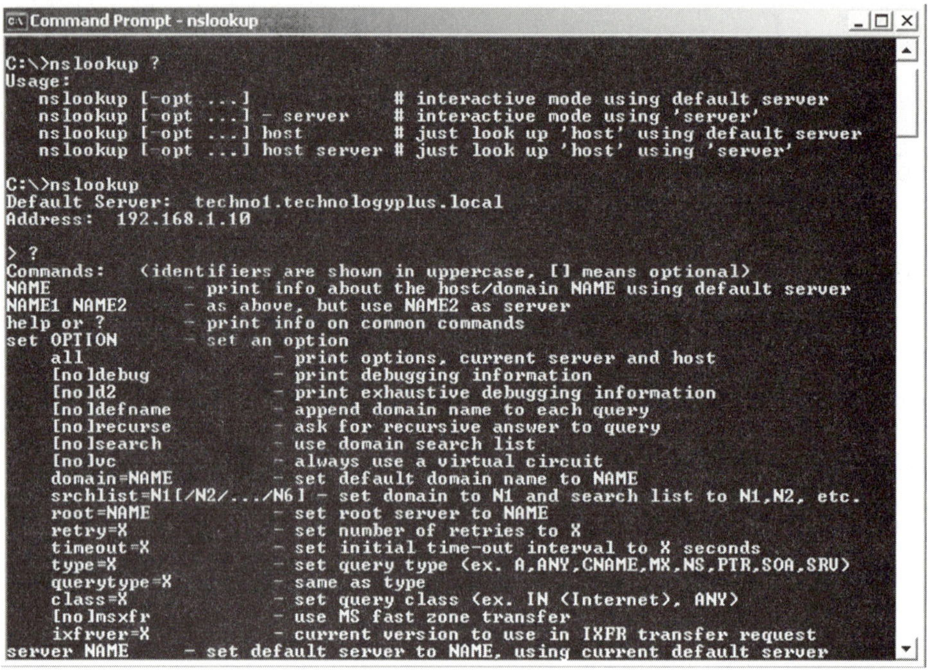

Figure 5-7: Using nslookup

There are two **nslookup** modes: interactive and non-interactive. If you only need a single piece of information, non-interactive mode works best. The syntax for a query is:

nslookup [[-option …] [computer to find]] | - [server]

You will know you are in interactive mode because the Command Prompt symbol will change to a greater-than sign. You can get back to the Command Prompt by typing Exit or Ctrl C.

1. Open the **Command Prompt** window.

2. Enter **nslookup,** then enter the IP address of your DNS server and press **Enter**. This returns the Fully Qualified Domain Name of the server with that IP address.

3. Now try out interactive mode. Enter **nslookup** without a name or IP address after it.

4. What docs just entering **nslookup** return? What happens if you enter a question mark at the greater-than sign?

_____

_____

_____

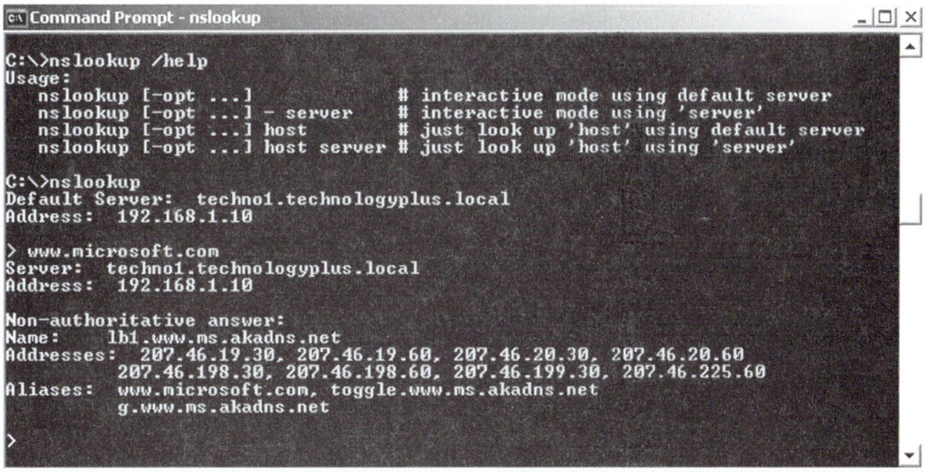

```
C:\>nslookup /help
Usage:
   nslookup [-opt ...]              # interactive mode using default server
   nslookup [-opt ...] - server     # interactive mode using 'server'
   nslookup [-opt ...] host         # just look up 'host' using default server
   nslookup [-opt ...] host server  # just look up 'host' using 'server'

C:\>nslookup
Default Server:  techno1.technologyplus.local
Address:  192.168.1.10

> www.microsoft.com
Server:  techno1.technologyplus.local
Address:  192.168.1.10

Non-authoritative answer:
Name:     lb1.www.ms.akadns.net
Addresses:  207.46.19.30, 207.46.19.60, 207.46.20.30, 207.46.20.60
            207.46.198.30, 207.46.198.60, 207.46.199.30, 207.46.225.60
Aliases:  www.microsoft.com, toggle.www.ms.akadns.net
          g.www.ms.akadns.net

>
```

Figure 5-8: Using nslookup in interactive mode

5. When you are in interactive mode and you enter www.microsoft.com what is returned?

_____

_____

■ **Part E: View DNS records using the DNS console**

1. Open the **DNS** console.

2. Select the plus sign on the left of the DNS server name and the plus sign **for Forward Lookup Zones**. Highlight the DNS server name and then right-click (Figure 5-9).

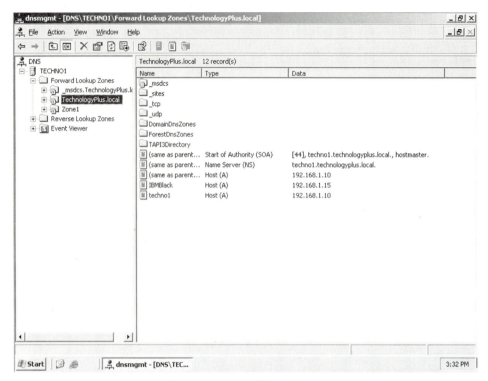

Figure 5-9: The DNS console

3. What are two ways to clear the DNS server's cache from within the DNS console?

_____

_____

4. Highlight the zone name and then highlight the Host (A) record of one of the computers listed. Why does the DNS server have a Host (A) record?

_____

_____

■ **Part F: View command-line tools: ipconfig, ping, NET, netstat, tracert and pathping**

1. Open the **Command Prompt** window.
2. Enter **ipconfig /?** Look carefully at the options available. Do you notice any settings for managing NetBIOS or DNS? **Note:** Be sure to add a space between the **ipconfig** command and the front slash questionmark **/?**. Also notice that some options begin with a hyphen and some with a front slash.
3. Enter **ping /?** View the options available. Notice any settings for NetBIOS or DNS.
4. Enter **NET /?** View the options available.

5. Enter **netstat /?** View the options available.

6. Enter **tracert /?** View the options available.

7. Enter **pathping /?** View the options available.

8. You have used the **ipconfig /all** utility to view network configuration information. Which two **ipconfig** utility options allow you to manage the local DNS cache?

_____

_____

9. Enter **ipconfig** and use the option to purge the DNS cache. Then enter the option to show the cache. Next, minimize the **Command Prompt** and open your browser. Go to several websites and then close your browser. Go back to the **Command Prompt** and enter **ipconfig** with the option to show the cache again. What has changed?

_____

_____

■ **Part G: View Network Monitor and other packet analyzers**

1. Click **Start**, select **Administrative Tools**, and then select **Network Monitor**. Open the **Capture** menu and then select **Start** to begin a capture. Go to your client computer and select **My Network Places** and then **Microsoft Windows Network** and attempt to connect to a share on the Windows server. If you are successful, you can copy a file to the client. Stop the capture in Network Monitor by selecting **Stop** and **View**.

2. Examine the frames you have captured. You can also save your capture.

3. Notice in Figure 5-10 that the client **IBMBlack** is making a session request using NBT protocol (NetBIOS over TCP/IP). Notice the line **Calling Name = IBMBlack**.

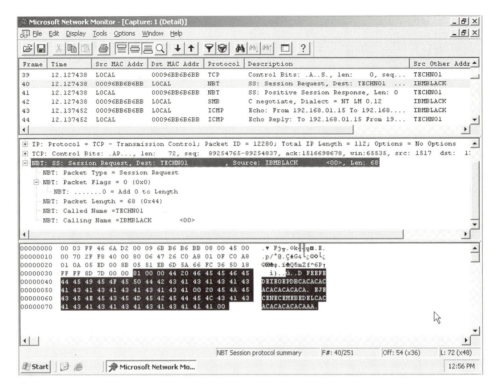

Figure 5-10: Network Monitor capture detail

4. What does the <00> mean after the name IBMBlack?

_____

_____

Project 5.2	Investigating Failures
Overview	Before you set off to solve network name resolution problems with all of the tools and utilities discussed in Project 5.1, you want to keep in mind the various processes that impact network traffic. You don't want to reconfigure your DNS server's zones only to find out that you have entered a static IP address incorrectly.
Outcomes	After completing this project, you will know how to: ▲ recognize where to begin when a name resolution failure occurs ▲ evaluate the output of resolution tools ▲ understand events in Event Viewer
What you'll need	To complete this project, you will need: ▲ a Windows Server 2003 computer with DNS installed and connected to a network

	▲ a client computer
Completion time	15 minutes
Precautions	None

■ Part A: Recognize where to begin

It might seem like you know the answer to your resolution problem but first, take a few minutes to gather a little information.

1. Begin your investigation by carefully viewing the current configuration and writing down what you see. Don't change any settings until you have documented the current set up.

2. Use **ipconfig** and **nslookup** and write down the information currently showing.

3. Open **Network Monitor** and do a capture of the traffic between the client computer and server. Try to determine if the client is having connection or resolution problems. Use **ping** to see what computers respond with a reply to the client computer.

4. If you sit at a client computer and can ping the IP address of another computer on the local network, what basic information do you know?

   _____

   _____

5. If you sit at a client computer and can ping the computer name of another computer on the local network, what does this tell you?

   _____

   _____

6. If you sit at a client computer and view **Microsoft Windows Network** and do not see a specific server listed, what might cause this problem?

   _____

   _____

■ Part B: Evaluate the output

1. Begin narrowing down the possible causes of the problem one at a time.

2. Take a careful look at any error messages. What does the error say or is there an error displaying? Be sure you entered the command and option properly.

3. For server errors, look at **Event Viewer** and possibly set up log files.

4. Review Figure 5-11. This warning indicates a DNS configuration error.

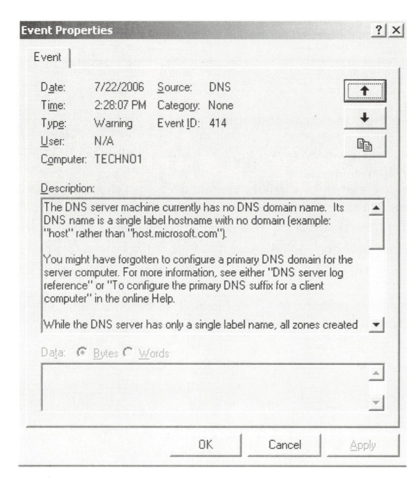

Figure 5-11: A warning in the Event Properties dialog box

5. What would you suggest doing to solve this particular error?

_____

_____

Project 5.3	Diagnosing and Monitoring Name Resolution Errors
Overview	Being a successful network administrator can be challenging, requiring a lot of trial and error. These activities create NetBIOS and DNS errors so you can see the effect.
Outcomes	After completing this project, you will know how to: ▲ recognize how configuration errors impact NetBIOS and DNS name resolution

	▲ use tools and utilities to examine configurations for errors
What you'll need	To complete this project, you will need: ▲ a Windows Server 2003 computer with DNS installed and connected to a network ▲ a client computer
Completion time	20 minutes
Precautions	None

■ Part A: Create a NetBIOS failure

1. Open the **WINS console**. The WINS console displays the name of the WINS server. Highlight **Active Registrations**. Right click and select **Display Records**. If there were hundreds of WINS entries you would want to filter this list. Select the **Find Now** button at the bottom. Look through this list and select a client computer's Host (A) record and right click. Select **Properties**.

2. You will enter an incorrect IP address in this record, leaving the computer name the same. For example, Figure 5-12 shows the IBMBlack computer with an IP address of 192.168.1.**25**. The local configuration for this computer is statically set for 192.168.1.**15**.

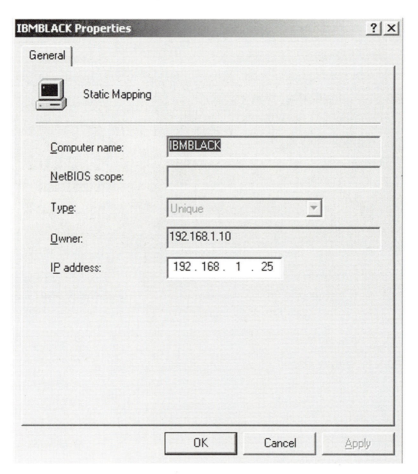

Figure 5-12: Wrong IP address

3.   Next you will open the **Command Prompt** window and investigate the result of this error. Enter **nbtstat** −c and press **Enter**.

4. Look carefully at Figure 5-13.

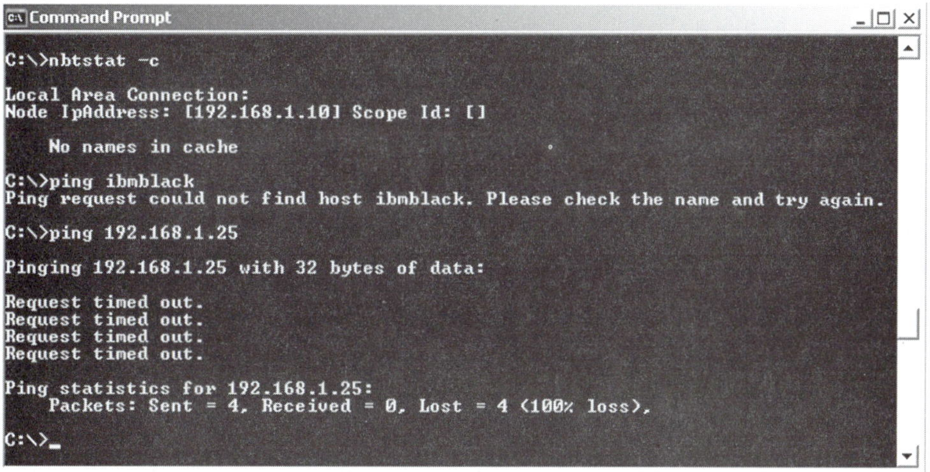
Command Prompt
C:\>nbtstat -c
Local Area Connection:
Node IpAddress: [192.168.1.10] Scope Id: []
No names in cache
C:\>ping ibmblack
Ping request could not find host ibmblack. Please check the name and try again.
C:\>ping 192.168.1.25
Pinging 192.168.1.25 with 32 bytes of data:
Request timed out.
Request timed out.
Request timed out.
Request timed out.
Ping statistics for 192.168.1.25:
Packets: Sent = 4, Received = 0, Lost = 4 (100% loss),
C:\>_

Figure 5-13: Using nbtstat -c

6. Describe what you see.

____

____

____

7. Using nbtstat, you may try troubleshooting the error by entering the computer's IP address 192.168.1.**15** (Figure 5-14).

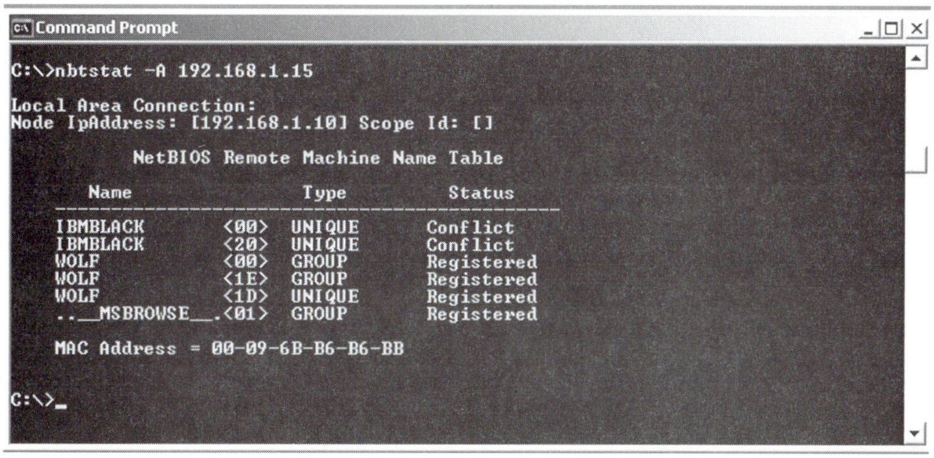
Command Prompt
C:\>nbtstat -A 192.168.1.15
Local Area Connection:
Node IpAddress: [192.168.1.10] Scope Id: []
NetBIOS Remote Machine Name Table
Name Type Status
IBMBLACK <00> UNIQUE Conflict
IBMBLACK <20> UNIQUE Conflict
WOLF <00> GROUP Registered
WOLF <1E> GROUP Registered
WOLF <1D> UNIQUE Registered
..__MSBROWSE__.<01> GROUP Registered
MAC Address = 00-09-6B-B6-B6-BB
C:\>_

Figure 5-14: Using nbtstat -A

7. With the 192.168.1.**25** IP address error configured in the WINS database, what does this query show?

_____

_____

_____

■ Part B: Create a DNS failure

1. Open the DNS console. Open the **Forward Lookup Zones** and open the zone name. Highlight the **NS record** for the zone. Right click and select **Properties**, then select **Edit**.

2. Edit the entry for the NS record or delete it. Clear the DNS cache. What tools would you use to verify this error?

_____

_____

_____

■ Part C: Troubleshoot common failures

As mentioned before, begin your investigation of name resolution failures by trying to determine if the problem is with NetBIOS or DNS. Gather information before making any changes to the configuration. Then, only make <u>one</u> configuration change at a time. Then check to see if the problem is resolved. Follow the resolution chain and if the name is not resolvable via nslookup, get verification from your ISP that there is not a problem with their DNS.

Project 5.4	Packet Analysis with Network Monitor
Overview	You have captured traffic using Network Monitor looking at the interaction between two computers. In this project a file is requested and sent from the server to the host.
Outcomes	After completing this project, you will know how to: ▲ capture network traffic using Network Monitor ▲ examine frames including the text sent
What you'll need	To complete this project, you will need: ▲ a Windows Server 2003 computer with DNS and Network Monitor

	installed and connected to a network ▲ a client computer
Completion time	20 minutes
Precautions	None

■ Part A: View Network Monitor traffic

Reviewing the actual traffic between two computers enables you to track communications, however it can be overwhelming.

1. Click **Start**, select **Administrative Tools**, and then select **Network Monitor**. This displays the **Capture** window. Minimize **Network Monitor**.

2. Next, click **Start**, point to **All Programs**, point to **Accessories**, and select **Notepad**. Create a file with a single line of text that you can identify in a frame (see Figure 5-15). Name your file and save it in the server's share.

Figure 5-15: Text in Notepad

3. Maximize **Network Monitor** again, open the Capture menu and select **Start**. Go back to your client computer and select **My Network Places** and then **Microsoft Windows Network** and attempt to connect to the share on the Windows server. When you see the file you created, copy it to your client computer.

4. Open the **Capture** menu again, and select **Stop and View**.

5. A careful review of the capture in Figure 5-16 shows two computers negotiating name resolution in order to create the packets required to request and send a file.

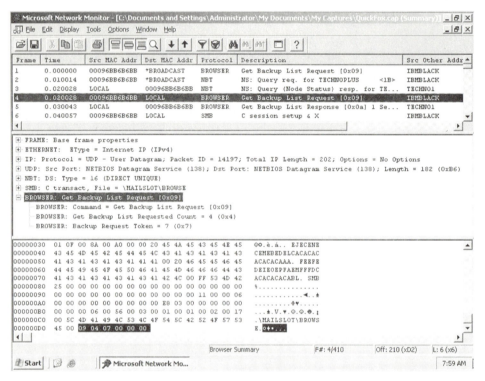

Figure 5-16: Capture in Network Monitor

6. Explain what has occurred in Figure 5-16. Is this request a broadcast? Was there a request prior to the one in Frame 4? Was there a response?

_____

_____

_____

7. Review Figure 5-17.

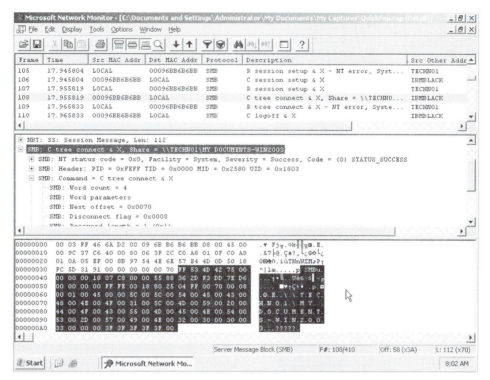

Figure 5-17

8. What is the name of the share?

_____

9. Review Figure 5-18.

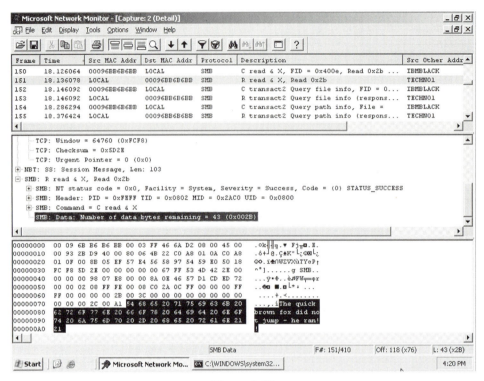

Figure 5-18

10. What is the status of Frame 151? What was the data that was sent?

Project 5.5	Packet Analysis with Ethereal or Etherpeek
Overview	You may want to investigate using a packet analyzer other than Network Monitor. There are numerous choices from vendors. Two examples are listed below. Ethereal, which is an open source packet analyzer and runs on Unix, Linux and Windows systems, is free to download and has some sample captures. You can find Ethereal at http://www.ethereal.com/. Etherpeek from Wildpackets is another protocol analyzer. You can find information about Etherpeek at: http://www.wildpackets.com/products/etherpeek/overview.
Outcomes	After completing this project, you will know how to: ▲ choose other packet analyzers ▲ examine packet analyzer features

What you'll need	To complete this project, you will need:
	▲ a computer with an Internet connection
Completion time	15 minutes
Precautions	None

■ Part A: Evaluate features of other packet analyzers

1. Go to http://www.ethereal.com/

2. Select the FAQ tab and then look for the question "Does Ethereal work on Windows XP?" What is the answer?

   _____

3. What is the current version of Ethereal? How many protocols can it analyze? List at least three features of Ethereal below.

   _____

   _____

   _____

4. Download Ethereal and then view sample captures at http://wiki.ethereal.com/SampleCaptures.

5. Review the information that you can find about Etherpeak at http://www.wildpackets.com/products/etherpeek/overview.

6. Compare and contrast the various features of Ethereal, Etherpeak and Network Monitor.

   _____

   _____

   _____

   _____

   _____

   _____

   _____

   _____

6
UNDERSTANDING DHCP RESOLUTION

PROJECTS

130

Project 6.1	Understanding DHCP
Overview	If you could be paid for all the hours that dynamic host configuration protocol (DHCP) has saved network administrators, this automatic configuration protocol would be worth a fortune. DHCP centralizes the process of handing out IP addresses so administrators do not have to sit down at each client computer on the network and configure the addresses manually.
	Another advantage of DHCP is the "dynamic" part, which means that if an IP address is handed out (actually it is called a *lease*) from a pool of addresses (called a *scope*) and if the computer doesn't use it for a specific amount of time, the lease expires and the IP address is free to be given to another computer. This conserves IP addresses.
	To use the DHCP service, you must install a DHCP server (or servers) on your network. Then, you need to authorize the server to assign valid IP addresses to clients. Next, on the DHCP server, you create scopes (from a range of valid IP addresses) that enable the server to lease the IP addresses in the scope to specific clients.
	Let's review the four-step DHCP process from the client's perspective. If the TCP/IP properties in the client computer have been configured to "Obtain an IP address automatically", it is considered a DHCP client. When the client computer starts, it will broadcast a DHCP discover message. It will wait for a response from the DHCP server. Any DHCP server that receives the discover message and has valid addresses to lease will respond with a lease offer. The client then answers the lease offer by accepting the lease with a message called a *lease request*. The server acknowledges the acceptance of its lease with a lease acknowledgment message. An easy way to remember this process is the mnemonic DORA – discover, offer, request, acknowledgment. All DHCP messages are sent using user datagram protocol (UDP). DHCP clients listen on UDP port 67. DHCP servers listen on UDP port 68.
	If a computer has multiple network adapters, the DHCP process occurs separately for each network adapter configured to obtain an automatic TCP/IP address until each network adapter has its own IP address configuration.
	The DHCP server stores the leased IP address information in a central database with additional configuration information sent along with the IP address, including settings for the subnet mask, IP address of the default gateway, and addresses of DNS servers. These configurations are called *options*.

Project 6.1	Understanding DHCP
Outcomes	After completing this project, you will know how to: ▲ explain DHCP functions ▲ examine TCP/IP properties of and use ipconfig on a client computer ▲ determine if DHCP has been installed on Windows Server 2003 computer ▲ install DHCP
What you'll need	To complete this project, you will need: ▲ a client computer ▲ a Windows Server 2003 computer connected to a local network ▲ an IP address and name to use for the DHCP server
Completion time	45 minutes
Precautions	None

■ Part A: Examine a client computer for DHCP configuration

1. Turn on the client computer and open the **Control Panel**. Select **Network Connections**, right-click **Local Area Connections**, and then select **Properties**. Highlight **Internet Protocol (TCP/IP)** and click the **Properties** button. Is the **Obtain an IP address automatically** radio button selected?

   _____

2. Close the dialog boxes and open a **Command Prompt** window. Enter **ipconfig /all** and press **Enter**. What does this tell you about this client's DHCP configuration?

   _____

3. View Figure 6-1. Is this client computer configured as a DHCP client? Will it broadcast for an IP address?

   _____

   _____

   _____

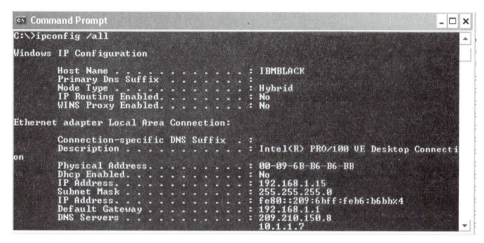

Figure 6-1: Determining a client's DHCP configuration using ipconfig

4. If a client computer is configured as a DHCP client, what will the client do when it first boots up on the network?

_____

_____

_____

_____

■ Part B: Install DHCP on a Windows Server 2003 computer

1. Turn on the Windows Server 2003 computer and log on as an administrator.

2. If you installed Active Directory using the wizard, DHCP has already been installed. You can verify this by selecting **Start**, pointing to **Administrative Tools**, and selecting **DHCP**.

3. If you do not see **DHCP** in the **Administrative Tools** window, you need to install it.

4. Open the **Control Panel**, select **Add or Remove Programs**, and then click **Add/Remove Windows Components**. The **Windows Components Wizard** opens.

5. Select **Networking Services** (Figure 6-2) and click the **Details** button.

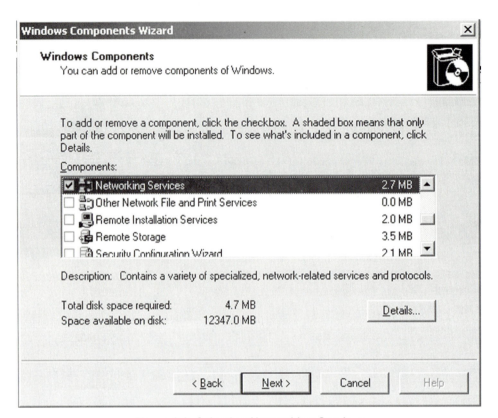

Figure 6-2: Selecting Networking Services

6. Check **Dynamic Host Configuration Protocol (DHCP)** (Figure 6-3) and click **OK**.

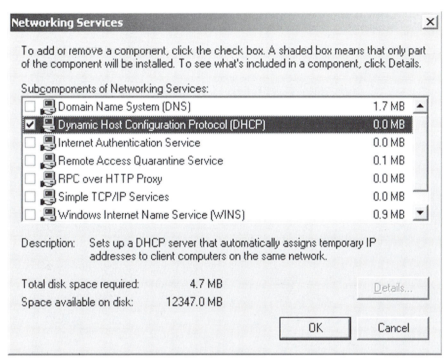

Figure 6-3: Selecting Dynamic Host Configuration Protocol (DHCP)

7. Click **Next** to advance to the **Configuring Components** screen, where Setup will configure the changes you selected.

8. If your server has been using a dynamically assigned IP address, a message box will display and prompt you to change the address to a static IP address. The **Optional Networking Components** dialog box will display. Click **OK** to open the **Local Area Connection Properties** dialog box and configure the static IP address (Figure 6-4). When you have finished assigning this address and close the **Local Area Connection Properties** dialog box, the wizard will complete the **Configuring Components** phase.

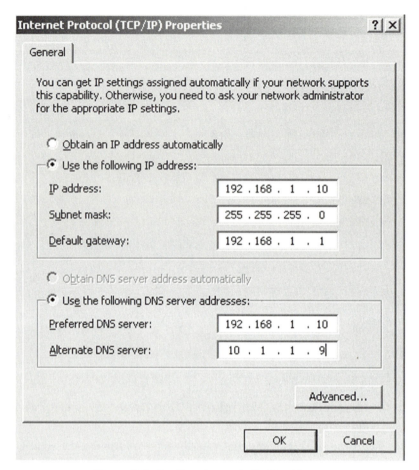

Figure 6-4: Configuring a static IP address

9. Click **Finish** on the **Completing the Windows Components Wizard** screen to close the wizard.

10. Close the **Add or Remove Programs** window.

11. Select **Start**, point to **Administrative Tools**, and select **DHCP** to open the **DHCP** console.

12. Right-click **DHCP** in the left pane and select **Manage authorized servers** from the pop-up menu (Figure 6-5).

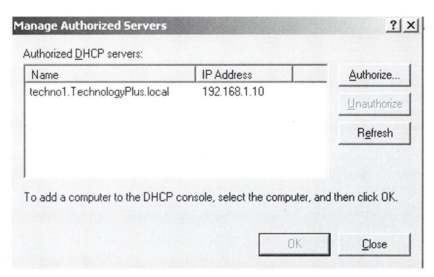

Figure 6-5: Manage Authorized Servers dialog box

13. Click the **Authorize** button and enter the IP address or the name of the DHCP server (Figure 6-6). **Note:** The fully qualified domain name (FQDN) of the DHCP server cannot exceed 64 characters.

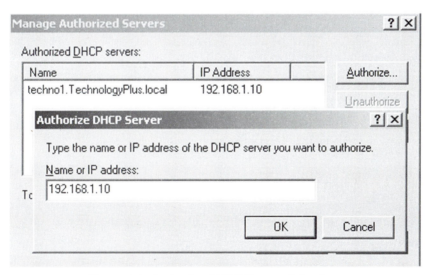

Figure 6-6: Authorize DHCP Server dialog box

14. The **Confirm Authorization** dialog box opens, displaying the name and IP address of the server you selected. Close the DHCP console. Now, open the DHCP console again and look carefully at the DHCP server name on the left. There was a small red arrow in a circle pointing down before this server was authorized. There should now be a small green arrow pointing up. If Active Directory is not running on this network, then there will be no authorization.

15. Explain the reason a DHCP server needs to be authorized.

    _____

    _____

    _____

16. If you use **ipconfig /all** on a client computer and the IP address shows as **169.254.x.y**, what does this indicate?

    _____

    _____

    _____

17. What other configuration information can a DHCP client receive when it obtains its IP address?

    _____

    _____

Project 6.2	Creating and Configuring Scopes, Superscopes, and Options
Overview	In this project, you will create and configure a DHCP scope and a superscope. A *scope* is a contiguous range of IP addresses. To simplify administration, you can group two or more scopes together and create a *superscope*. The superscope allows the DHCP server to provide multiple logical subnet addresses to DHCP clients on a single physical network. You can only have one superscope per server. DHCP *options* are additional IP configuration information such as default gateway and DNS server addresses that a DHCP server can supply to a client. There are four types of options: server options, scope options, class options, and reserved options. Server options are assigned to all scopes and clients of a particular server. A server option setting will be given to all DHCP clients unless a more specific option (scope, class, or client) is assigned. Options commonly set at the server level include the list of DNS servers to be used by the client, the DNS domain suffixes to be used by the client, the WINS servers to be used by the client, and the NetBIOS node type for NetBIOS name resolution. Scope options are settings that apply only to clients in a certain subnet. For example, it is common to specify different routers for different physical subnets. Class options enable different types of computers to obtain settings specific to those computers. Finally, client options enable you to create a specific setting for an individual client. By default, client options override class options, class options override scope options, and scope options override server options.
Outcomes	After completing this project, you will know how to: ▲ create and configure a DHCP scope ▲ configure lease duration and basic scope options ▲ create and configure a DHCP superscope
What you'll need	To complete this project, you will need: ▲ a client computer ▲ a Windows Server 2003 computer connected to a local network ▲ IP addresses to use for the scopes and superscopes
Completion time	1 hour for the scope configuration and 30 minutes for the superscope configuration
Precautions	If you already have a DHCP server on your network, be sure you know the configuration settings in its scope(s) to avoid any overlap in assigning IP addresses. Also note that you can only have one superscope per server.

■ **Part A: Create and configure a DHCP scope**

1. Open the **DHCP** console.

2. Select the name of your DHCP server on the left side of the console.

3. Right-click the server and then select **New Scope** (Figure 6-7) to open the **New Scope Wizard**.

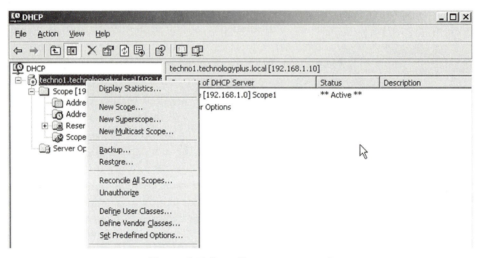

Figure 6-7: New Scope command

4. Click **Next** to open the **Scope Name** screen. Enter a name in the **Name** text box that will help you identify the scope easily. Enter a description of the scope in the **Description** text box (Figure 6-8).

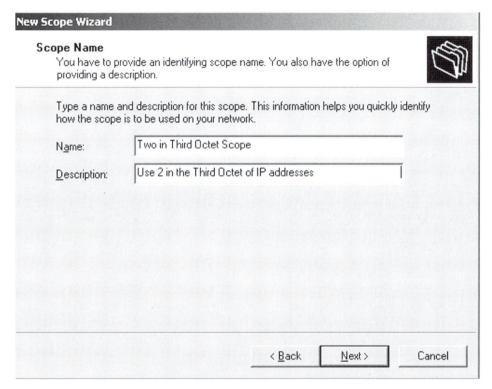

Figure 6-8: Scope Name screen

5. Click **Next** to open the **IP Address Range** screen (Figure 6-9). Enter the first address in your DHCP scope in the **Start IP address** text box. Enter the last address in the range in the **End IP address** text box.

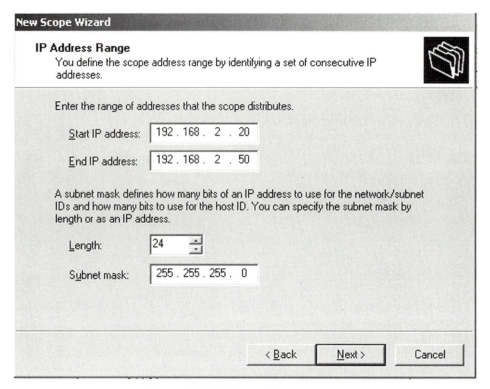

Figure 6-9: IP Address Range screen

6. The subnet mask should be set automatically in the bottom half of the **IP Address Range** screen. If you need to change the subnet mask, you can specify it in terms of length (number of bits) or as an IP address (255.255.255.0).

7. Click **Next** to open the **Add Exclusions** screen. On this screen, you can exclude addresses in the specified range from the scope. Exclusions allow you to maintain static addresses within the scope, such as the address of the DHCP server and other servers. If you don't want to add any exclusions here, you can configure them later.

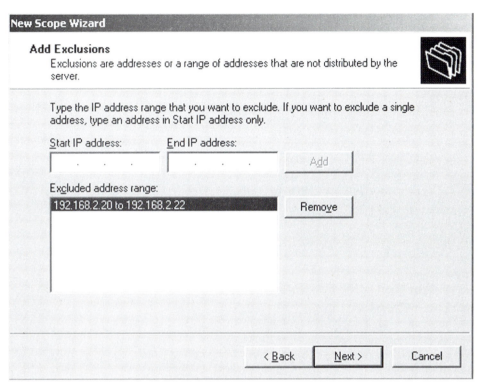

Figure 6-10: Add Exclusions screen

8. In the **Start IP address** text box, enter the first address in the address range that you want to exclude from the scope. In the **End IP address** text box, enter the last address in the range that you want to exclude from the scope. If you want to exclude only one address, enter that address in the **Start IP address** text box only.

9. Click **Add** to add the range to the **Excluded address range** list box.

10. Click **Next** to open the **Lease Duration** screen. The default lease duration is 8 days. You may want to reduce the duration for networks that have portables and dial-up connections, and increase it for networks with desktops that rarely change.

11. Click **Next** to accept the default duration and open the **Configure DHCP Options** screen. Select the **Yes, I want to configure these options now** radio button to configure the IP addresses for default gateways, DNS servers, and WINS servers.

12. Click **Next** to open the **Router (Default Gateway)** screen (Figure 6-11). Enter the address of your network's default gateway in the **IP address** text box and click **Add**.

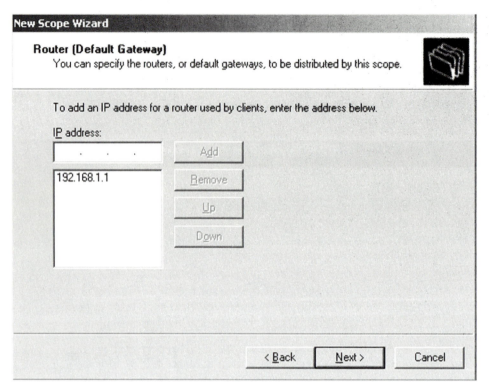

Figure 6-11: Router (Default Gateway) screen

13. Click **Next** to open the **Domain Name and DNS Servers** screen (Figure 6-12). Enter the name of the domain that you want your client computers to use for DNS name resolution in the **Parent domain** text box. Enter the name of the DNS server that you want your scope clients to use in the **Server name** text box and click **Resolve**, or simply enter the IP address of the server in the **IP address** text box.

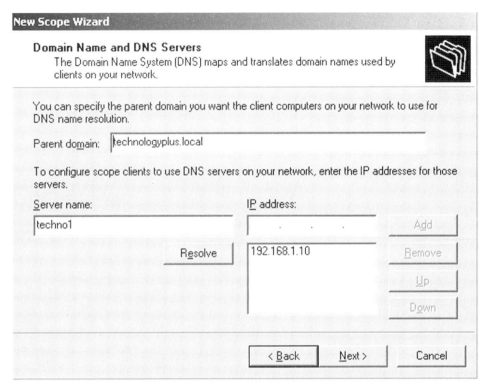

Figure 6-12: Domain Name and DNS Servers screen

14. Click **Add** to add the server address to the **IP address** list box.

15. Click **Next** to open the **WINS Servers** screen (Figure 6-13). If you are on a network that is using older Windows clients and NetBIOS name-to-IP address resolution is required, enter the name of a WINS server for this scope in the **Server name** text box and click **Resolve**. Alternatively, enter the address in the **IP address** text box.

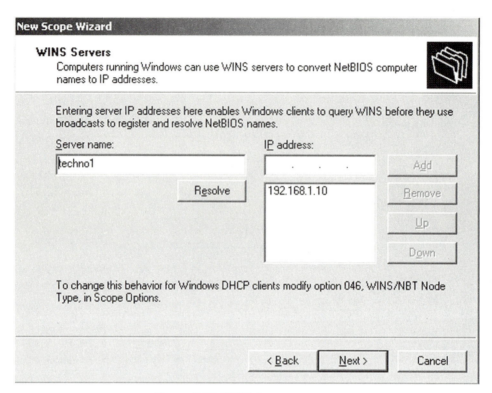

Figure 6-13: WINS Servers screen

16. Click **Add** to add the WINS server, then click **Next** to open the **Activate Scope** screen.

17. Select the **Yes, I want to activate this scope now** radio button or click **Cancel** if you are doing this as an exercise only.

18. Click **Next** to open the **Completing the New Scope Wizard** screen.

19. Click **Finish** to complete the creation of the new scope. The new scope is now listed in the DHCP console.

20. How do you know if your new scope is working?

_____

_____

_____

21. Is your new scope passing out addresses?

_____

22. Highlight your new DHCP scope on the left side of the console. Right-click and select **Display Statistics** (Figure 6-14).

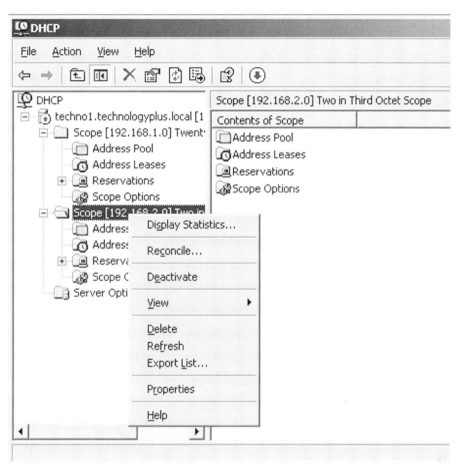

Figure 6-14: Display Statistics command

23. How many **Total Addresses** does it show?

_____

24. Close the scope statistics window. Select **Properties** on the pop-up menu for the scope. Verify the information you entered for your scope. Are the **Start IP address** and **End IP address** correct?

_____

_____

_____

25. What is the difference between a scope reservation and a scope exclusion?

_____

_____

_____

■ Part B: Create and configure a DHCP superscope

1. You need to create a second scope before you can create a superscope. Follow the steps in part A to create a second scope.

2. Highlight the DHCP server and right-click it. Select **New Superscope** (Figure 6-15).

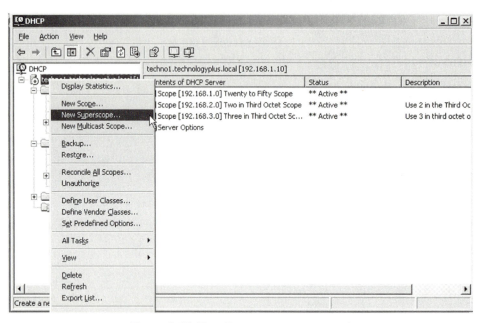

Figure 6-15: New Superscope command

3. The **Welcome to the New Superscope Wizard** screen displays (Figure 6-16).

Figure 6-16: Welcome to the New Superscope Wizard screen

4. The **Superscope Name** screen opens. Enter the superscope name in the **Name** text box and click **Next**.

5. The **Select Scopes** screen appears (Figure 6-17). Click the scopes in the **Available Scopes** list (use the **Ctrl** key to select two). Click **Next**.

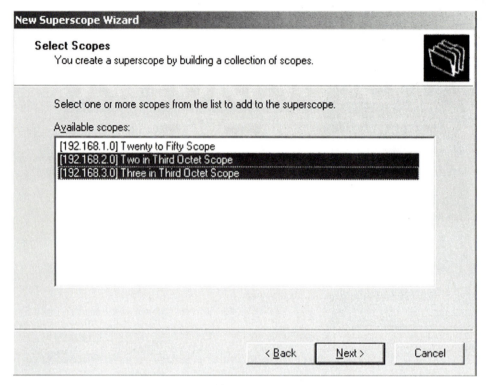

Figure 6-17: Select Scopes screen

6. The **Completing the New Superscope Wizard** screen opens (Figure 6-18).

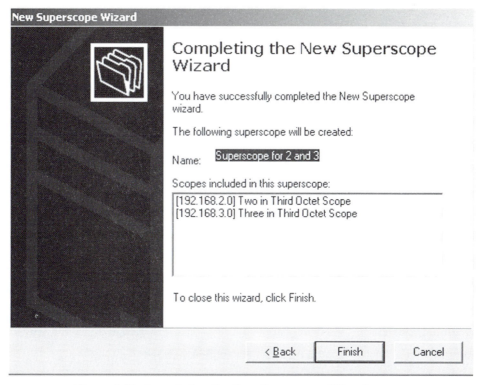

Figure 6-18: Completing the New Superscope Wizard screen

7. Click **Finish** to complete the process and close the DHCP console.

8. What do you do if you want to remove a scope from the superscope?

    _____

    _____

9. You have entered two IP addresses for DNS servers in your scope options. One client computer in that scope is having DNS connection problems. What might be the cause?

    _____

    _____

■ Part C: Set server options

Instead of configuring each scope with a DNS server option, you can configure the DHCP server with a DNS server option.

1. Highlight the **DHCP server** and right-click it. Select **Set Predefined Options** (Figure 6-19)

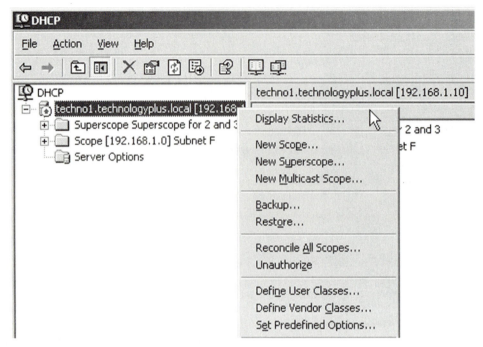

Figure 6-19: Set Predefined Options

2. The **Predefined Options and Values** dialog box opens. Click the down arrow next to the **Option name** text box and select **006 DNS Servers** (Figure 6-20).

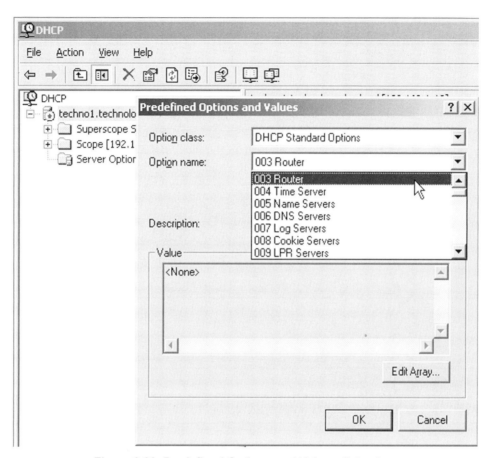

Figure 6-20: Predefined Options and Values dialog box

3. Click the **Edit Array** button.
4. In the **IP address** text box, enter the IP address provided to you by your instructor and click **Add**.
5. Click **OK** to save the setting, and then click **OK** again.
6. Close the **DHCP** console.

Project 6.3	Administering DHCP Servers
Overview	Your DHCP server is installed with several scopes and the clients have begun leasing IP addresses. Now you need to practice a few more skills to ensure that your DHCP server continues to run smoothly. For instance, there may be times when the DHCP service needs to be paused or stopped to perform maintenance tasks. One such task is to create a manual backup to a location other than the local drive. The DHCP service makes an automatic backup of the DHCP database by default every hour.
Outcomes	After completing this project, you will know how to: ▲ review administration tasks ▲ pause and restart the DHCP service ▲ perform manual backup of the DHCP server database ▲ manually compact the DHCP database
What you'll need	To complete this project, you will need: ▲ a client computer ▲ a Windows Server 2003 computer connected to a local network
Completion time	30 minutes
Precautions	Be careful not to delete the cfg file in the Dhcp\backup directory.

■ Part A: Review administration tasks

One place to find a list of DHCP administration tasks is to review the Help feature.

1. From the DHCP console, select **Help** on the menu bar. Select **Help Topics**.

2. The MMC will display showing **DHCP** listed under **Contents**. Select the plus sign (**+**) in front of DHCP and select **New ways to do familiar tasks**. Review the different methods of doing administration. Select **How to...** and review the topics.

3. What does **Help** say under **Managing Scopes** about **Excluding an address from a scope**?

_____

_____

_____

_____

■ Part B: Pause the DHCP server

To perform a backup of a DHCP server database, you should change the status of the server.

1. Open the **DHCP** console and highlight the **DHCP server** on the left-side pane.

2. Right-click and select **All Tasks**, and then select **Pause** (Figure 6-21). You can also find the **Pause** command on the **Action** menu.

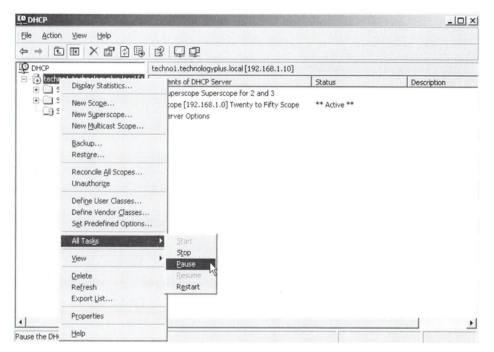

Figure 6-21: Pause command

3. To resume the DHCP service, select **All Tasks** and **Restart**.

■ Part C: Perform a manual backup of a DHCP server database

If the DHCP database becomes corrupted, you may need to restore it from a backup you save to a different location. As with all data files, it is important for administrators to schedule regular backups.

1. In the **DHCP** console, highlight the DHCP server on the left-side pane.

2. Right-click and select **Backup**.

3. The **Browse for Folder** dialog box opens. The default folder for saving a DHCP database during backup is **<systemroot>\WINDOWS\system32\Dhcp\backup**. You may change this location, but the backup must be saved to a local folder.

4. Click **OK** to save the backup to the specified location. To verify that you have created a backup successfully, navigate to the folder in which you saved the database and find the **DhcpCfg** file (Figure 6-22).

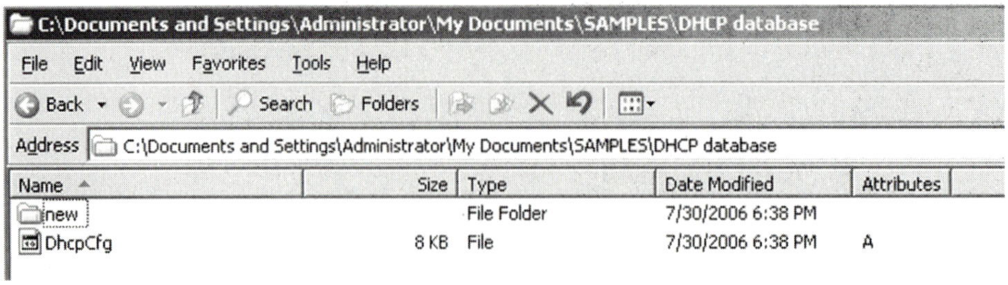

Figure 6-22: DhcpCfg file

5. What happens, by default, when the system detects a problem with the DHCP database?

_____

_____

■ Part D: Manually compact the DHCP database

1. Open the **DHCP** console, highlight the **DHCP server** on the left-side pane.
2. Right-click and select **Stop**.
3. Open the **Command Prompt** window and change directories (**cd**) until you reach **<systemroot> \WINDOWS\system32\dhcp**. Press **Enter**.
4. Next, you will enter the command to use a utility called **JETPACK.exe**. This utility will compact the DHCP database. The correct syntax for **Jetpack.exe** is:

```
JETPACK.EXE <database name> <temp database name>
```

In the example above, **<temp database name>** should be a file name (**TMP.MDB**) **Jetpack.exe** uses as a temporary database file. Another example of this command is:

```
CD %SYSTEMROOT%\SYSTEM32\DHCP
NET STOP DHCPSERVER
JETPACK DHCP.MDB TMP.MDB
NET START DHCPSERVER
```

In this example, the DHCP server can be stopped and started within the **Command Prompt** window.

5. Enter **jetpack dhcp.mdb compactdhcp.mdb** and press **Enter**. (In this command, the **compactdhcp.mdb** is the temporary file name used by **JETPACK.exe**.)
6. Close the **Command Prompt** window.

7. Start the **DHCP Server service** by either opening the DHCP console again, or, if needed, open the **Administrative Tools** window, select **Services**, and then highlight the **DHCP Server** and open the **Action** menu. Select **Start**.

Project 6.4	Dynamic DNS Configuration
Overview	When the IP addresses of DHCP clients are updated dynamically, the DNS server must be notified so it can update the client name-to-IP address and IP address-to-name mapping in the DNS database. Windows Server 2003 allows you to integrate these two functions. Even if your DNS service is not managed on Windows Server 2003, you can still integrate DHCP with DNS. For Windows Server 2003, you have several choices on how the dynamic update process is accomplished. By default, Windows XP, 2000, and 2003-based DHCP clients are configured to request that they register the Host (A) resource record and the DHCP server register the PTR resource record. You can also configure the DHCP server to update both the DNS A and the PTR records. There are two ways to enable DHCP for dynamic updates: at the server level and at the scope level. By enabling it at the server level, DHCP will dynamically update all scopes and superscopes.
Outcomes	After completing this project, you will know how to: ▲ integrate DHCP with DNS on a Windows Server 2003 system
What you'll need	To complete this project, you will need: ▲ a client computer ▲ a Windows Server 2003 computer connected to a local network
Completion time	15 minutes
Precautions	None

■ **Part A: Integrate DHCP with DNS**

1. Open the **DHCP** console.
2. Right-click the **DHCP server**. Select **Properties**.
3. Select the **DNS** tab.
4. Select the **Enable DNS dynamic updates according to the settings below** check box (if it isn't already checked) (Figure 6-23).

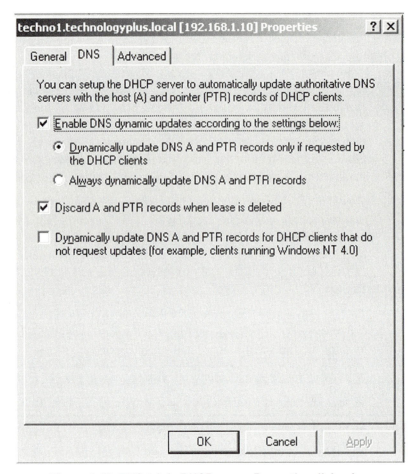

Figure 6-23: DNS tab in DHCP server Properties dialog box

5. You have a choice of allowing the DHCP clients to determine when their records are updated (i.e., by request) or having the DHCP server update all DHCP client records automatically. The default is to have the client request registration.

6. What happens to the dynamic update if the client is not running Windows XP, 2000, or 2003?

_____

_____

7. When a DHCP client lease expires and it is not renewed by the client, what happens to the entry in DNS?

_____

_____

8. Should a DHCP server be configured as a DHCP client to dynamically update the DHCP server's DNS records?

_____

_____

Project 6.5	Planning a Redundant DHCP Infrastructure
Overview	One of the disadvantages of DHCP is that it can become a single point of failure if you don't plan properly. Remember, DHCP does not share its database with any other servers. If you only have one DHCP server and it is unavailable, clients will not be able to obtain a new or renewing lease and will eventually be without network access. So why not just put DHCP on all the servers on your network? The answer is that multiple DHCP servers can create problems if they have conflicting scope ranges. Planning for a redundant DHCP infrastructure means creating exclusions on each server to avoid overlap. To configure two DHCP servers on the same subnet to increase fault tolerance, set up the two scopes using an exclusion design. To review, an exclusion is an address or address range that should never be offered by the DHCP server. A DHCP scope consists of a pool of IP addresses on a single subnet, such as 192.168.1.2 through 192.168.1.254, which the DHCP server can lease to DHCP clients. Each physical network can have only one DHCP scope or superscope with a continuous range of IP addresses. You can use a 50/50, 75/25, or 80/20 design. For example, distribute the IP addresses in each scope range by having 50% of the addresses available for lease in one DHCP server's scope and the other 50% of the addresses excluded in the other DHCP server's scope. That way, if there is a DHCP failure, the operating server will be able to continue leasing addresses. In your plan, two DHCP servers, one for backup, can support numerous DHCP clients; however, you may want to provide DHCP services on both sides of a remote link. Another thing to consider is the broadcast limitation of your network.
Outcomes	After completing this project, you will know how to: ▲ plan a redundant DHCP structure
What you'll need	To complete this project, you will need: ▲ two Windows Server 2003 computers with DHCP installed
Completion time	15 minutes
Precautions	Creating exclusions on a DHCP server that has been in operation can create

a problem for clients who already have an IP address leased from the range.

■ Part A: View the current exclusion range in a scope

Before setting up a second DHCP server, view the scope(s) for the current system.

1. Open the **DHCP** console.

2. In the left pane of the window, select the plus sign (**+**) in front of the **DHCP server** name. Select the plus sign (**+**) in front of **Scope**.

3. Highlight **Address Pool**. The Start IP address and End IP address range will display along with any exclusion Start IP address and End IP address range (Figure 6-24).

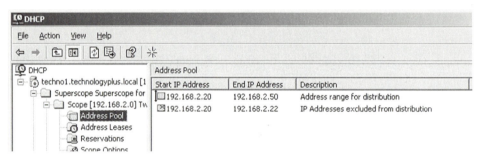

Figure 6-24: Address Pool

■ Part B: Plan an exclusion range for two DHCP servers on the same subnet

1. To plan a redundant structure, write down the IP address pool for the subnet.

2. Determine the percentage of addresses you want each DHCP server to manage (i.e., 50/50, 80/20).

3. Using the percentage, write down the IP address range for each server, being careful not to overlap any IP addresses.

4. Determine the Start IP address and End IP address range for both scopes. Determine the Start IP address and End IP address for the exclusion for both scopes.

5. Create a scope (see Project 6-2) on DHCP Server A and DHCP Server B. (**Note:** You must have two DHCP servers to do this; however, you can write the two ranges in the space below).

6. What is the IP address range for DHCP Server A?

_____

_____

7. What is the IP address range for DHCP Server B?

_____

_____

8. What is the exclusion range for DHCP Server A?

_____

_____

9. What is the exclusion range for DHCP Server A?

_____

_____

Project 6.6	Using DHCP on a Multisegment Network
Overview	It is a fairly simple process for a DHCP client on the local network to broadcast for the DHCP server, but what about a client who is not local?
	If you want to use DHCP on a multiple physical segment network, you must install another DHCP server, install a DHCP Relay Agent on each segment, or ensure that the router(s) between the networks can forward Bootstrap Protocol (BOOTP) broadcasts.
	DHCP network traffic does not cross subnets because DHCP messages are broadcasts. Many, but not all, routers include options to forward DHCP broadcast messages on to connected network segments. A relay agent passes DHCP/BOOTB messages that are broadcast on a physical network to a specific DHCP server. The agent fills in the 0.0.0.0 address on the packet with the relay agent or router's IP address and then forwards the message to the DHCP server. The DHCP server receives the message and examines the gateway IP address field to determine which DHCP scope to use to assign the client's IP address.
	Windows Server 2003 includes the DHCP/BOOTP Relay Agent service; however, you will not find the relay agent configuration on the DHCP console. The installation and configuration of a DHCP Relay Agent is managed through the Routing and Remote Access console.
Outcomes	After completing this project, you will know how to:
	▲ install DHCP Relay Agent using Routing and Remote Access
What you'll need	To complete this project, you will need:
	▲ a Windows Server 2003 computer with DHCP and Routing and Remote Access installed

	▲ the IP address of the DCHP server that will receive the relayed messages
Completion time	15 minutes
Precautions	None

1. Open the **Start** menu, point to **Administrative Tools**, and select **Routing and Remote Access** to open the **Routing and Remote Access** console.

2. Select the plus sign (**+**) to the left of the server name to expand it. Select the plus sign (**+**) to the left of **IP Routing** to expand the **IP Routing** node.

3. Right-click **General** and select **New Routing Protocol**.

4. In the **New Routing Protocol** dialog box, select **DCHP Relay Agent** (Figure 6-25) and click **OK**.

Figure 6-25: New Routing Protocol dialog box

5. Right-click **DHCP Relay Agent** and select **Properties** to open the **DHCP Relay Agent Properties** dialog box.

6. Add the IP address(es) of the DHCP server(s) that will receive relayed messages in the **Server address** text box (Figure 6-26), click **Add**, and then click **OK** to close the dialog box.

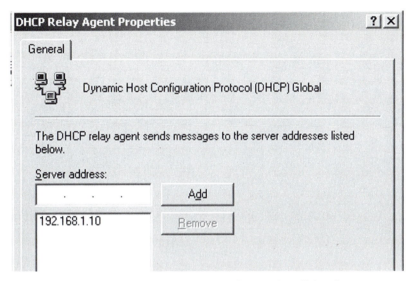

Figure 6-26: DCHP Relay Agent Properties dialog box

7. In the **Routing and Remote Access** console, enable the interface for the relay agent by right-clicking **DHCP Relay Agent** again and selecting **New Interface**.

8. In the **New Interface for DHCP Relay Agent** dialog box, select the interface through which you want the relay agent to be enabled and click **OK**.

9. Close the **Routing and Remote Access** console.

10. How can you determine if your router supports DHCP/BOOTP relay?

_____

_____

7

TROUBLESHOOTING DHCP

PROJECTS

Project 7.1	Troubleshooting DHCP Server Configuration
Overview	The more familiar you become with the DHCP service, the easier it will be to pinpoint problems.
	Errors that occur with DHCP addressing rarely originate at the client because client configuration is simple and straightforward. However, because configurations on DHCP servers and DHCP configuration for routers and switches can be tricky, they cause almost all failures.
	Recognizing and resolving problems before clients are unable to connect to the network involves monitoring the DHCP service. However, if problems do occur, there are a number of logical steps you can follow to find solutions.
Outcomes	After completing this project, you will know how to:
	▲ investigate DHCP problems using the console
	▲ isolate server configuration errors
What you'll need	To complete this project, you will need:
	▲ a client computer
	▲ a Windows Server 2003 computer connected to a local network
Completion time	45 minutes
Precautions	None

■ Part A: Examine the Manage Authorized Servers dialog box

As you have learned, there are a number of configurations you should examine to determine the current DHCP settings. Once you understand how this installation of DHCP is configured, you can then concentrate on troubleshooting addressing problems.

1. Open the **Start** menu, point to **Administrative Tools**, and select **DHCP** to open the **DHCP** console.

2. Right-click **DHCP** at the top of the left pane and select **Manage Authorized Servers**(Figure 7-1).

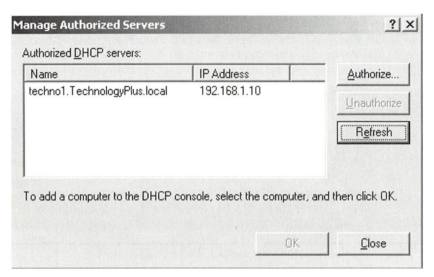

Figure 7-1: Manage Authorized Servers dialog box

3. What can you determine from the **Manage Authorized Servers** dialog box?

_____

_____

_____ ■ **Part B: Examine the Add Server dialog box**

1. Right-click **DHCP** at the top of the left pane and select **Add Server**.

2. The **Add Server** dialog box appears, allowing you to select a server to add to the console (Figure 7-2).

3. Click the **Browse** button.

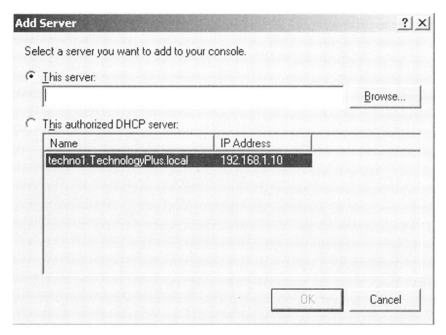

Figure 7-2: Add Server dialog box

4. How can this dialog box help you explore available DHCP servers?

_____

_____

■ Part C: Examine the DHCP server Properties dialog box

1. Highlight the first **DHCP** server on the list in the left pane of the console. Notice the server's FQDN and IP address (Figure 7-3).

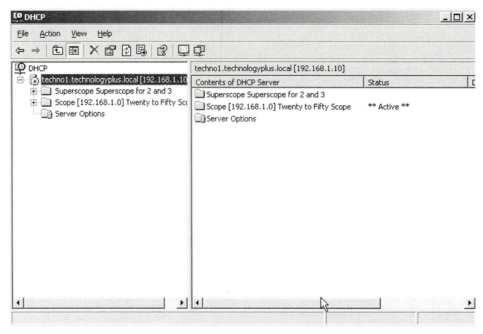

Figure 7-3: DHCP server's FQDN and IP address

2. Right-click the DHCP server to display the pop-up menu and select **Properties**. The DHCP server **Properties** dialog box displays, showing three tabs.

3. On the **General** tab (Figure 7-4), you can configure the time interval for the automatic update of statistics; enable audit logging, which will write data to a log file; and enable the display of the **BOOTP Table** folder in the DHCP console tree. Also, notice that you can see the green up arrow in a circle on the server icon.

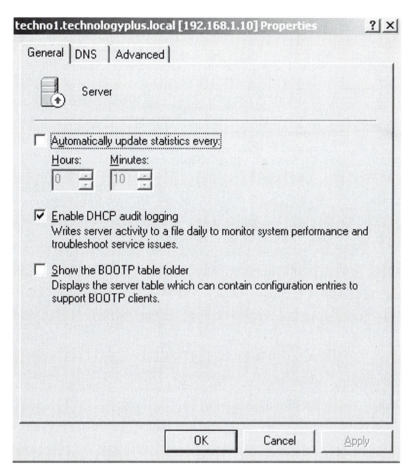

Figure 7-4: General tab of the DHCP server Properties dialog box

4. What does a green up arrow on the server icon mean?

    _____

    _____

5. Why would you want to enable audit logging? What is the default location for the audit log file?

    _____

    _____

6. Select the **DNS** tab on the DHCP server **Properties** dialog box (Figure 7-5). This tab enables you to configure DNS dynamic updates.

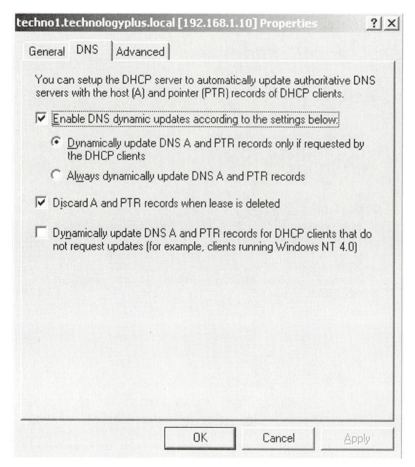

Figure 7-5: DNS tab in the DHCP server Properties dialog box

7. Next, select the **Advanced** tab (Figure 7-6). There are a number of configurations on this tab. You can do the following:

   • set the number of times the DHCP server attempts to resolve an address conflict

   • configure the paths to the folders that hold the audit log, database, and backup database

   • specify the connections (LAN interfaces) on which the DHCP server service is listening for DHCP messages.

   • set the authorization credentials for DNS dynamic updates

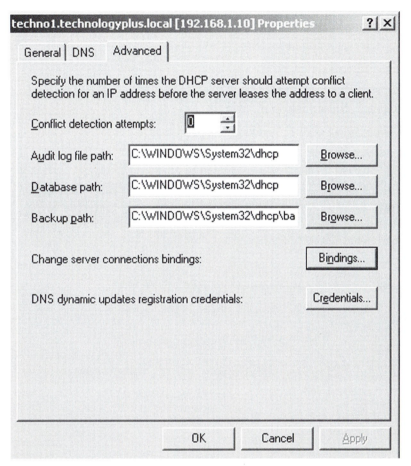

Figure 7-6: Advanced tab in the DHCP server Properties dialog box

8. What happens to the DHCP server database if the path to **Dhcp.mdb** is moved or deleted?

_____

_____

9. Click the **Bindings** button on the **Advanced** tab. The **Bindings** dialog box is displayed (Figure 7-7).

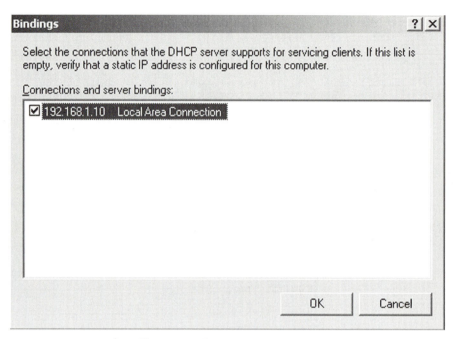

Figure 7-7: Bindings dialog box

10. What does it mean if there is no IP address in this box? What if there is no checkmark in the box for this connection?

_____

_____

11. Close the **Bindings** dialog box, and then click the **Credentials** button on the **Advanced** tab (Figure 7-8).

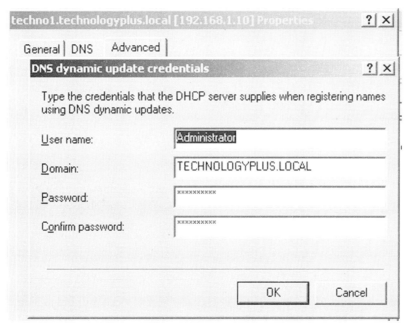

Figure 7-8: DNS dynamic update credentials dialog box

12. Why is it important to manage the credentials of the account that registers DNS dynamic updates?

_____

_____

13. Review Figure 7-9 and notice that this warning indicates a security risk when the DNS dynamic update service is not using the proper credentials.

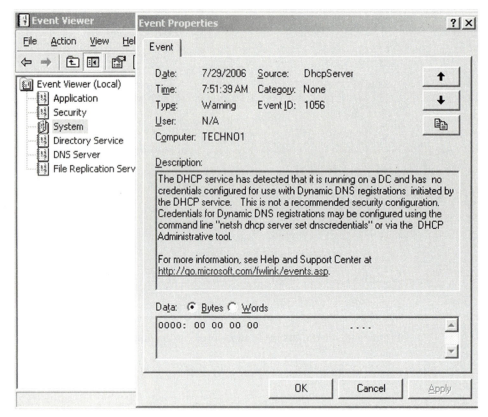

Figure 7-9: Warning

■ **Part D: Troubleshoot client address failures**

One common error that occurs in client configurations is the use of a static client IP address.

1. On the client computer, open the **Control Panel** and select **Network Connections**.

2. Right-click **Local Area Connection** and select **Properties** to open the **Local Area Connection Properties** dialog box. Select **Internet Protocol** and click the **Properties** button.

3. Review Figure 7-10. This shows that this client has a static IP address in the private IP range – 192.168.1.x.

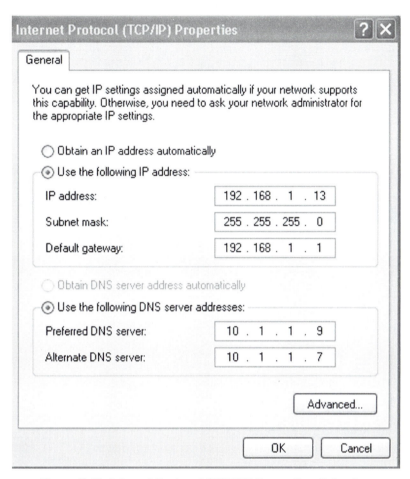

Figure 7-10: Internet Protocol (TCP/IP) Properties dialog box

4. What happens to DHCP configuration information when the client's IP address is set manually?

_____

_____

5. If you use **ipconfig /all** and see that a client's IP address falls in the 169.254.0.1 to 169.254.255.254 range, what does it indicate?

_____

_____

■ Part E: Troubleshoot scope configuration failures

1. Defining and activating a DHCP scope enables the DHCP server to provide clients with IP addresses in a single subnet. How can you determine if the scope has been activated?

_____

_____

Project 7.2	Troubleshooting Switch and Router Configuration Problems
Overview	On networks where clients are separated by a switch or a router, configurations must take into account DHCP broadcast messages. By default, switches forward broadcast messages (using the MAC address) to all the ports on the switch. Due to the implementation of spanning tree protocol (STP) for reduction of bridging loops, broadcast traffic may be blocked at the port unless properly configured.
	By default, routers do not pass broadcast messages to another subnet and, although this is beneficial in most cases, it prevents DHCP clients on a subnet without a DHCP server from sending and receiving DHCP broadcast addressing messages.
Outcomes	After completing this project, you will know how to: ▲ create and configure a DHCP scope ▲ verify scope configurations and exclusions ▲ confirm the DHCP server's address ▲ examine client configurations for broadcast paths ▲ understand DHCP configurations for a relay agent
What you'll need	To complete this project, you will need: ▲ a client computer ▲ a Windows Server 2003 computer connected to a local network
Completion time	30 minutes
Precautions	In the future, if you suspect that the routers and switches are causing DHCP errors, you may need to contact the administrator for assistance.

■ Part A: Examine common problems configuring DHCP subnets

Selecting the IP address range for a subnet is a straightforward process as long as you follow certain guidelines. In Project 6.2, you created a new DHCP scope. You indicated a consecutive range of IP addresses for a single subnet. For this activity, you will examine current scope configurations.

1. Open the **DHCP** console and highlight the **Scope** folder. You may need to select the plus sign (**+**) in front of the DHCP server.

2. Right-click the folder and select **Properties**. The **Scope Properties** dialog box displays, showing the **Scope name**, the **Start IP address**, the **End IP address**, and the subnet mask (which may appear grayed out) (Figure 7-11).

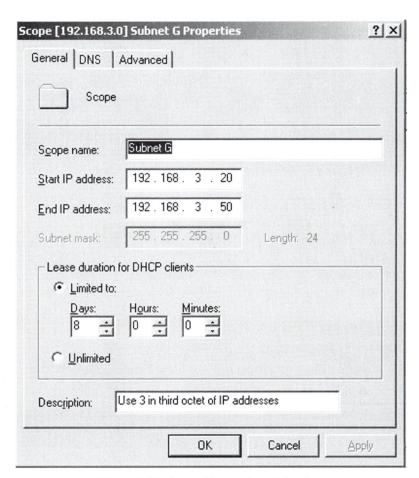

Figure 7-11: Scope Properties dialog box

3. If there is no exclusion range for this scope, you can add one by entering the Start IP address and the End IP address.

4. Why would you want to add an exclusion range for a scope? Can you add more than one exclusion range? What value does an excluded address have?

_____

_____

_____

5. If you have two consecutive ranges of IP addresses for a subnet, how do you configure the scope?

_____

_____

6. How can you determine if the IP address of a DHCP server is properly configured?

_____

_____

■ Part B: Verify DHCP service for a subnet

BOOTP (the predecessor to DHCP) and DHCP depend on broadcast messages to communicate with clients. Because routers normally do not forward broadcast messages from one subnet to another, how can a DHCP message pass between subnets? There are several answers to this question. First, the router may be configured to allow DHCP/BOOTP forwarding, which enables it to determine the IP address of the DHCP server. Second, there may be a DHCP Relay Agent located on the client's subnet. This relay agent can run on another client or server computer and will listen on the subnet for DHCP messages. It will then pass those messages directly to the DHCP server on the other subnet.

1. Open a **Command Prompt** window on the DHCP client.
2. At the command prompt, enter **ipconfig /all** and press **Enter** (Figure 7-12).

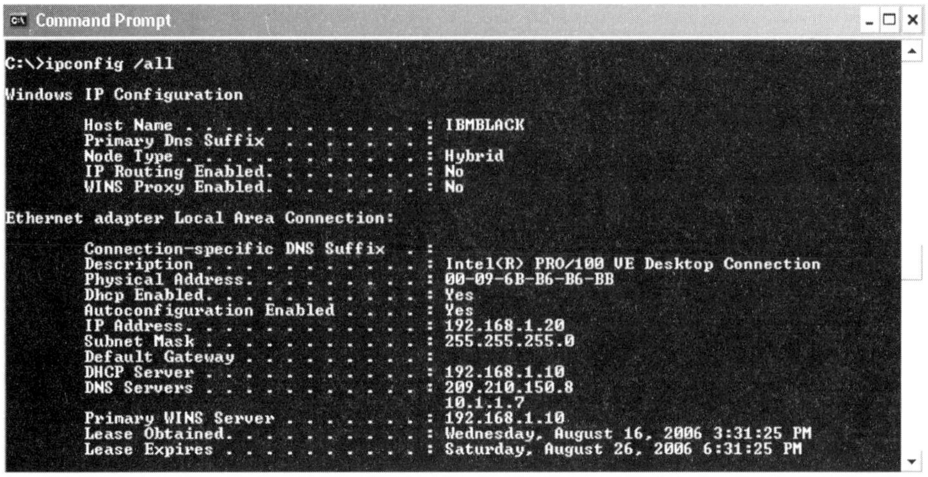

Figure 7-12: Using ipconfig /all

3. How can checking the IP address of the DHCP server on the client provide information about where a client is receiving its DHCP lease?

_____

_____

4. How can the TCP/IP utility **pathping** help you troubleshoot a client that is unable to obtain an IP address? **Note:** You have verified that the client is configured to **Obtain an IP address automatically**.

_____

_____

■ Part C: Troubleshoot switch configurations

As mentioned, switch configurations may cause a DHCP client's request for an IP address to go unheard because the switch has placed a block on the port. Switches that have settings for the STP may be configured to avoid bridging loops by blocking ports that send broadcasts. You can verify that the client is sending and receiving DHCP broadcast traffic by doing a capture.

1. Open **Network Monitor** on the DHCP server. **Start** a network capture.
2. Open a **Command Prompt** window on the DHCP client.
3. At the command prompt, enter **ipconfig /release** and press **Enter**.
4. Wait a few minutes and then **Stop** the capture.
5. Review Figure 7-13. Notice the protocol and the description of the highlighted frame.

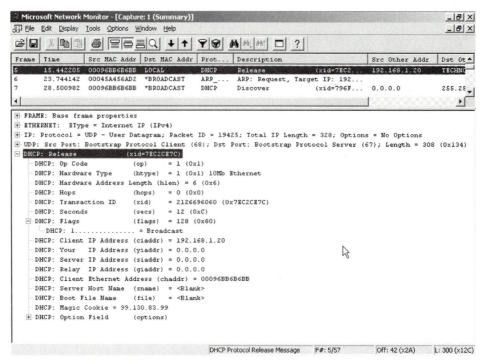

Figure 7-13: A capture

6. Is the DHCP release command a broadcast message? How can you determine if the client is on a different subnet?

_____

_____

7. Next, **Start** another network capture.

8. At the command prompt, enter **ipconfig /renew** and press **Enter**.

9. Wait a few minutes and then **Stop** the capture. Examine the capture. View the traffic for renewing the IP address.

10. Is the DHCP **renew** command a broadcast message? What does this tell you about the client's port on the switch?

_____

_____

_____

■ Part D: Troubleshoot router configurations

There are some basic guidelines to follow when you suspect a router is causing DHCP failures. First, determine if the client is on a different subnet than the DHCP server. Next, confirm whether the router on the client's network is performing DHCP services itself by passing out IP addresses. In this case, the router, by default, may be using private IP addresses in the 10.0.0.0 range, the 172.16.0.0 to 172.31.0.0 range, or the 192.168.0.0 to 192.168.255.0 range. Because it is a common practice to use these private IP addresses on internal networks (networks that have network address translation [NAT] or a proxy server), you should determine just where the client obtained its address.

1. Open a **Command Prompt** window on the DHCP client.
2. At the command prompt, enter **ipconfig /all** and press **Enter**.
3. Write down the client's IP configuration information (if available).

_____

_____

4. Open the **DHCP** console. Select the plus sign (**+**) in front of a **Scope**.
5. Select the **Address Leases** folder. Any IP address lease for this DHCP server in this scope will be shown in the right-hand pane (Figure 7-14).

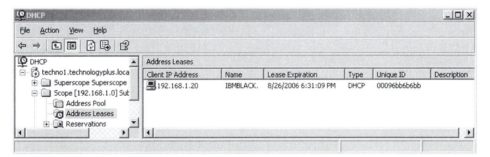

Figure 7-14: IP Address Leases

6. Compare the client's IP address to IP addresses shown in each scope's **Address Leases** folder. What can you conclude if the client's IP address does not appear in any of the scopes on this DHCP server?

_____

_____

■ Part E: Troubleshoot DHCP configurations for a relay agent

Clients on subnets that do not have a DHCP server will be unable to obtain an IP address unless the router is configured to pass DHCP traffic or a DHCP Relay Agent is installed. Most routers today are capable of recognizing DHCP messages; however, if you need to configure the DHCP relay service, you need to make sure the DHCP server is configured properly.

1. The relay agent device or software is physically located on a subnet that is connected to the network. It is configured with the static IP address of your DHCP server. (**Note:** You do *not* install it on your DHCP server.)

2. On your DHCP server, open the **DHCP** console. Highlight the **DHCP server**, and right-click to open the **New Scope** dialog box.

3. Configure a new scope that matches the network address on the other side of the router where the relay agent is located.

4. Include a default gateway that is not the same IP address as the router that separates the client's subnet. Do not include this scope in a superscope. The relay agent will forward DHCP/BOOTP messages through the router to the DHCP server.

5. You want to add the Windows Server 2003 DHCP Relay Agent on a server connected to a second subnet and have your DHCP server manage IP addressing for the second subnets clients. What is the first thing you must do?

_____

_____

_____

Project 7.3	Monitoring DHCP Services
Overview	Just as car owners should check their oil to avoid engine failure, DHCP administrators should review the DHCP events and logs. Periodically checking the processes that make up the DHCP services allows the IT professional to avoid unnecessary downtime in the network. Once it is configured properly, DHCP usually needs little maintenance, but it must be monitored on a regular basis.
Outcomes	After completing this project, you will know how to: ▲ review DHCP events in Event Viewer ▲ use the DHCP built-in monitoring tools ▲ perform manual backup of the DHCP server database ▲ read DHCP log files
What you'll need	To complete this project, you will need: ▲ a client computer ▲ a Windows Server 2003 computer connected to a local network
Completion time	30 minutes
Precautions	None

■ Part A: Use Event Viewer for error detection

1. Open the **Start** menu, point to **Administrative Tools**, and select **Event Viewer** to open the **Event Viewer**.
2. Highlight **System** in the left pane and view the event entries on the right.
3. Notice the headings on each column. By default, **Event Viewer** sorts events by the most recent date.
4. Click the box with the column title **Source**.
5. The events will sort alphabetically by source. View any DHCP events.
6. What DHCP events did you find? Figure 7-15 shows a warning event. Why would this event be considered a warning?

_____

_____

_____

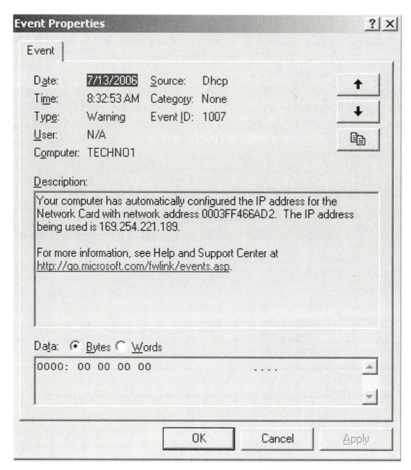

Figure 7-15: DHCP warning event

■ Part B: Use DHCP built-in tools

You can use the netsh command-line utility to manage DHCP. Its name stands for network shell, and DHCP commands can be added to it to allow you to configure servers. This utility has two advantages: less overhead when managing DHCP servers across a slow link, and the automation of commands using scripts for multiple DHCP servers.

1. Open a **Command Prompt** window.

2. At the command prompt, enter **netsh dhcp server** and press **Enter**. This shows the various commands available (Figure 7-16).

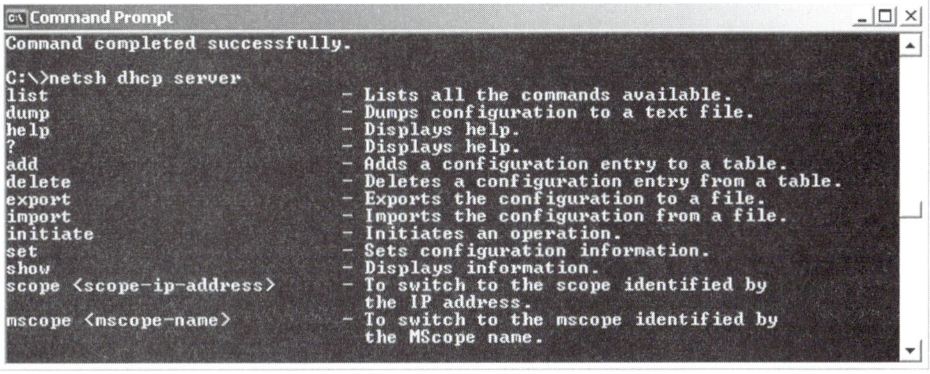

Figure 7-16: Using netsh dhcp server

3. Add the **dump** command and all of the DHCP configuration information will display.

4. Write this information to a text file by adding a text file name to the end of the command; for example, **netsh dhcp server dump >dhcpstuff.txt** of the DHCP (Figure 7-17).

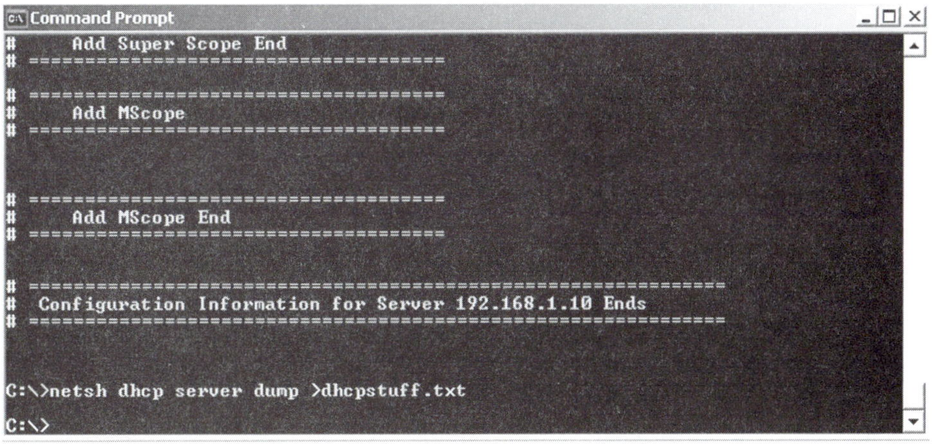

Figure 7-17: Using the dump command

5. Review the text file using **Notepad** (Figure 7-18).

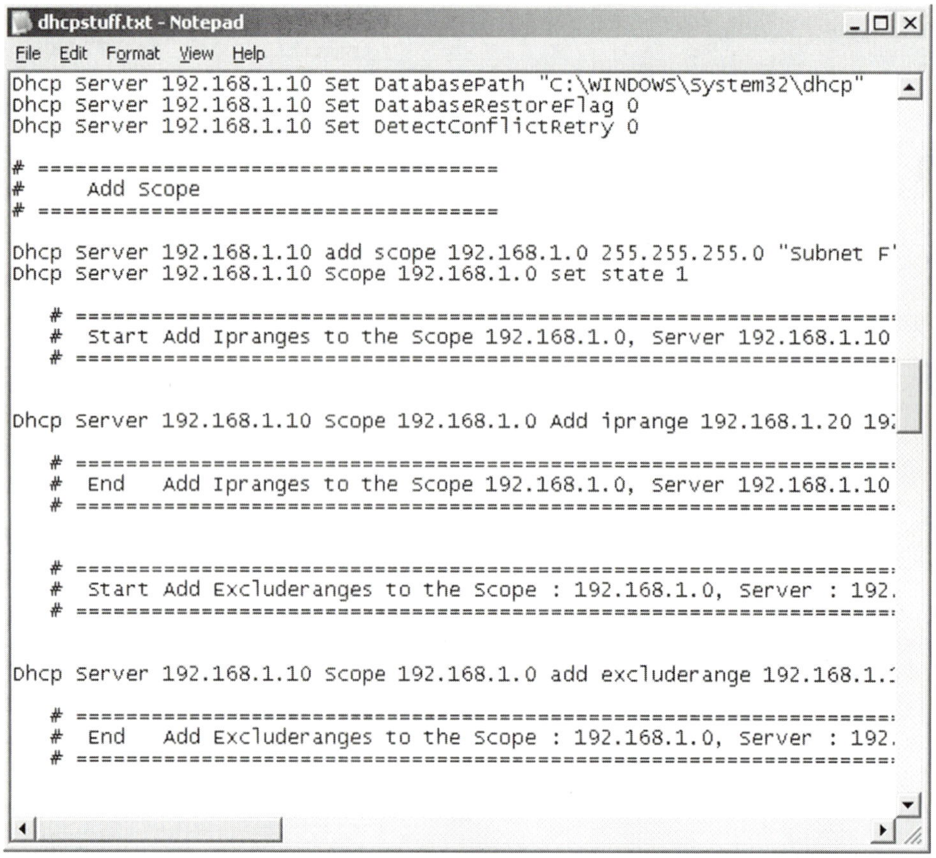

```
dhcpstuff.txt - Notepad                                    _ |□| x|
File  Edit  Format  View  Help
Dhcp Server 192.168.1.10 Set DatabasePath "C:\WINDOWS\System32\dhcp"  ▲
Dhcp Server 192.168.1.10 Set DatabaseRestoreFlag 0
Dhcp Server 192.168.1.10 Set DetectConflictRetry 0

# ====================================
#     Add Scope
# ====================================

Dhcp Server 192.168.1.10 add scope 192.168.1.0 255.255.255.0 "Subnet F'
Dhcp Server 192.168.1.10 Scope 192.168.1.0 set state 1

  # ================================================================:
  # Start Add Ipranges to the Scope 192.168.1.0, Server 192.168.1.10
  # ================================================================:


Dhcp Server 192.168.1.10 Scope 192.168.1.0 Add iprange 192.168.1.20 19:

  # ================================================================:
  # End   Add Ipranges to the Scope 192.168.1.0, Server 192.168.1.10
  # ================================================================:


  # ================================================================:
  # Start Add Excluderanges to the Scope : 192.168.1.0, Server : 192.
  # ================================================================:


Dhcp Server 192.168.1.10 Scope 192.168.1.0 add excluderange 192.168.1.:

  # ================================================================:
  # End   Add Excluderanges to the Scope : 192.168.1.0, Server : 192.
  # ================================================================:
                                                                   ▼
◄|                                                               ►|
```

Figure 7-18: Text file in Notepad

6. What are two configuration settings you found in the text file?

_____

_____

■ Part C: Create and view DHCP log files

The DHCP server logs are stored daily as a text file and can be viewed with Notepad.

1. Open the **DHCP** console. Highlight the **DHCP server** and right-click. Select **Properties** from the pop-up menu.
2. Confirm there is a checkmark in the box next to **Enable DHCP audit logging.**
3. Select the **Advanced** tab and view the **Audit log file path**.
4. Open **Notepad** and select **File** and then **Open** from the menu.
5. Select **All Files** from the **Files of Type** at the bottom of the dialog box.
6. The log files are named for the day of the week and have a **.log** file extension (Figure 7-19).

Figure 7-19: DHCP server log files

7. What is the Event ID shown for Authorized (servicing) on a DHCP server? Approximately how often does Event 24 – IP address cleanup operation run?

_____

_____

Project 7.4	Managing the DHCP Database
Overview	The DHCP database design incorporates a number of features that make it easy to manage. You have seen the process of compacting the database to remove unused space, and you know the database does a backup automatically every hour.
Outcomes	After completing this project, you will know how to: ▲ reconcile DHCP scopes ▲ restore the compacted database from a file ▲ monitor DHCP server performance
What you'll need	To complete this project, you will need: ▲ a client computer ▲ a Windows Server 2003 computer connected to a local network
Completion time	30 minutes
Precautions	None

■ Part A: Reconcile DHCP scopes

Due to the addition and deletion of client leases, scopes can become inconsistent. The DHCP database stores records in several places and includes a Reconcile feature to cross-check the contents.

1. Open the **DHCP** console and highlight the **Scope** name.
2. Right-click and select **Reconcile** on the pop-up menu.
3. Select the **Verify** button. If the database is consistent, you will see Figure 7-20. If there are any inconsistencies, the dialog box will list them and allow you to repair them. You can also reconcile all scopes by selecting the DHCP server, right-click to bring up the pop-up menu, and select **Reconcile All Scopes**.

Figure 7-20: DHCP message box

4. What is the difference between reconcile and refresh?

_____

_____

5. You can also reconcile scopes to recover from a corrupt DHCP database. First remove the database files, and then reconcile the server's scopes.

■ Part B: Restore the DHCP database from the compacted file

There may be times when you need to restore the entire DHCP database due to corruption or loss. Again, follow the Best Practices recommendation and have a current copy of the DHCP database saved on another computer.

1. Open the **DHCP** console and highlight the **DHCP server** name.
2. Right-click and select **Restore**.
3. Browse the folder for the location of the backup database files.
4. You will receive a warning that the DHCP service must be stopped and then restarted (Figure 7-21).

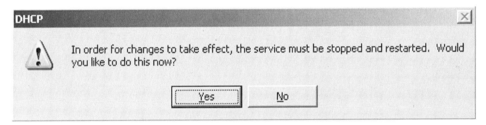

Figure 7-21: DHCP warning

5. Where are the backup DHCP files stored? What is the file name for the database file? When you restore the database files, will scope options, exclusions, and reservations restore as well?

_____

_____

_____

■ Part C: Monitor DHCP server performance

DHCP servers are an essential component on the network, and it is a good idea for network administrators to regularly monitor their performance. Starting with a baseline measure, you can compare server performance over time and respond to performance degradation.

1. Open the **Start** menu, point to **Administrative Tools**, and select **Performance**.

2. Select **System Monitor** in the left pane

3. To add DHCP server performance counters, select the button with the plus sign (**+**).

4. The **Add Counters** dialog box displays (Figure 7-22). Choose **DHCP Server** as the **Performance object**.

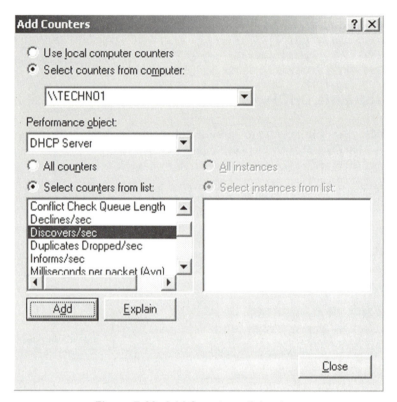

Figure 7-22: Add Counters dialog box

5. Add several counters, including the **Packets Received/sec**, **Discovers/sec**, and **Packets Expired/sec**, and view the DHCP server's performance in graph form and as a report (using the **Report** button to the left of the **Add** button on the menu).

6. Describe a situation where you would want to monitor DHCP performance to compare your baseline performance measures with current performance.

_____

_____

Project 7.5	Examining DHCP Packets
Overview	No examination of DHCP would be complete without taking a careful look at the traffic DHCP generates on your network. Using Network Monitor, you can capture frames sent to and from DHCP clients and servers. By analyzing this traffic, you can diagnose and prevent network problems.
Outcomes	After completing this project, you will know how to: ▲ examine DHCP frames in Network Monitor ▲ filter and evaluate DHCP traffic ▲ spot DHCP problems using packet analysis
What you'll need	To complete this project, you will need: ▲ a client computer ▲ a Windows Server 2003 computer connected to a local network
Completion time	30 minutes
Precautions	None

■ Part A: Examine DHCP frames in Network Monitor

You can use Network Monitor to verify that a client can actually connect to the DHCP server and begin the four-step process. For this activity, you will use a DHCP client that needs a new IP address.

1. Open **Network Monitor** on the DHCP server. **Start** a network capture.

2. On a computer that has *not* been a DHCP client previously, configure the TCP/IP configuration to **Obtain an IP address automatically**. Click **OK**.

3. Go back to the DHCP server, wait a few minutes, and then **Stop** and **Save** the capture.

4. Review the four DHCP entries in the capture.

5. You should see entries similar to those in Figures 7-23 to 7-25 and 7-27. These illustrate the four-step process on a new DHCP client.

6. Review **Frame 7** in Figure 7-23. How can you identify the client who is sending this message? How can you verify this information on the client? Can we determine if there was a relay agent to forward this message?

_____

_____

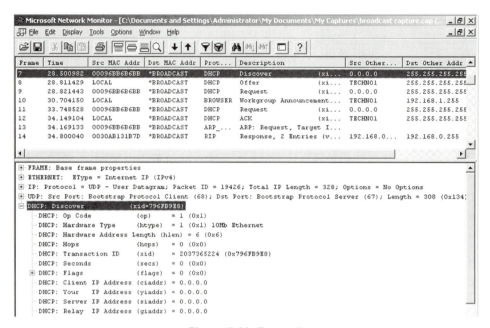

Figure 7-23: Frame 7

7. Review **Frame 8** in Figure 7-24. What IP address is the DHCP server offering? Review the DHCP Offer frame on your system, what IP address is your DHCP server offering the client?

_____

_____

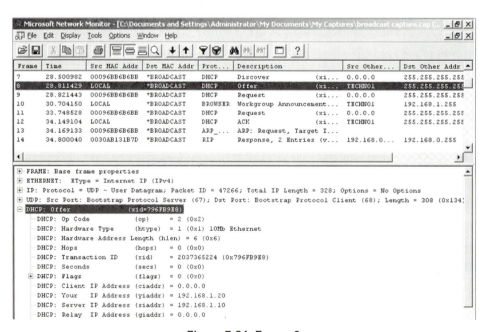

Figure 7-24: Frame 8

8. Review **Frame 9** in Figure 7-25. What is the client's host name? What can you determine about DNS from this figure?

_____

_____

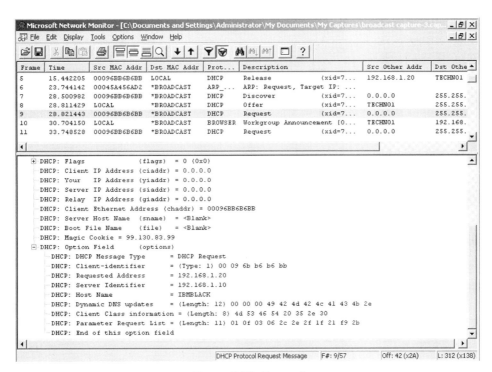

Figure 7-25: Frame 9

9. Review **Frame 12** in Figure 7-26. How long is the lease? What option did the client receive with the IP address?

_____

_____

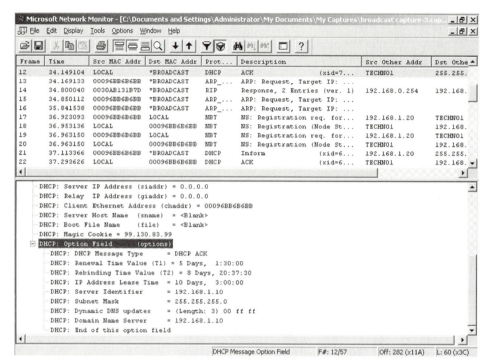

Figure 7-26: Frame 12

■ **Part B: Filter and evaluate DHCP traffic**

The process of reviewing a long Network Monitor capture can be time consuming. You can easily filter a capture for DHCP traffic.

1. Open **Network Monitor**. Open the **File** menu and select **Open**. Browse to the folder where you saved the capture in the previous activity. Open your **xxx.cap** file.

2. Open the **Display** menu and then select **Filter** (or use the **Filter** button) (Figure 7-27).

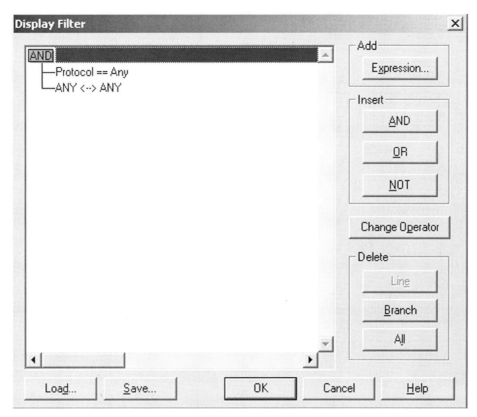

Figure 7-27: Display Filter dialog box

3. Select the **Expression** button on the top right.

4. In the **Expression** dialog box, select the **Protocol** tab (Figure 7-28). All the **Enabled Protocols** will be listed on the left.

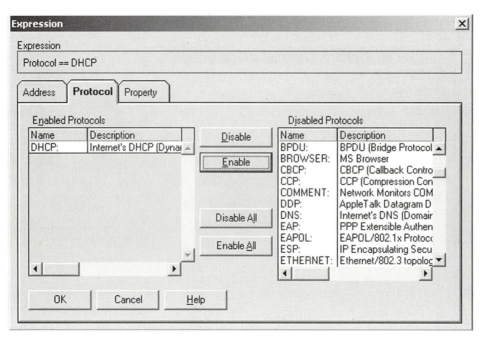

Figure 7-28: Expression dialog box

5. Select **Disable All**. Now find DHCP in the list on the right and highlight it. Select **Enable**.

6. In the **Display Filter** dialog box, note that **Protocol = = DHCP** (Figure 7-29).

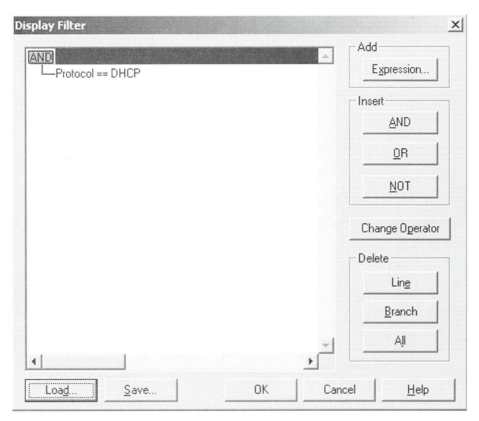

Figure 7-29: Display Filter dialog box

7. Select **OK**. Note that you can now save this filter to use on any capture.
8. Select **Save** and give your filter a name (Figure 7-30).

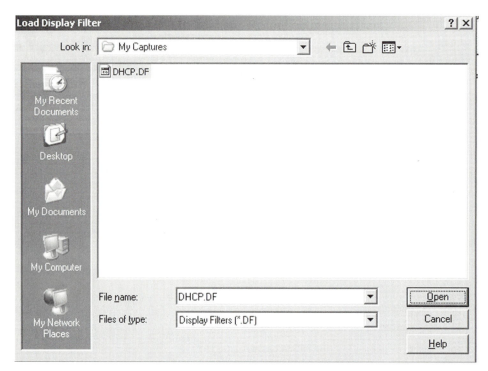

Figure 7-30: Saving the Filter

9. Now open the **Display Filter** dialog box again and select the **Load** button on the bottom left.

10. Highlight your new DHCP filter (**xxx.DF**) and select **Open**. Now select **OK** to apply the filter to your capture. Only the DHCP Protocol frames show in the window (Figure 7-31). To cancel the filter, select the **Disable Filter** on the menu, the **Toggle Filter** button, or reset the filter to **Any <= => Any**.

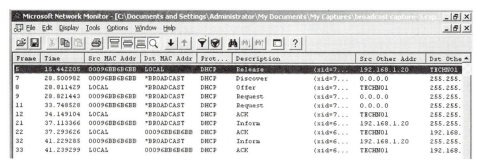

Figure 7-31: DHCP filter

11. Can you filter for DHCP traffic from the server to the client? What other filters could you use to troubleshoot DHCP client problems?

_____

_____

■ Part C: Examine DHCP frames

You have examined frames created by the DHCP four-step process. Now look at some others. Along with the four-step message exchange, DHCP uses four other messages. The server can use the **DHCPNack** to inform the client that the requested TCP/IP configuration is invalid. The client uses the **DHCPRelease** to tell the DHCP server that it no longer needs its IP address, and the **DHCPDecline** to decline a specific the server's TCP/IP configuration. Finally, there is the **DHCPInform** message, which can be sent by a workgroup DHCP server acting as a client or by a client asking for local configuration parameters. A DHCP server that receives a **DHCPInform** message constructs a **DHCPACK** message with local configuration parameters without allocating a new IP address.

1. Review **Frame 21** in Figure 7-32. What computer sent this message? Was it sent directly to the DHCP server?

_____

_____

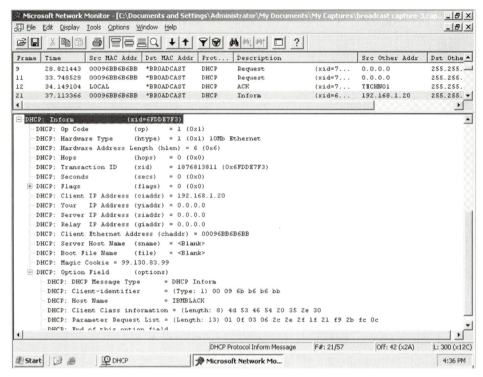

Figure 7-32: Frame 21

8

MANAGING SECURITY

PROJECTS

Project 8.1	Understanding Users and Groups
Overview	Active Directory is the directory service for Windows 2000 and Windows Server 2003. So what is a *directory service*? An example of a *directory* would be a telephone book with each name and phone number being an object. If you know the person's name, you can look up the person's phone number. However, knowing the phone number without knowing the person's name would be of little value. Also, even if you know the person's name, the phone book listing will not provide the name of the person's nearest relative. Because Active Directory is a *directory service*, the objects in Active Directory have a relationship to each other and the hierarchical structure greatly simplifies the process of finding an object. Plus, objects can be secured with individual security permissions for their use.

As you know, one of the main reasons for using a network is to enable users to share network resources. Active Directory increases user productivity by simplifying the way users find and access resources such as printers and servers, and it provides a centralized hierarchical structure for security administration of user access. Network management is simplified by allowing administrators to organize users into groups. Using security groups, administrators can assign access permissions and can delegate administrative privileges and rights to a number of users at once.

Although this sounds extremely beneficial, the design of the Active Directory hierarchy takes careful planning. Active Directory stores access control information on each object, which, when applied, determines which users can access that object and what they can do with it.

Once Active Directory is installed, you can manage users, groups, and computers from the management console. Users can log on with a single user name and password (called *single-sign on*) and, if given permission, can access resources located on servers throughout the domain. |
| Outcomes | After completing this project, you will know how to:

▲ create a user account
▲ isolate server configuration errors
▲ review Administrator account group membership
▲ create a group and add a user |
| What you'll need | To complete this project, you will need:

▲ a client computer
▲ a Windows Server 2003 computer connected to a local network |
| Completion time | 45 minutes |
| Precautions | If you are using a Windows Server 2003 system that already has new user account entries, consult the network administrator for guidelines. |

■ Part A: Create a user account

Networks restrict who can gain access to network resources by setting up a user account for anyone who wants to log on. In fact, users should not be able to access your network without first establishing their identity. Active Directory stores user information such as first name, last name, logon name, and password in the form of user account attributes. Attributes are a person's height and weight as shown on the person's driver's license; these attributes enable authorities to recognize individuals. When you set up a user account, you are creating a security principal in Active Directory that identifies a specific user. When the user logs on to the network by entering security credentials such as username and password, they are authenticated by Active Directory. Administrators can then either grant or deny access to network resources based on that specific user's needs.

1. Open the **Start** menu, point to **Administrative Tools**, and then select **Active Directory Users and Computers** (Figure 8-1).

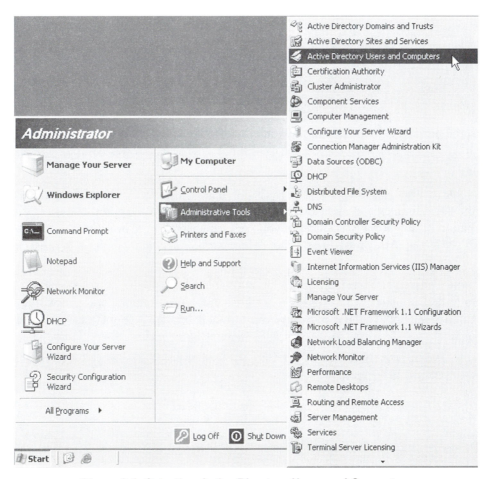

Figure 8-1: Selecting Active Directory Users and Computers

2. The **Active Directory Users and Computers** console will display (Figure 8-2).

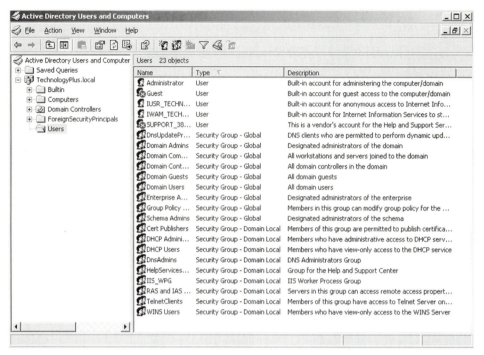

Figure 8-2: Active Directory Users and Computers console

3. Select the plus (**+**) sign in front of the domain name in the left pane.

4. Highlight **Users**. The list of users will display in the right pane. Notice that there are a number of entries already in this folder.

5. Select the column heading **Type**. The list will sort alphabetically, showing **User** at the bottom. Click on the heading again and it will show the **User** type at the top. If this is a new installation of Windows Server 2003, you will see several built-in users, the most important of which is the **Administrator**. The Administrator account has full permission to use computer resources.

6. You will also see a **Guest** account that is disabled by default. This account allows users access to the computer even if they do not have a unique username and password. Although you can rename both of these accounts, you cannot delete the Administrator or Guest built-in accounts.

7. Be sure **Users** is highlighted in the left pane and right-click. Select **New** on the pop-up menu and then **User** (Figure 8-3).

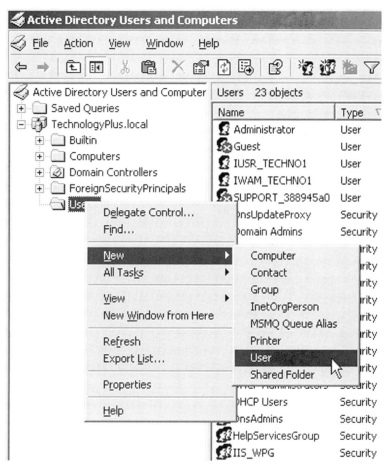

Figure 8-3: Creating a new user

8.   The **New Object - User** dialog box displays (Figure 8-4).

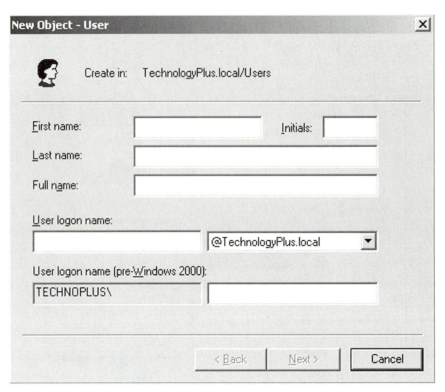

Figure 8-4: New Object - User dialog box

9. Enter a **First name** and a **Last name** (both will appear in the **Full Name** text box) and the **User logon name**. Record what you entered:

    Full name: _____

    User logon name: _____

10. Click **Next**. Enter a password in the **Password** text box. By default on domain controllers, passwords must be at least seven characters and contain three of the following four categories: uppercase characters, lowercase characters, digits (0–9), and nonalphabetic characters (i.e., $, &, %). Password complexity requirements are enforced when passwords are changed or created. If you do not enter the password as required by password policy, an error message will display (Figure 8-5).

    Record the password you selected: _____

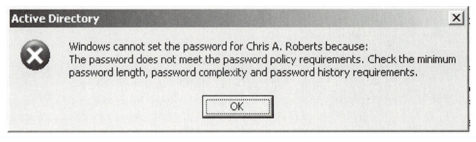

Figure 8-5: Password complexity warning message

11. Reenter the identical characters in the **Confirm password** text box. Notice that there is a check in the box for **User must change password at next logon**. This enables users to manage the creation of their passwords.

12. When you create a new user account on a domain controller, where is that user's information stored? If you create a new user account on a Windows XP computer, where will it be stored?

_____

_____

■ Part B: Increase security for the Administrator account

By default during Windows Server 2003 installation, the name Administrator is given to the account with full control over the computer. This account can never be deleted or removed from the Administrators group. Active Directory assigns new accounts, including built-in accounts, a globally unique identifier (GUID). A security identifier (SID) is also assigned for logon authentication and access to resources. SIDs contain both domain values (relative identifiers [RIDs]) and unique values. The Administrator account on all systems is assigned a RID of 500, which makes it easy to spot by hackers if they can obtain a list of the computer's SIDs. Because there are a number of hacking programs that can extract SIDs, it is a good idea to make it harder for a hacker to find that account.

As a Best Practice, you should use the Administrator account during the initial system setup and then never use it again. You can rename it, but that will not hide its RID. It makes more sense to both rename it and disable it. However, understand that even if the Administrator account is disabled, it can still be used to gain access to a domain controller using Safe Mode. If you need to use the Recovery Console, you must to know the password for this account. Set a long and complex password. Windows Server 2003 by default has a lockout policy for the Administrator account of five bad attempts to log in remotely or over the network; however, local login (at the keyboard) does not have this restriction. Once you have renamed and disabled the original Administrator account, create a dummy account with Administrator as the name, and give it a complex password and no permissions. You can audit this "Administrator" account to see if there are internal users who may be trying to practice their hacking skills.

1. Open the **Active Directory Users and Computers** console. Select **Users** in the left pane.

2. Highlight **Administrator** in the right pane.

3. Right-click and select **Rename** on the pop-up menu (Figure 8-6).

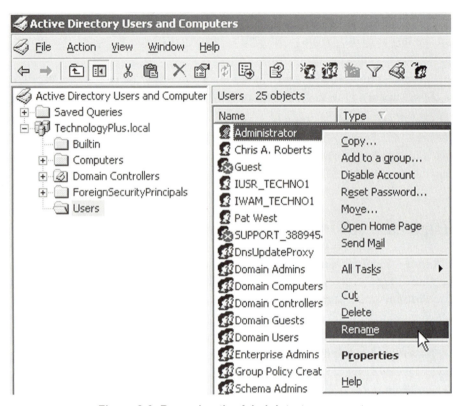

Figure 8-6: Renaming the Administrator account

4. A box will appear around **Administrator** and you will be able to change the name.

5. WRITE DOWN THE NEW NAME!

_____

6. Highlight the new name and select **Copy** from the pop-up menu. Create a new Administrator account with a different name. WRITE DOWN THE NEW ADMINISTRATOR ACCOUNT NAME AND PASSWORD!

_____

Note: You will not be able to log on without knowing this name and password.

7. Now highlight the old Administrator (renamed) account and right-click to open its **Properties** dialog box. Select the **Account** tab and under **Account options**, select **Account is disabled**.

8. Log off (you do not need to shut down the server) and log back on using the new account and password.

9. What other information in the Administrator account would you want to update in Active Directory?

_____

_____

■ Part C: Review Administrator account group membership

By default, the Administrator account that you just renamed is a member of a number of groups.

1. Log on using the account you just renamed and open the **Active Directory Users and Computers** console.
2. Select **Users** in the left pane and highlight the renamed **Administrators** account in the right pane.
3. Right-click and select **Properties**.
4. Select the **Member Of** tab (Figure 8-7).

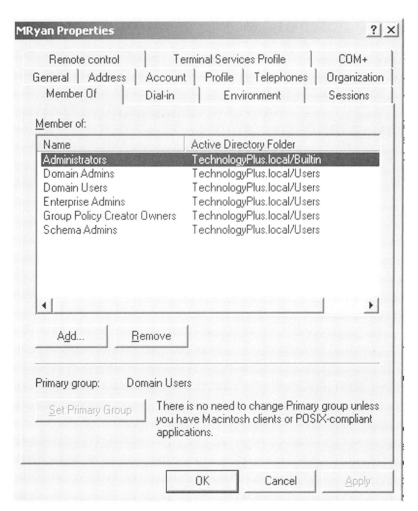

Figure 8-7: Member Of tab

5. In Active Directory, there are two types of user accounts: domain user accounts and built-in user accounts. *Domain user accounts* are used to grant or deny access to resources on a network. *Built-in user accounts* are created automatically during installation. You have just seen an example of a built-in user account – the Administrator account. There are local user accounts on Windows Server 2003 computers that are *not* domain controllers. Local user accounts can only be used to grant or deny access to local resources on that computer. Once a server has been promoted to a domain controller, a user who logs on at a domain controller's keyboard is authenticated by Active Directory; in other words, domain controllers do not have local accounts.

6. What other account could you add to increase security for Windows Server 2003?

_____

_____

■ Part D: Create a Global group

Until now, the new user accounts you created were members of built-in groups such as the Administrators group or the Account Operators group. These groups have default permissions that are already assigned. However, your Active Directory design will likely need to be more closely aligned with your own organization's structure. You can do this by creating groups to simplify administration and assign permission to the whole group at once. A group can contain user accounts, computers, contacts, and other groups. As you have learned, organizational units (OUs) are primarily used to organize objects, while groups are specifically used to grant access to resources. Remember, you cannot assign permissions to an OU, but you can assign permissions to the users or computers in a group. In this activity, you are going to first create an OU and then add a group to that OU.

1. Open the **Active Directory Users and Computers** console.

2. Select the domain and right-click. The pop-up menu will display.

3. Select **New** and **Organizational Unit** (Figure 8-8).

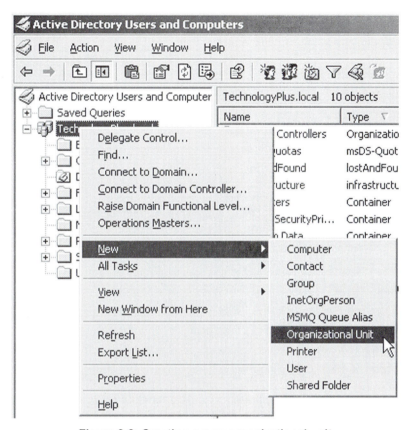

Figure 8-8: Creating a new organizational unit

4. The **New Object - Organizational Unit** dialog box appears. Enter the name of your new OU. Figure 8-9 shows the creation of a Customer Service OU. If you decide later to move your OU under another OU, it is simple process.

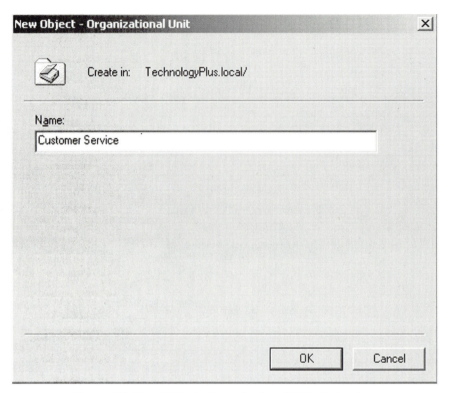

Figure 8-9: New Object - Organizational Unit dialog box

5.   Click **OK** and the new OU will display in the left pane.
6.   Highlight the new OU and right-click. Select **New** and then **Group** (Figure 8-10).

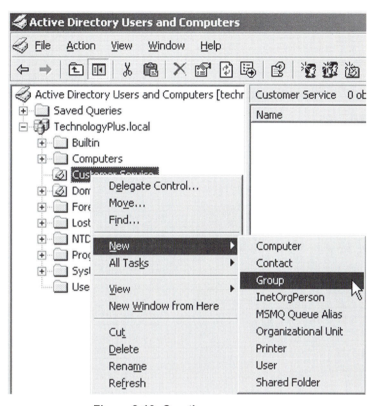

Figure 8-10: Creating a new group

7. The **New Object - Group** dialog box displays (Figure 8-11).

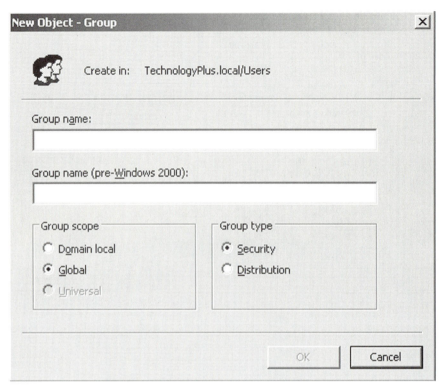

Figure 8-11: New Object - Group dialog box

8. Select a group name and shortened pre–Windows 2000 name, if necessary. Record the group name you selected.

_____

9. Leave the default selections in **Group scope (Global)** and **Group type (Security)** as is (Figure 8-12).

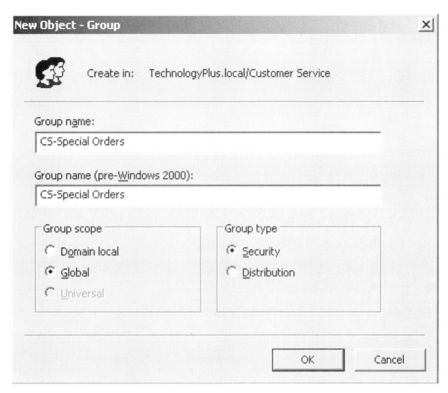

Figure 8-12: Selecting a Group name, Group scope, and Group type

10. Click **OK**. The new group will appear in the right pane (Figure 8-13).

Figure 8-13: New group

11. The group you just created is a Global group. What is Microsoft's recommendation for adding users to a Global group? Can you add other groups to a Global group?

_____

_____

_____

Project 8.2	Using the RunAs Command
Overview	Logging on to a Windows Server 2003 with full administrator credentials can create a security risk for your Windows Server 2003 system, so Microsoft recommends that administrators create two user accounts – one with broad administrative credentials, and one regular account that is restricted for nonadministrative tasks. However, to avoid logging off and back on, you can log on with the regular user account and then use the RunAs command to access administrative tools that require the account with full administrator credentials. (RunAs is sometimes referred to as *secondary logon*.)
Outcomes	After completing this project, you will know how to: ▲ review the RunAs command ▲ use the RunAs command with a regular account ▲ create a RunAs shortcut
What you'll need	To complete this project, you will need: ▲ a client computer ▲ a Windows Server 2003 computer connected to a local network
Completion time	20 minutes
Precautions	None

■ Part A: Review the RunAs command

The Administrator account is identified by Active Directory as an object with credentials to perform system- and domainwide administrative tasks. Groups that use administrative credentials include Administrators, Domain Admins, and DNS Admins. If a hacker can acquire the name and password for this account, all information on the network can be compromised.

1. Log on using the renamed **Administrator** account.
2. Open the **Active Directory Users and Computers** console.
3. Select **Users** and then highlight a regular user account. Check this regular user's group membership by selecting the **Member Of** tab. This account should *not* be a member of the Administrators group; however, the account does need logon interactively rights if you are using it to log on sitting at the keyboard of your domain controller. Otherwise, it does not need logon interactively rights. If this user does not have logon interactively rights, the logon will fail and a logon interactively error will display (Figure 8-14).

Figure 8-14: Logon Message

4. The user in Figure 8-15 is a member of the Account Operators built-in group. This user can logon interactively but is restricted from using specific tools such as Network Monitor.

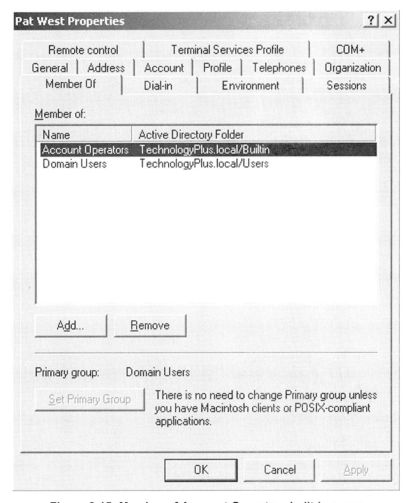

Figure 8-15: Member of Account Operators built-in group

5. Log out of the system and log back in using the regular user's account.

6. Select **Administrative Tools** and then **Network Monitor**.

7. The regular user will receive an error message (Figure 8-16)

Figure 8-16: Error message

8. Highlight **Network Monitor** in the **Administrative Tools** list and right-click. Select the **Run as** command on the pop-up menu (Figure 8-17).

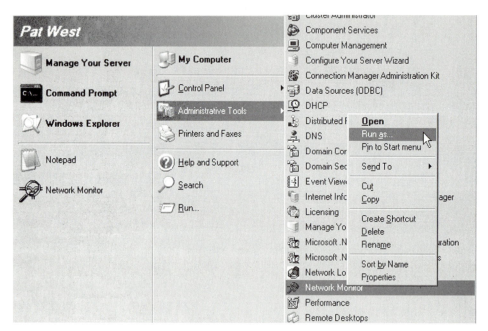

Figure 8-17: Selecting the Run as command

9. The **Run As** dialog box displays, asking **"Which user account do you want to use to run this program?"** (Figure 8-18). You can also use **runas** from the command prompt.

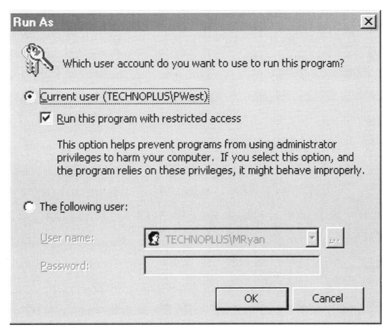

Figure 8-18: Run As dialog box

10. Why would you want to control who has interactive logon?

_____

_____

■ Part B: Create and use a RunAs shortcut

You may want to create a RunAs shortcut icon to easily access the RunAs command from your desktop.

1. Log on using your regular user account that does not have permission to access **Active Directory Users and Computers**.

2. Select an area on the desktop where there are no icons.

3. Right-click, point to **New** and then select **Shortcut**(Figure 8-19).

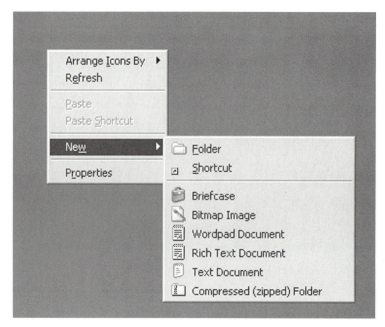

Figure 8-19: Creating a Desktop shortcut

4. The **Create Shortcut** wizard displays.

5. Enter **Runas */user:administrator@domainxxx.local* "mmc dsa.msc"** (modify this entry for the administrator's login and for your domain name) (Figure 8-20).

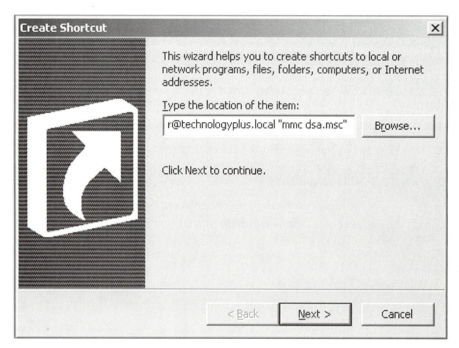

Figure 8-20: Create Shortcut wizard

6. Select **Next** and then give the shortcut a name (Figure 8-21).

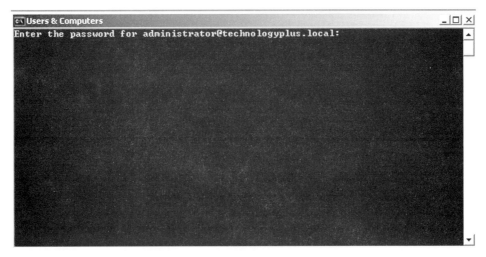

Figure 8-21: Naming the shortcut

7. Select **Finish**.

8. The shortcut icon will show on the desktop. Double-click the icon. A **Users & Computers** password prompt window will appear (Figure 8-22).

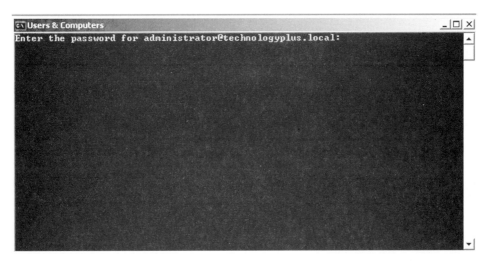

Figure 8-22: Users & Computers password prompt window

9. Enter the password for the administrator at the prompt. (**Note:** When you type the password, it will not display for security purposes.) Then, press **Enter**.

10. If you log on as your regular account and want to create a shortcut icon for Network Monitor, what would you do?

_____

_____

Project 8.3	Managing Users
Overview	Organizations are always changing, which means users will move and change responsibilities. Therefore, you need to learn how to modify user status on the network. You have learned how to create a new user and how to rename the Administrator account. This project discusses effective ways to manage users.
Outcomes	After completing this project, you will know how to: ▲ review user properties ▲ reset passwords ▲ create a home folder
What you'll need	To complete this project, you will need: ▲ a client computer ▲ a Windows Server 2003 computer connected to a local network
Completion time	30 minutes
Precautions	None

■ **Part A: Review the properties of a user account**

When you create a new user account, you can set a number of personal and network properties.

1. Open **Active Directory Users and Computers**. Select **Users**. Select the new user you created in the previous activity or create a new user.
2. Once the new user is shown in the right-hand pane, highlight the new user's name.
3. Right-click and select **Properties**. Select the **Member Of** tab.
4. The user in Figure 8-23 is a member of only one group, the **Domain Users** group, which is the default.

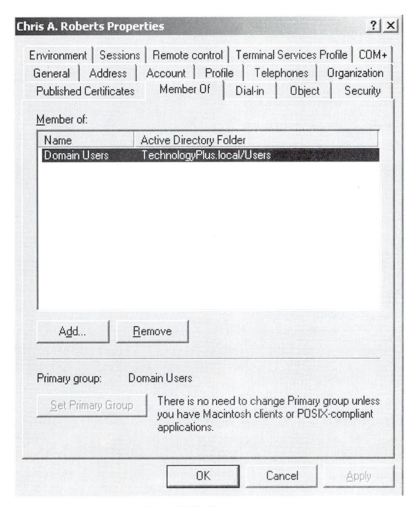

Figure 8-23: User account

5. Select the **Account** tab (Figure 8-24).

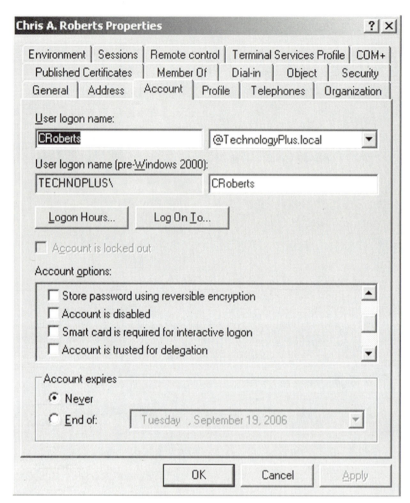

Figure 8-24: Account tab

6. Review the various **Account options** by scrolling down the list. Notice the **Account is disabled** selection. You may want to create a new user such as a temporary worker and then disable the account until the day the temporary worker starts. You can also disable an account for users who take a leave of absence. If you disable the account, a red **X** will display on user's name and **Enable Account** will display on the pop-up menu. List the different account options here and explain their function.

_____

_____

_____

_____

7. Select the **Logon Hours** button. The **Logon Hours** dialog box for the user account appears (Figure 8-25). Because this is a temporary worker who only works 8 to 5, you may

want to restrict the time this user can log on to the network. Then close the Logon Hours dialog box.

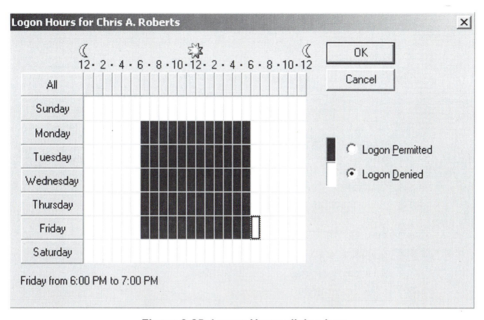

Figure 8-25: Logon Hours dialog box

8. Select the **Log On To** button on the **Account** tab of the user account's **Properties** dialog box. The **Logon Workstations** dialog box appears (Figure 8-26). You can use this dialog box to limit this temporary worker to specific workstations.

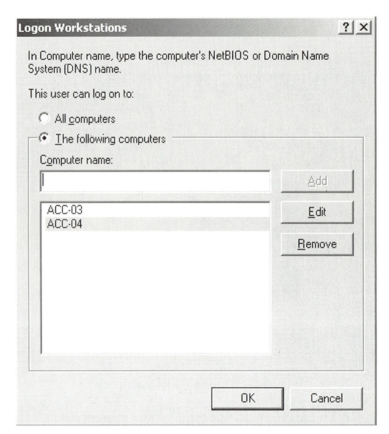

Figure 8-26: Logon Workstations dialog box

9. What are some other situations in which you would want to limit which computers could be used?

_____

_____

■ Part B: Reset user passwords

1. Highlight the user account and right-click. The pop-up menu displays. Note that the command to reset a password is on this menu and *not* in **Properties** (Figure 8-27). You can also see a number of other selections.

Figure 8-27: Reset Password command

2.   Notice that the **Copy**, **Move**, and **Rename** commands are located here. If the user account is disabled, **Enable Account** will also be in this list (Figure 8-28).

Figure 8-28: Enable Account command

3. Select **Move** and the **Move** dialog box displays, allowing you to select where to move the user account (Figure 8-29).

Figure 8-29: Move dialog box

4. If you manage a large number of temporary workers, what would be an easy way to create new user accounts?

_____

_____

■ Part C: Create a home folder

Setting up home folders allows users to save their work to a network server instead of locally on a hard disk. Home folders should be created on an NTFS volume. One advantage of home folders is that these files will be included in the regular backup of servers.

1. Before you can set up a home folder for your user, you need to create a **Users** folder on a network server and share it (there will be more information about shares in chapter 9). Using the **%username%** will create a folder with the user's name and give them Full Control permission of the folder. It will also remove the Administrator account Full Control permission from the folder.

2. Open **Active Directory Users and Computers**. Select **Users** and highlight your new user in the right pane.

3. Right-click and select **Properties**. Select the **Profile** tab (Figure 8-30).

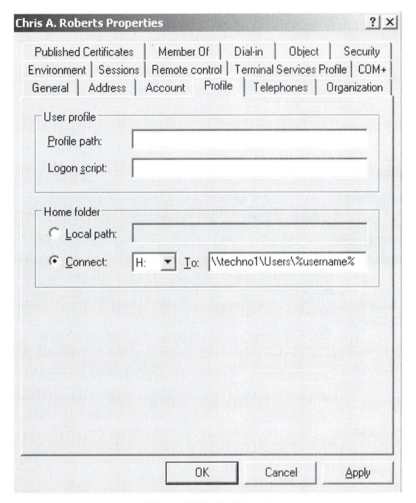

Figure 8-30: Profile tab

4. Under **Home folder**, select the **Connect** radio button.

5. Select the drive letter and then enter the server name and the folder as follows:
    \\servername\Users\%username%

6. Can you name one disadvantage of using home folders?

    _____

    _____

Project 8.4	Managing Groups
Overview	Before getting too deep into groups, let's step back a little and make certain you understand the structure of Active Directory. *Domains* are the main units of organization – the big box that holds all the objects. In fact, many companies need only one domain.
	OUs are containers used to organize objects within a domain. OUs can contain users, computers, groups, and other Active Directory objects. OUs are logical administrative units that are used to delegate administrative rights. OUs enable you separate the domain into more manageable parts, letting other administrators be responsible for their part.
	A *group* is a container for managing user accounts. The most important aspect to understand about groups is that you can assign permissions to them, rather than granting permissions to a lot of individual users. While an OU can help organize user accounts for administration, a group enables you to reduce your workload by "batching" the process of providing users access to resources.
	Active Directory provides two types of groups: distribution groups, which are used with e-mail, and security groups, which let you assign permissions to shared resources. We will use security groups in the activities below.
	Groups have a *scope* that identifies the extent of the group's function. There are three group scopes: universal, global, and domain local. Before you create a group, you need to determine its purpose. Will the group hold users from more than one domain? Will the group be used to assign permissions for a particular resource?
	You have seen some of the built-in security groups that are created automatically, such as the Domain Users or Domain Admins group. Along with these, there are built-in groups that have a specific purpose such as performing certain tasks. When you add a user to one of these groups, the user receives all user rights assigned to the group or permission to use a shared resource.
	What is the difference between rights and permissions? User *rights* allow a user to do a task such as backup files or add new accounts. User rights are most often assigned to network administrators. *Permissions* are similar to a ticket that enables a user to gain access to and perform functions at certain levels such as reading a document or making a change to a document. All shared resources on the network have permissions assigned to them even if the resource is open to any user. Active Directory holds the permission list for each resource object in a discretionary access control list (DACL) and compares a user's credentials to that list when the user attempts to access the resource. That's the reason these groups are called *security* groups.

Project 8.4	Managing Groups
Outcomes	After completing this project, you will know how to: ▲ review a built-in group for security settings ▲ add a user to a group
What you'll need	To complete this project, you will need: ▲ a client computer ▲ a Windows Server 2003 computer connected to a local network
Completion time	30 minutes
Precautions	None

■ Part A: Review a built-in group for security settings

When you add a user to an existing group, the user receives the rights and/or permissions of that group.

1. Open **Active Directory Users and Computers**. Highlight the **Users** folder in the left pane. (Some groups may have been moved to other folders.)

2. Sort the list by clicking on the **Type** column heading. Select **Domain Admins**, which is a **Security Group - Global** type (Figure 8-31).

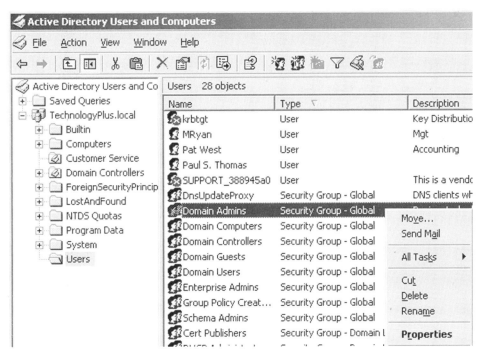

Figure 8-31: Domain Admins group

3. Select **Properties** and then select the **Security** tab. By default, the Domain Admins group is a member of the Administrators group on all domain controllers, all domain workstations, and all domain member servers at the time they are joined to the domain. By default, the Administrator account is a member of this group. Because the group has full control in the domain, add users with caution!

4. Highlight **Administrators** and look at the **Permissions for Administrators**. Select the **Advanced** button. The **Advanced Security Settings for Domain Admins** dialog box displays (Figure 8-32).

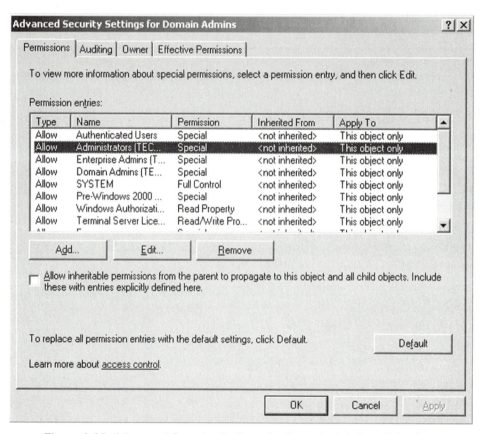

Figure 8-32: Advanced Security Settings for Domain Admins dialog box

5. Select the **Effective Permissions** tab (Figure 8-33).

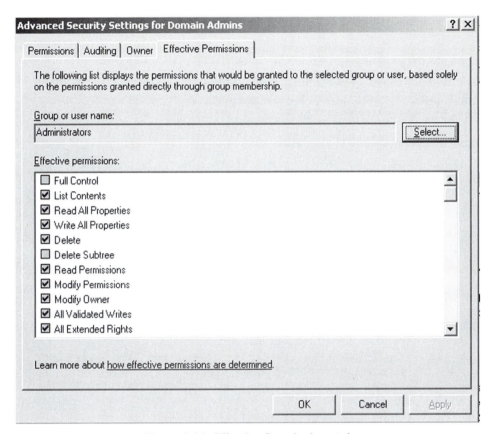

Figure 8-33: Effective Permissions tab

6. Click the **Select** button. Enter **Administrators** in the **Enter the object name to select** text box. Click the **Check Name** button. Click **OK**.

7. Effective permissions for the Administrators group will display. As you can see, there is an extensive list. Review Microsoft's documentation to fully understand the default user rights, such as accessing this computer from the network and allowing logon locally.

8. Using groups simplifies the assignment of permissions. Why would you create a group if there is currently only one user that would be in the group?

_____

_____

■ Part B: Add a user to a group

Managing groups includes adding and removing users.

1. Open **Active Directory Users and Computers**. Highlight the **Users** folder in the left pane. Select a new user. If you need to create a new user, follow the steps above.

2. Right-click on the user and select **Properties**.

3. Select the **Member Of** tab. Click **Add**.

4. Click the **Advanced** button. Click the **Find Now** button. The **Select Groups** dialog box displays (Figure 8-34)

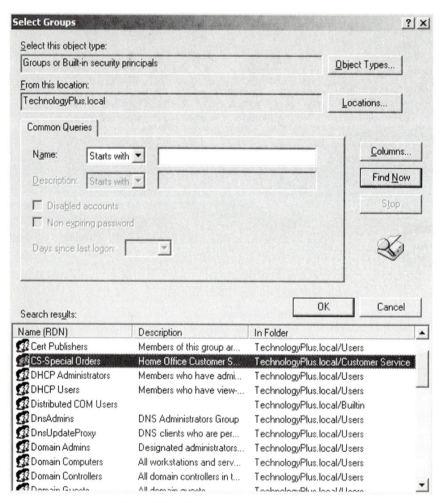

Figure 8-34: Select Groups dialog box

5. Select the new group in the **Search results** list. Click **OK**, **OK**, and then **Apply**. The new group (in this case, **CS-Special Orders**) will be shown in the **Member of** list (Figure 8-35).

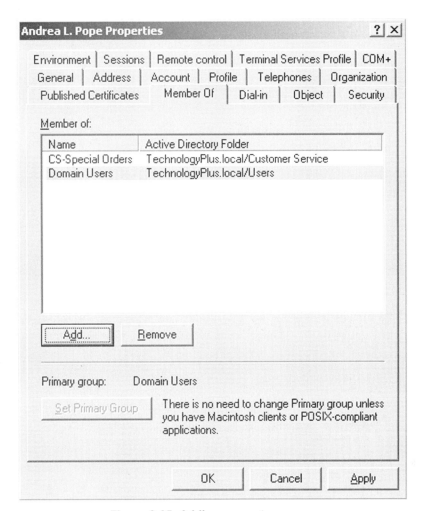

Figure 8-35: Adding a user to a group

Project 8.5	Understanding Group Policy
Overview	Managing the user environment is an important task for any administrator. In large organizations, it can be difficult to manually maintain consistent user and computer settings. Active Directory includes a feature called Group Policy *(don't confuse Group Policy with Active Directory security groups!)*. Group Policy allows administrators to automatically deploy user and computer settings, in turn easing the burden of controlling the computing environment. Group Policy is implemented using one or more *Group Policy Objects* (GPOs). A GPO is an Active Directory object that contains a collection of Group Policy settings.
	GPOs can be applied to various Active Directory containers, such as sites, domains, and OUs. GPOs can exist at any or all of these containers. As a result, there is a potential for conflicting settings. To deal with this, there is a specific order in which GPOs are processed. The order in which GPOs are processed is as follows: local, site, domain, OUs (LSDOU).
	Just as with other Active Directory objects, it is possible to delegate administrative control to individual GPOs, dispersing the administrative burden associated with GPO administration.
Outcomes	After completing this project, you will know how to: ▲ understand the function of Group Policy ▲ view Group Policy Objects in the GPMC
What you'll need	To complete this project, you will need: ▲ a client computer ▲ a Windows Server 2003 computer connected to a local network
Completion time	20 minutes
Precautions	None

■ Part A: Understand the function of Group Policy

To take advantage of Group Policy, an administrator needs a good understanding of the different components of a GPO, as well as the different settings that can be applied by a GPO. A GPO consists of two components. One part is a *Group Policy Container* (GPC). A GPC is an Active Directory component that contains GPO attributes, extensions, and version information. Each GPO has a corresponding GPC that is stored in the System\Policies folder of the Active Directory Users and Computers console. The name of the GPC corresponds with the GUID of the GPO. The second part of a GPO is the *Group Policy Template* (GPT). A GPT is a collection of folders stored in %SYSTEMROOT%\SYSVOL\sysvol\domainname\Policies on each Windows Server 2003 domain controller. Like the GPC, the GPT folder is also named after the GUID of the GPO.

There is an updated management tool for Group Policy called the Group Policy Management console. If you do not have it, you can download it from the Microsoft Web site. It does require Windows Server 2003 or Windows XP Professional with Service Pack 1, and some of its features require a domain controller.

1. Open **Administrative Tools**. Look for **Group Policy Management** (Figure 8-36).

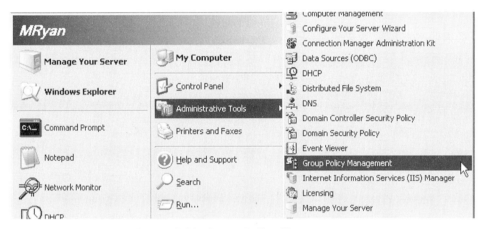

Figure 8-36: Group Policy Management

2. Open the **Group Policy Management** console.

3. Select **Domains**, and then select the domain name (Figure 8-37).

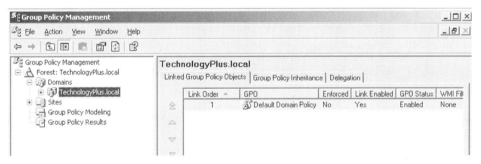

Figure 8-37: Group Policy Management console

4. Right-click and review the list of commands on the pop-up menu (Figure 8-38).

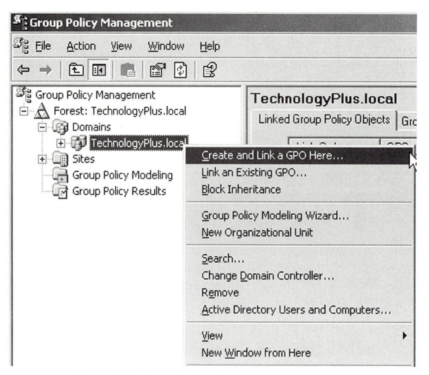

Figure 8-38: Group Policy Management commands

5. Select the plus sign (**+**) in front of the domain and select **Default Domain Policy**. This GPO applies to the entire domain. You will receive a warning (Figure 8-39).

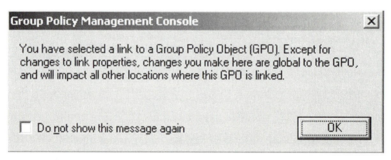

Figure 8-39: Group Policy Management Console warning

6. Click **OK**.
7. The **Default Domain Policy** will display in the right pane (Figure 8-40).

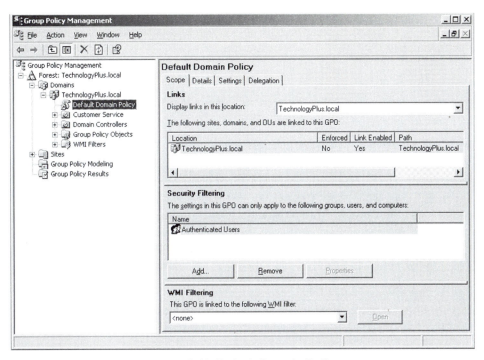

Figure 8-40: Default Domain Policy

8. Select the **Settings** tab (Figure 8-41). You will see the settings for **Computer Configuration**, **Windows Settings**, **Security Settings**, and **Account Policies/Password Policy**.

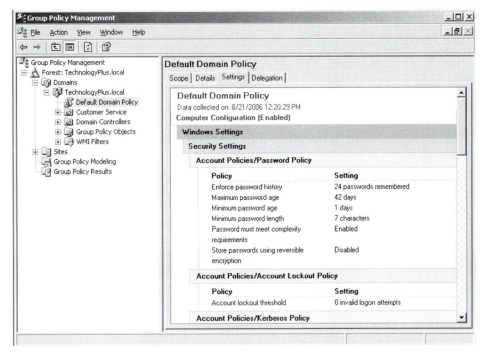

Figure 8-41: Settings tab in the Default Domain Policy

9. When you first created a user account, what settings in this list were applied?

_____

_____

Project 8.6	Using the Delegation of Control Wizard
Overview	The Delegation of Control Wizard enables you to delegate responsibility for a variety of administrative tasks. To use this tool, you must be a member of the Domain Admins or Enterprise Admins group and you must have been delegated the appropriate authority. By delegating administration, you can allow groups within your organization to take more control of their local network resources. This also limits the accidental damage an administrator can do to a certain area.
Outcomes	After completing this project, you will know how to: ▲ delegate responsibility of the administration of an OU ▲ verify that the group has been assigned permission of the OU
What you'll need	To complete this project, you will need: ▲ a client computer ▲ a Windows Server 2003 computer connected to a local network
Completion time	20 minutes
Precautions	None

■ Part A: Delegate responsibility of the administration of an OU

You can offload some of the responsibility for administrative tasks by delegating responsibility to another administrator.

1. Open **Active Directory Users and Computers**. Highlight an OU in the left pane that you have created. In this example, the **Customer Service OU** is selected. Right-click and select **Delegate Control** (Figure 8-42).

Figure 8-42: Delegate Control command

2. The **Delegation of Control Wizard** displays (Figure 8-43).

Figure 8-43: Delegation of Control Wizard

3. Click **Next**. On the **Users or Groups** screen, click the **Add** button.

4. The **Select Users, Computers, or Groups** dialog box appears (Figure 8-44).

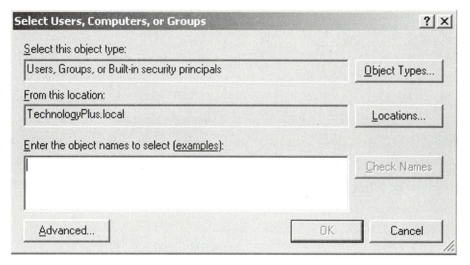

Figure 8-44: Select Users, Computers, or Groups dialog box

5. Click the **Advanced** button, and then select **Find Now**.

6. View the **Search results** and select the group that you want to manage the OU.

7. Click **Next**. The **Tasks to Delegate** screen appears (Figure 8-45).

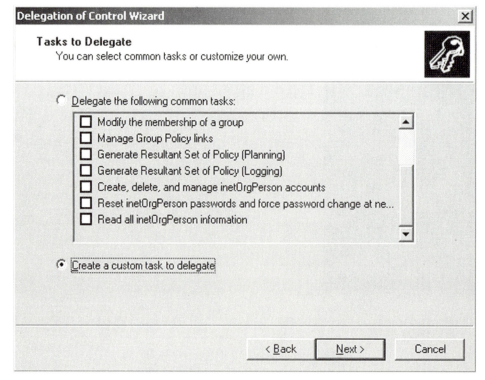

Figure 8-45: Tasks to Delegate screen

8. Select the **Create a custom task to delegate** radio button.

9. Click **Next** and on the **Active Directory Object Type** screen, select the radio button for **This folder,...** (Figure 8-46).

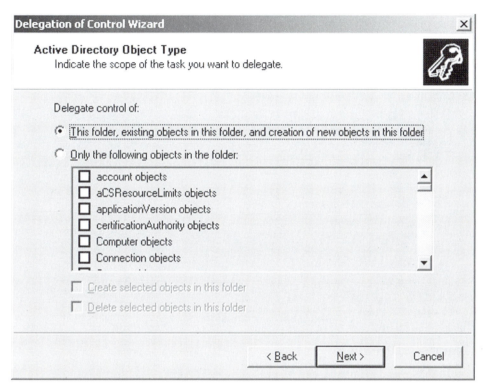

Figure 8-46: Active Directory Object Type screen

10. Click **Next**, and on the **Permissions** screen, select **General** and **Full Control** (Figure 8-47).

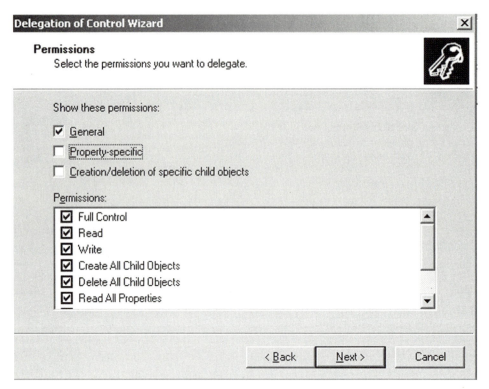

Figure 8-47: Permissions screen

11. Click **Next** and then **Finish**.

12. When you delegate control of an OU, can you determine what the administrator(s) will be responsible for?

_____

_____

■ Part B: Verify that the group has been assigned permission of the OU

After running the wizard, you will want to verify that the responsibility has been assigned. You can review the access control setting for the group.

1. Select the OU and right-click. Select **Properties**.

2. Select the **Security** tab and highlight the group (Figure 8-48).

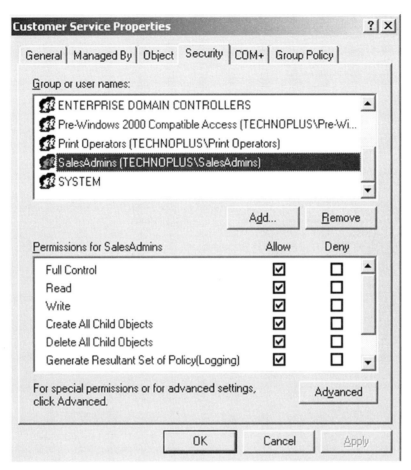

Figure 8-48: Security tab in the Group Properties dialog box

3. Click **Advanced**.
4. On the **Permissions** tab, note the permission entry for the group (Figure 8-49).

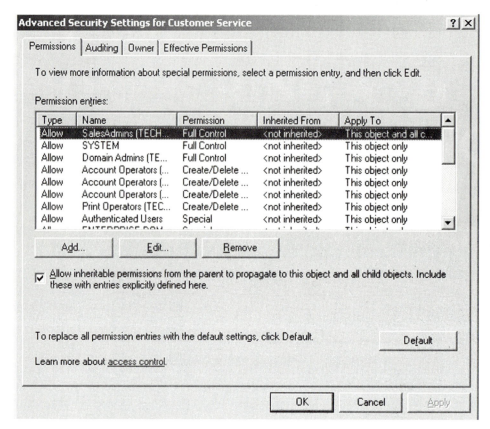

Figure 8-49: Permissions tab in the Advanced Security Settings dialog box

9
MANAGING PERMISSIONS

PROJECTS

Project 9.1	Understanding File and Folder Permissions
Overview	Despite the emphasis on security these days, weekly reports of personal data loss continue to make the headlines. In truth, the release of sensitive employee or customer data can ruin an administrator's career. For this reason, an understanding of access control of network files and folders continues to be a top priority for administrators.

Stored with each file and folder that uses Microsoft's NTFS file system is an access control list (ACL), which contains all of the user and group accounts that have been granted or denied access. When a user attempts to gain access to a file or folder, the user's credentials are compared to the list. If the user is a member of multiple groups, the user's effective permission for the file or folder is the sum of all the NTFS permissions they have been granted.

Although this seems fairly straightforward, setting permissions on NTFS takes careful consideration. Here are some of the constraints:

- Folders and files carry slightly different permissions. If file permissions conflict with folder permissions, file permissions take priority.
- NTFS security is in effect if a user sits at the keyboard of the computer or gains access across the network.
- Deny access overrides any Allow permission.

By default, files and subfolders inherit permissions from the folder above them – the parent folder. In other words, any permissions set on the parent folder will also apply to any subfolder and file created underneath it unless you prevent inheritance. When you create a new volume, default permissions are set that are inherited by any folder you create.

Users attempting to access a file or folder across the network will not be able to see a folder on a file server unless the folder has been shared. On older file systems, the use of shared folders (discussed below) was the only way to secure access. However, on Windows systems, shared folders can be used in conjunction with NTFS permissions to allow network users to view and connect to folders across the network. Remember, if you share a folder and do not set permissions either at the share level or through NTFS, anyone who has access to the network can view and access the folder. |
| Outcomes | After completing this project, you will know how to:

▲ describe the NTFS permission structure
▲ view NTFS default settings
▲ examine user and group permissions on NTFS folders and files |

Project 9.1	Understanding File and Folder Permissions
What you'll need	To complete this project, you will need: ▲ a client computer ▲ a Windows Server 2003 computer connected to a local network
Completion time	30 minutes
Precautions	None

■ Part A: Review NTFS folder permissions

When you create a new folder on a volume that has been formatted with NTFS, you can modify the access a user or group has to that folder by setting one or more of six folder permissions. Folder permissions include Full Control, Modify, Read & Execute, List Folder Contents, Write, and Read. Permission settings are shown in the Properties dialog box for the folder. You use a check box to either Allow or Deny the permission. If the permission has a check in the box that is gray, this permission has been inherited from a parent folder. (**Note:** Special permissions are discussed in Project 9.2.)

- **Full Control:** Users or groups can change permissions, take ownership, and delete subfolders and files, as well as perform actions permitted by all the other NTFS folder permissions (below). Users or groups with Full Control permission on a folder can delete any file in the folder, regardless of the permissions protecting the file!

- **Modify:** Users or groups can delete the folder, as well as perform actions permitted by Write and Read & Execute (below).

- **Read & Execute:** Users or groups can move through folders even if they do not have permission to those folders. They can perform Read and List Folder Contents permissions.

- **List Folder Contents:** Users or groups can see the names of files and subfolders in the folder. This permission only displays when you view *folder* permissions.

- **Write:** Users or groups can create new files and subfolders within the folder, change folder attributes, and view folder ownership and permissions.

- **Read:** Users or groups can open and read files and subfolders. They can view folder ownership, permissions, and attributes (Read-Only, Hidden, Archive, and System).

1. Open the **Start** menu, point to **All Programs**, point to **Accessories**, and select **Windows Explorer,** *or* you can just right-click the **Start** button and select **Explore**.

2. Highlight a folder, or if you do not have a folder created, create one by highlighting a drive and then selecting **File** from the menu. Select **New**, and then **Folder**. Name the folder and then highlight it.

3. Right-click the folder and select **Sharing and Security** (or **Properties**) to open the **Properties** dialog box for the folder. Select the **Security** tab.

4. In Figure 9-1, you will notice that there are four groups listed in the upper box of the **Security** tab. Notice that in the lower box, **Permissions for Administrators**, there are **seven** selections with either **Allow** or **Deny** check boxes. The seventh selection is **Special Permissions**. We discuss those in a later project. The **Allow** check boxes are gray with checks in the boxes. This indicates that those permissions were inherited from a parent folder.

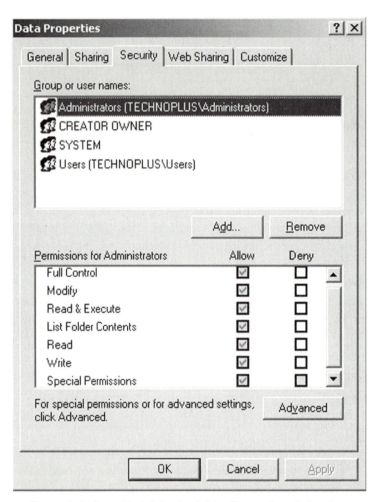

Figure 9-1: Security tab in the folder Properties dialog box

5. Will a user be able to access a folder if the user has **Read** permission for the folder and is a member of a group that has been denied **Full Control**?

_____

_____

6. Windows Server 2003 has updated the default NTFS permissions for the **Everyone** group. This group no longer includes anonymous users. What default permissions does this group have for a new volume?

_____

_____

7. If a user without administrator permissions selects the local disk, the **Add** and **Remove** buttons are grayed out (Figure 9-2). The user will still be able to view permissions, but not make modifications.

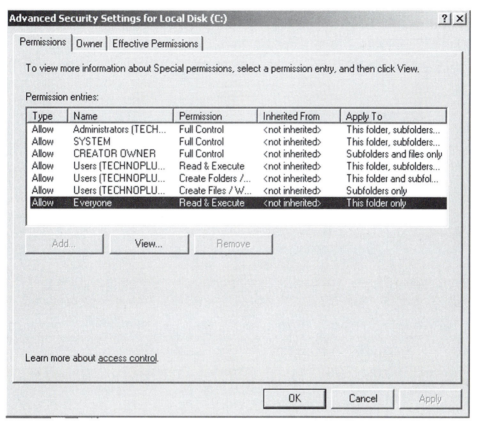

Figure 9-2: Add and Remove buttons grayed out

■ Part B: Review NTFS file permissions

Users create files using hundreds of different kinds of applications and then store those files on either their own hard disk or on a network server. If they store the file on an Active Directory file server, access permissions for the file are stored along with it. The user who saves the file becomes the file owner with Full Control permission; however, there are four other permissions you can set to control user and group access to files.

- **Full Control:** Users or groups can change permissions, take ownership, and perform actions permitted by all other NTFS file permissions (below).
- **Modify:** Users or groups can modify and delete the file, as well as perform actions permitted by Write and Read & Execute (below).
- **Read & Execute:** Users or groups can run executable files, including scripts, and perform Read.

- **Read:** Users or groups can read the file and view attributes, ownership, and permissions for the file.

- **Write:** Users or groups can overwrite the file, change file attributes, and view file ownership and permissions.

1. Start **Windows Explorer**. Highlight the name of a file and right-click. Select **Properties** to open the **Properties** dialog box for the file.

2. Select the **Security** tab. Highlight the file owner. Figure 9-3 shows permissions for the owner.

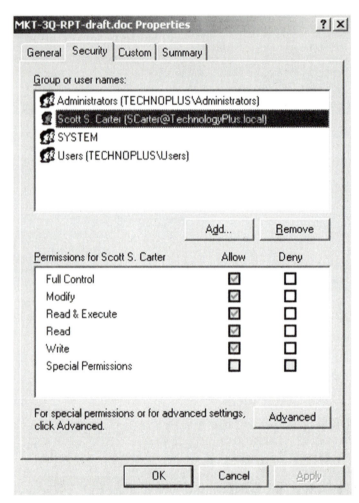

Figure 9-3: Security permissions for the file owner

3. Click the **Advanced** button to view the **Advanced Security Settings** dialog box for the file (Figure 9-4). The owner has **Full Control**, and users have **Read & Execute**.

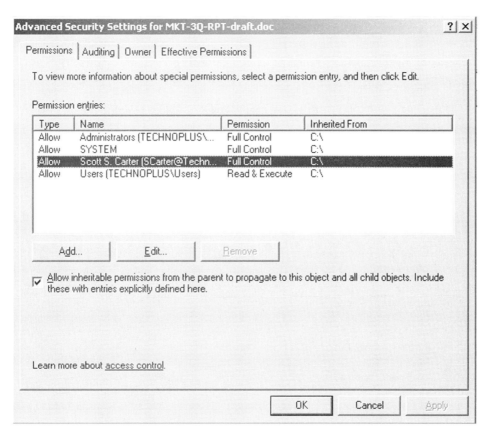

Figure 9-4: Advanced Security Settings dialog box

4.   Select the **Owner** tab (Figure 9-5). The current owner is displayed, and the lower box shows who could take ownership of the file.

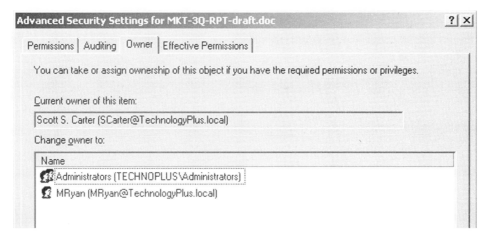

Figure 9-5: Owner tab in the Advanced Security Settings dialog box

5. Select the **Effective Permissions** tab. This tab enables you to display the cumulative NTFS permissions granted to a selected group or user. Click the **Select** button on the right. Enter the name of the user or group, or select the **Advanced** button to bring up the Select User, Computer, or Group list. Select **Find Now**. Choose a user or group and click **OK** (Figure 9-6).

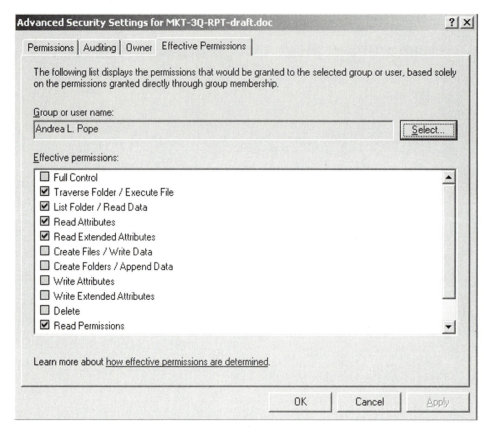

Figure 9-6: Effective Permissions tab in the Advanced Security Settings dialog box

6. If you view this file from a Windows XP workgroup computer, the file's **Properties** dialog box does not include the **NTFS Security tab** (Figure 9-7).

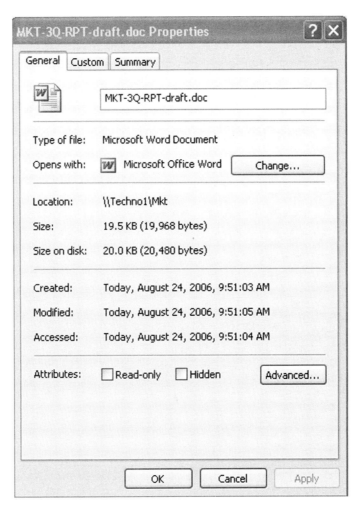

Figure 9-7: Viewing the file from a Windows XP workgroup computer

7. If you want to view a file's security settings from a Windows XP computer that is not joined to a domain, select **Folder Options** in the **Control Panel**. Select the **View** tab, and then uncheck the **Use simple file sharing [Recommended]** check box in the list of **Advanced Settings** (Figure 9-8).

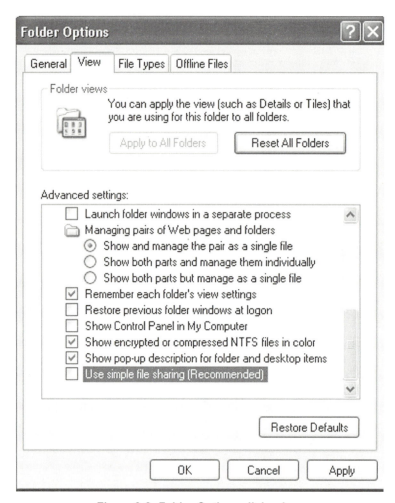

Figure 9-8: Folder Options dialog box

8. Click the **Apply** button to apply the setting and then highlight the file name again. This time the **Properties** dialog box will display the **Security** tab (Figure 9-9).

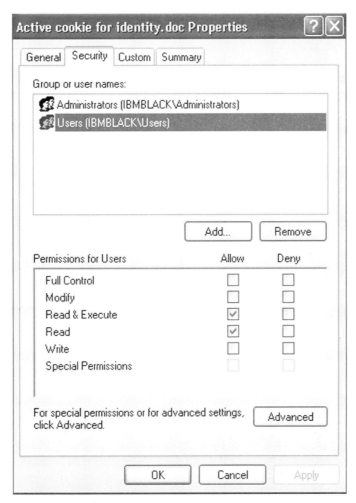

Figure 9-9: Security tab

9. If a user does not have permission to save a file in a specific directory, an error message will display (Figure 9-10)

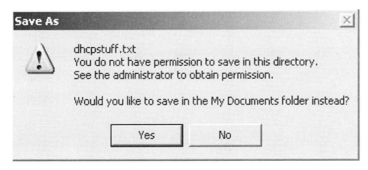

Figure 9-10: Error message

10. If an employee leaves the company and they have owner permission to important files, what steps should the administrator take?

   _____

   _____

11. Where should you look if you want to review all of the permissions a specific user or group has to a file or folder?

   _____

   _____

Project 9.2	Using Special Permissions
Overview	The standard file and folder permissions normally provide enough flexibility that Special Permissions are unnecessary. That said, there may be a few cases when they provide the specific level of access that is necessary.

Special Permissions include:

- Traverse Folder/Execute File (folders only)
- List Folder/Read Data (folders only)
- Read Attributes
- Read Extended Attributes
- Create Files/Write Data (folders only)
- Create Folders/Append Data (folders only)
- Write Attributes
- Write Extended Attributes
- Delete Subfolders and Files
- Delete
- Read Permissions
- Change Permissions
- Take Ownership
- Synchronize (multithreaded programs only)

The standard permissions are composed of a series of Special Permissions. For example:

- Read is composed of List Folder/Read Data, Read Attributes, Read Extended Attributes, Read Permissions, and Synchronize.
- Modify includes all of the special permissions, except Delete Subfolders and Files, Change Permissions, and Take Ownership.
- Change Permissions is helpful if you want administrators to manage file and folder permissions, but you *do not* want them to have Full Control to delete files or folders or write to files or folders.
- Take Ownership also provides an important function. As previously discussed, Windows assigns an owner/creator to all objects when the object is created, and it assigns this owner/creator Full Control permission. An administrator who wants to make permission changes to the file must Take Ownership of that file.

Project 9.2	Using Special Permissions
Outcomes	After completing this project, you will know how to: ▲ describe NTFS special permissions ▲ review Special Permissions set on folders or files ▲ create Special Permissions
What you'll need	To complete this project, you will need: ▲ a client computer ▲ a Windows Server 2003 computer connected to a local network
Completion time	30 minutes
Precautions	None

■ Part A: Review NTFS Special Permissions for a folder

Special Permissions can be accessed through the **Advanced Security Settings** dialog box.

1. Open **Windows Explorer.** Highlight the name of a folder and right-click. Select **Properties**.

2. Select the **Security** tab (Figure 9-11), and then click the **Advanced** button.

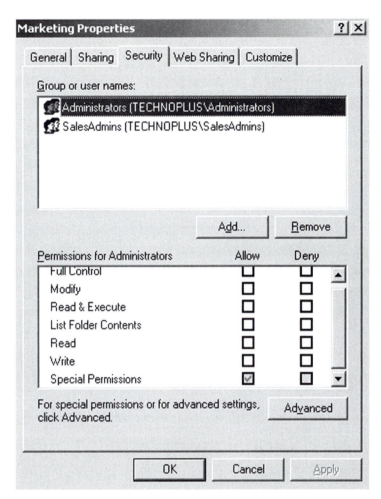

Figure 9-11: Advanced button on the Security tab of the folder Properties dialog box

3. The **Advanced Security Settings** dialog box for the folder opens (Figure 9-12). Click the **Edit** button.

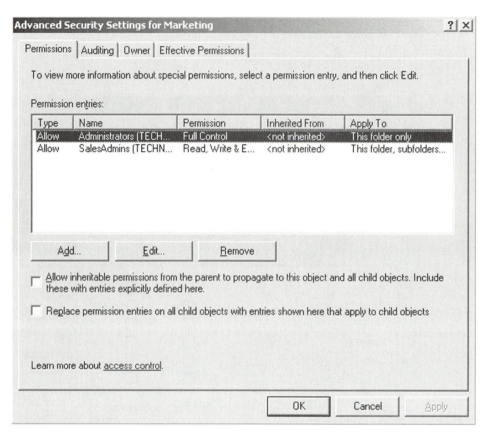

Figure 9-12: Edit button in the Advanced Security Settings dialog box

4. The **Permission Entry** dialog box displays, allowing you to select the **Name** of the user or group that will be assigned the special permissions. Select **Change** if the name does not appear in the box. Once you have the correct user or group, select **Apply onto** to designate where the permission will be applied. Next, enter checkmarks in the **Allow** check boxes beside the permissions to be applied. Figure 9-13 shows the SalesAdmins group has permissions for all but Full Control, Delete Subfolders and Files, Delete, Change Permissions, and Take Ownership.

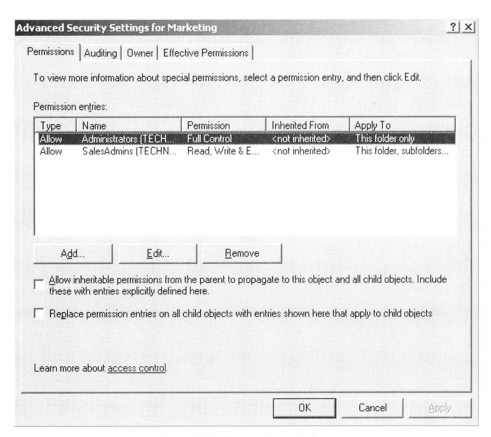

Figure 9-13: Special permissions

5. Can you describe a situation where you would limit the user's permission to delete a folder or its subfolders and files?

_____

_____

■ **Part B: Assign Take Ownership permission to a file**

The Take Ownership permission is accessed through the Advanced Security Settings dialog box. As you know, the Take Ownership permission allows the owner or a member of the Administrators group to assign another user the ability to take ownership. This permission can solve the problem of a file that has been created by someone who is no longer available.

1. Open **Windows Explorer**. Highlight a file name. (If you select a file in the **Users** folder that has Full Control assigned only to the owner, you will receive an Access Denied error.) Select **Properties**. Select the **Security** tab.

2. Click the **Advanced** button at the bottom of the dialog box. Select the **Owner** tab to review who owns the file. Figure 9-14 shows that the Administrators group is the owner of this file.

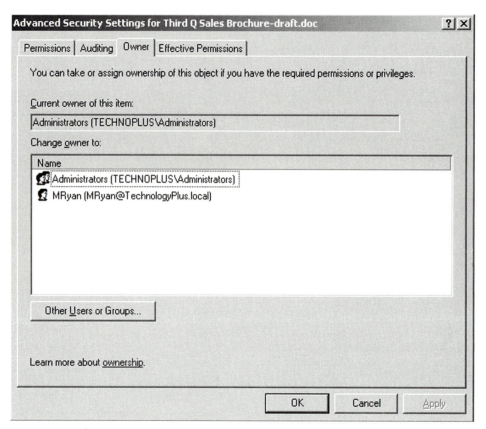

Figure 9-14: Owner tab

3. Select the **Effective Permissions** tab and enter the user or group you want to assign Take Ownership permissions. Figure 9-15 shows that this user has no permissions to this file.

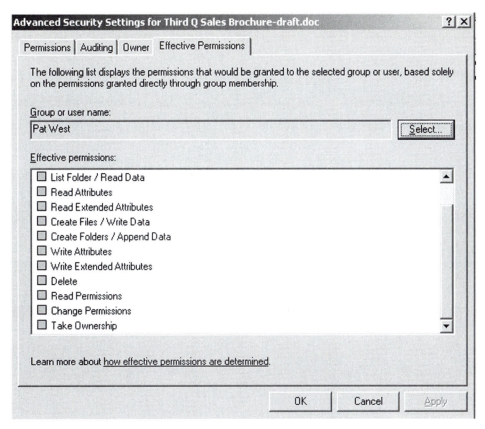

Figure 9-15: Effective Permissions tab

4. Select the **Permissions** tab and then click **Add**. Enter the name of the user or group *or* click the **Advanced** button to search for the name. Click **OK**.

5. Enter a checkmark in the **Allow** box to the right of **Take Ownership** (Figure 9-16) and click **OK**.

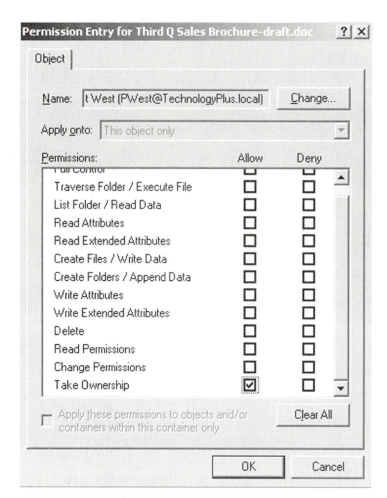

Figure 9-16: Permission Entry dialog box

6. Review the **Permissions** tab again in **Advanced Security Settings** dialog box (Figure 9-17). Click **OK**.

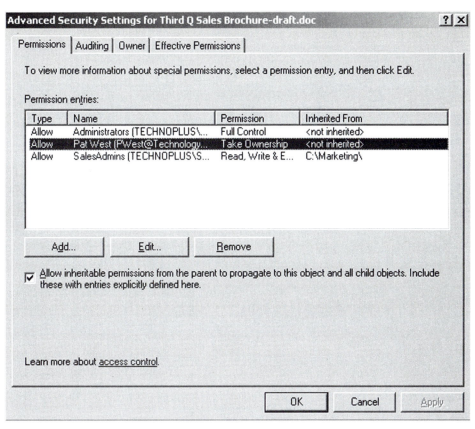

Figure 9-17: Permissions tab

7. Review the **Security** tab in the **Properties** dialog box. Note that **Special Permissions** on the bottom of the list on the **Properties** dialog box should show a gray box with a checkmark (Figure 9-18).

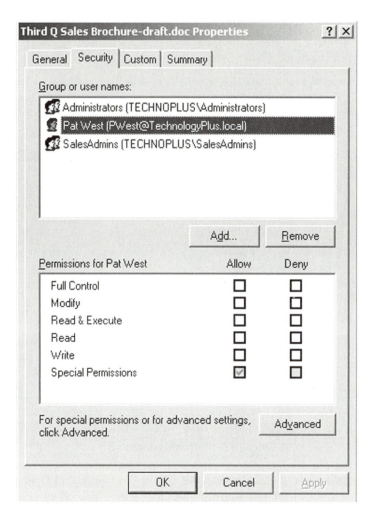

Figure 9-18: Special Permissions selected

8. Every object in Active Directory is assigned an owner (this is considered an attribute of the object and not a permission). Describe how the Take Ownership permission enables an owner to verify a file's usage.

_____

_____

_____

Project 9.3	Assigning NTFS Permissions
Overview	It is a network manager's job to lock down access to network data using NTFS file and folder permissions, and although this may seem like a routine administrative task, consider the consequences of a few incorrect settings. For example, the permission for the company's payroll folder is reset to Everyone – Full Control or the Sales Department's customer database (including customer financial information) is copied to a customer service representative's hard disk. Data loss, whether intentional or just human error, is a concern for all administrators. It is critical that you know the correct techniques for securing data and administering NTFS permissions.
	The following are recommended guidelines:
	• Assign the most restrictive NTFS permissions. If users can perform their jobs with Read & Execute permissions, do not assign Write. (This is sometimes called the *least privilege principle*.)
	• Assign permissions to folders, not files.
	• Review the default inheritance settings immediately after installation. The settings for Windows 2000 Server and Windows Server 2003 are different.
	• When possible, separate data into folders that require the same permissions.
	• Assign users Full Control for public data folders. This allows users to manage the folders and files they create.
	• Use the Deny permission only when necessary.
	It is recommended that you create a security policy outlining the way to administer NTFS permissions and implement it throughout the organization.
	You can also automate how NTFS permissions are set on the domain folders by using a security template. You then use the secedit command-line utility to schedule and apply the template to one or many computers.
Outcomes	After completing this project, you will know how to:
	▲ configure permissions for a new folder
	▲ configure recommended permissions for a file server
What you'll need	To complete this project, you will need:
	▲ a client computer
	▲ a Windows Server 2003 computer connected to a local network
	▲ administrative permission to create a folder and a user group that can be assigned permission to access to the new folder
Completion time	30 minutes
Precautions	None

■ **Part A: Configure permissions for a new folder**

1. Start **Windows Explorer**. Create a folder under the root of your system volume or another folder.

2. Highlight the new folder and select **Sharing and Security**. The **Do not share this folder setting** on the **Sharing** tab is the default. Select the **Security** tab. Review the default user or group names that were inherited when you created the folder (Figure 9-19).

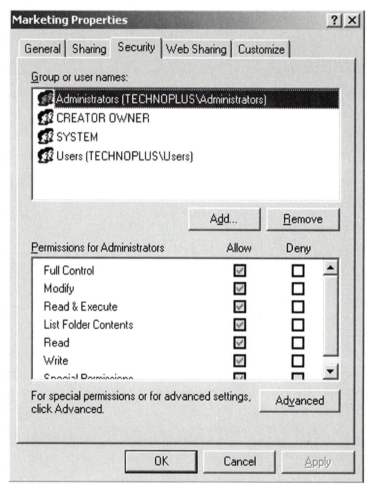

Figure 9-19: Security tab

3. Try to remove all users or groups except administrators. If you try to remove them *before* you uncheck the inheritance check box in the **Advanced Security Settings** dialog box, you will receive an error message (Figure 9-20).

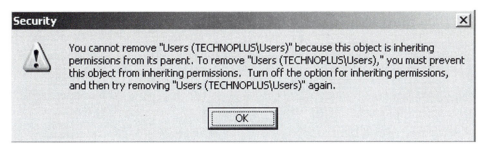

Figure 9-20: Error message

4. Click the **Advanced** button and then *uncheck* the **Allow inheritable permissions from the parent** check box. A **Security** message box opens giving you the choice of **Copy**, **Remove**, or **Cancel** (Figure 9-21). Click **Remove**.

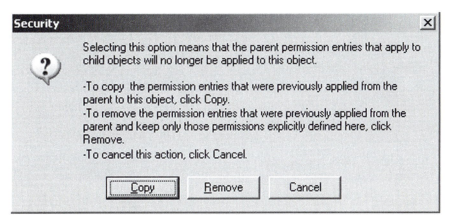

Figure 9-21: Security message box

5. The **Advanced Security Settings** dialog box for the folder appears (Figure 9-22). You can now select the default users or groups that *do not* need permission to this folder and remove them. Be sure to leave the administrators with Full Control.

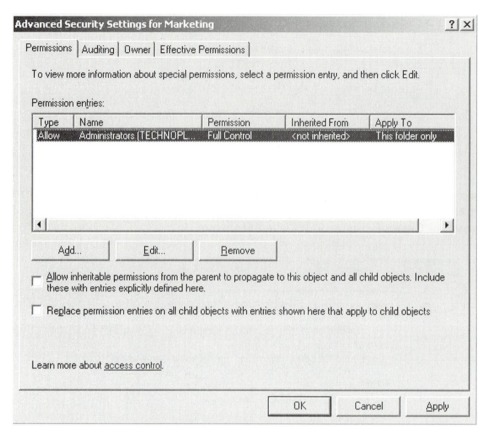

Figure 9-22: Advanced Security Settings dialog box

6. Click **Add**. The **Select User, Computer or Group** dialog box appears (Figure 9-23). Enter the name of the group you want to have access this folder in the **Enter the object name to select** text box, or select the **Advanced** button and you can choose **Find Now** to look for the name.

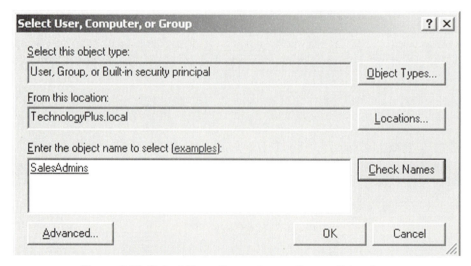

Figure 9-23: Select User, Computer, or Group dialog box

7. Enter checkmarks for the permissions you want the group to use to access the folder (Figure 9-24).

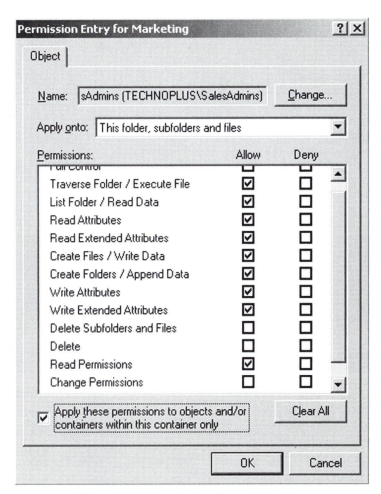

Figure 9-24: Permission Entry dialog box

Note: You will not be able to test the user or group permissions you have just assigned from your client computer unless you have enabled sharing on this folder. Shared folders are covered in Project 9.5.

■ Part B: Configure recommended permissions for a file server

Microsoft recommends the following permissions for certain types of common folders on network file servers with NTFS volumes:

Folder Type	Permission Setting
Public Folder – a folder that is accessed by all users	Set **Modify** permission to the Users group.
Drop folder – a folder that holds user's documents that only a manager can read	Set **Write** permission for the Users group that is applied to **This Folder only**.
Application folder – a folder containing applications that run over the network	Set **Read**, **Read & Execute**, and **List Folder Content** permissions to the Users group
Home folders – user's individual folders	Set **Full Control** permission for each user's folder.

Note: Users and groups with Full Control permission for a folder can delete files and subfolders within that folder, regardless of the permissions on those files and subfolders.

1. Create a single **Users** folder where all users' **Home folders** will be stored. Assign only **Read & Execute** permissions to the **Users** group for this folder.

2. Create an individual user's folder in the **Users** folder using the account name.

3. Assign this user **Full Control** permission (Figure 9-25). Remove all other permissions.

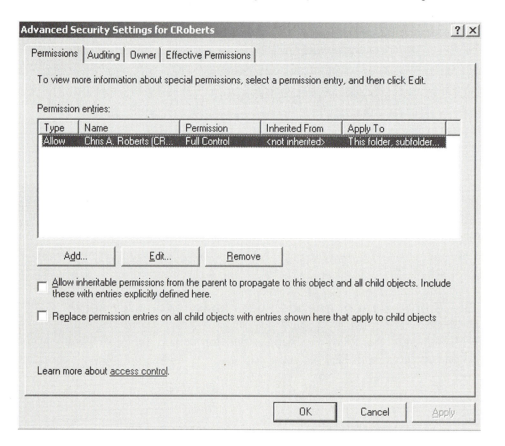

Managing Permissions   **275**

Figure 9-25: Full Control permission assigned

4.   Review the **Effective Permissions** for the Administrators group (Figure 9-26).

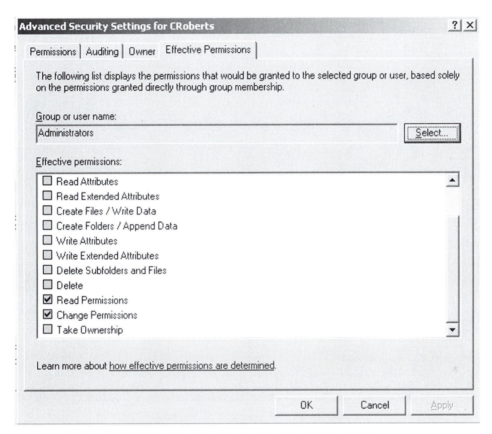

Figure 9-26: Effective Permissions for the Administrators group

5.   Review the **Properties** dialog box for the individual user's folder (Figure 9-27).

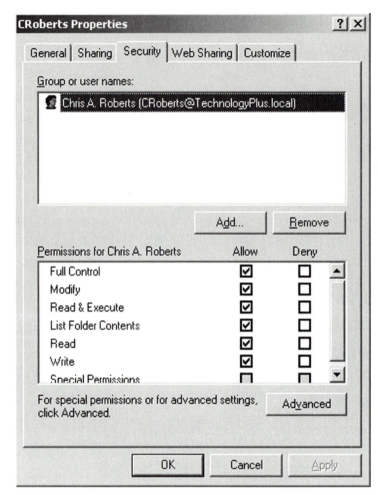

Figure 9-27: Properties dialog box

6. Using administrator credentials, attempt to *open* the user's folder. You will receive an error message denying access (Figure 9-28). Now, *highlight* the user's folder and right-click. You will be able to view the **Security** tab.

Figure 9-28: Error message

Note: You will not be able to test the user or group permissions you have just assigned from your client computer unless you have enabled sharing on this folder. Shared folders are covered in Project 9.5.

7. Will an administrator be able to open and view a file in a user's **Home folder** if Full Control permission is set to the user only?

_____

_____

8. You want a user who is currently on vacation to be the owner of a specific folder. What do you do?

_____

_____

Project 9.4	Copying and Moving Files and Folders
Overview	There is an aspect of managing files and folders we have not discussed and that is the ability of files and folders to be copied or moved to another location. As mentioned, Active Directory holds the ACL along with the file or folder. If this ACL includes permissions that are inherited from a parent folder, a user's credentials are compared to those permissions as well. You might ask then what happens when the parent folder has changed. The following NTFS guidelines apply: • If files or folders are *copied* into another folder, they inherit the permissions of the destination folder. • If files or folders are *moved* from one folder to another, they retain their permissions. However, this occurs only if the destination folder is *within the same volume*. You must have Write permission to the destination folder before you can copy or move files or folders into it. You must have Modify permission for the source folder or file before you can move it. Also, the account that actually copies or moves the file or folder becomes the owner. Note: It is a good idea to write down the ownership and permissions assigned to a file or folder BEFORE you copy or move it.
Outcomes	After completing this project, you will know how to: ▲ review the permissions of a copied file ▲ copy a file from one folder to another ▲ review the permissions of a moved file ▲ move a file from one folder to another
What you'll need	To complete this project, you will need: ▲ a client computer ▲ a Windows Server 2003 computer connected to a local network
Completion time	30 minutes
Precautions	None

■ Part A: Review the permissions of a copied file

1. Highlight a file, right-click and select **Properties** to open the **Properties** dialog box for the file. Select the **Security** tab. Review the permissions set for this file. Figure 9-29 shows that Pat West and SalesAdmins have permissions on the file.

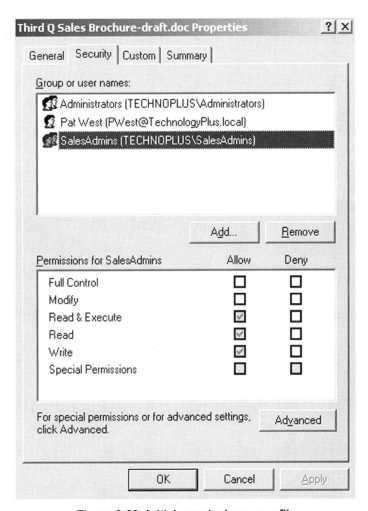

Figure 9-29: Initial permissions on a file

2. Highlight the file name, open the **Edit** menu, and select **Copy to Folder**.

3. The **Copy Items** dialog box opens (Figure 9-30). Select the folder to which you want to copy the file, and then select **Copy**.

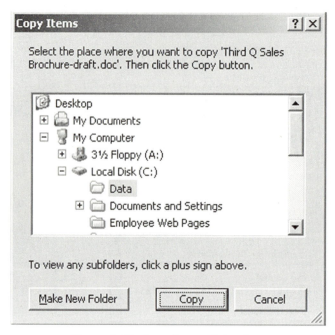

Figure 9-30: Copy Items dialog box

4. Select the destination folder and highlight the file. Select **Properties** to open the **Properties** dialog box, and then select the **Security** tab. Review the permissions. Figure 9-31 shows that Pat West and SalesAdmins are no longer listed.

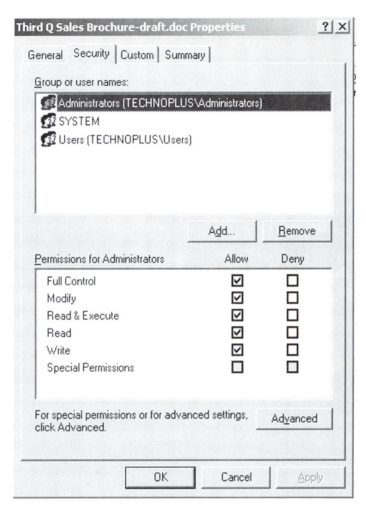

Figure 9-31: Permissions after file has been copied

5. Can you explain why a copied file's owner becomes the user who copies the file into the destination folder?

_____

_____

■ **Part B: Review the permissions of a moved file**

1. Highlight a file, right-click, and select **Properties** to open the **Properties** dialog box for the file. Select the **Security** tab. Review the permissions set for this file. Figure 9-32 shows Pat West and SalesAdmins have permissions on the file.

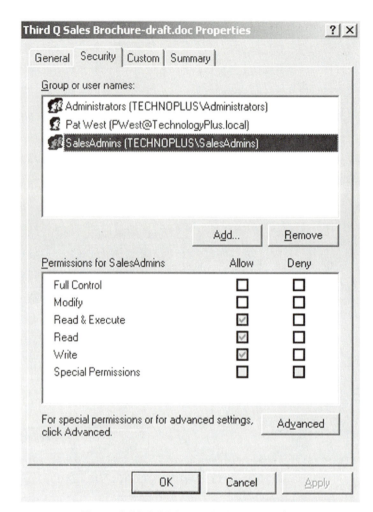

Figure 9-32: Initial permissions on a file

2. Highlight the file name and select **Edit** from the menu bar and **Move to Folder.**

3. The **Move Items** dialog box opens (Figure 9-33). Select the folder where you want to move the file. Select **Move**.

Figure 9-33: Move Items dialog box

4. Select the destination folder and highlight the file. Select **Properties** to open the **Properties** dialog box. View the **General** tab to see the destination folder (Figure 9-34).

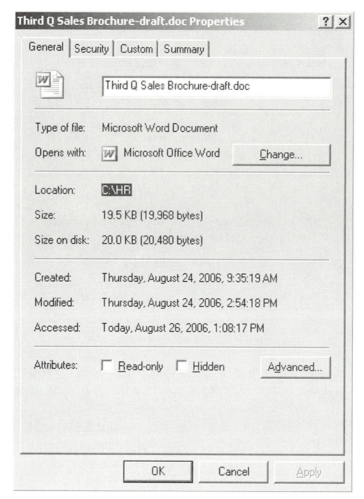

Figure 9-34: Destination folder

5. Select the **Security** tab. Review the permissions. Figure 9-35 shows that Pat West and SalesAdmins are listed with permissions.

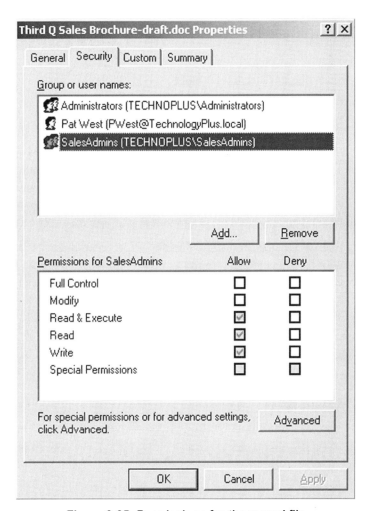

Figure 9-35: Permissions for the moved file

6. You need to revise a document that is stored on the file server. You select the file and select **Move To Folder**, moving the document to your client computer for editing. Why would you want to review the permissions when you put the document back on the file server?

_____

_____

Project 9.5	Managing Shared Folders
Overview	Up to this point, we have discussed only NTFS permissions. However, NTFS permissions *do not* provide network users the ability to view folders on network servers. How can this be? You assign Full Control NTFS permission to the Users group for a folder on the network file server and they can't see it?! Correct.

For files, folders, applications, and other objects to be viewed by network users, you must enable sharing. Think of network resources as being behind a tall, solid gate that limits the view inside. When the gate is open – a folder is shared – users can see the folder on their resources list (e.g., My Network Places) and can attempt to gain access to the folder contents.

Shares, sharing, and shared folders all refer to the process of offering network resources for users to view. You may also have heard of mapping. By sharing the folder on the file server, you allow users to 'map' a new drive letter on their computers under My Network Places to the shared folder – in other words, the map creates a path to that folder and it becomes another disk drive on the user's computer.

Shared folder guidelines:

- You must be an administrator to create shared folders.

- Once a folder is shared, all network users are able to view it. You cannot hide the folder from certain people – it is all or nothing.

- Shared folders can be assigned permissions.

- Shared folder permissions apply to folders, not individual files.

- Shared folder permissions do not restrict access to users who gain access to the computer at the keyboard (or through Terminal Services).

- Shared folder permissions combine – effective permissions are the combination of the user and group shared permissions (not NTFS).

- Shared folder permissions are the only way to secure network resources on a File Allocation Table (FAT) volume.

- A shared folder appears in Windows Explorer as an icon of a hand holding the shared folder.

- When you copy a shared folder, the copy is not shared. When you move or rename a shared folder, the folder is not shared.

- Share Permissions are *not* part of the NTFS Effective Permissions calculation.

There are three Allow choices and three Deny choices for shared folders: Full Control, Change, and Read.

Although share permissions are much simpler than NTFS permissions and |

Project 9.5	Managing Shared Folders
	only apply to users who attempt to connect across the network, share permissions do control *maximum* access. As an example, if the shared folder permission is set to Read, Read is the most the user can do with the folder. Even if that user has Full Control permissions in NTFS, the user will not be able to save a file to the shared folder. By default, on Windows Server 2003, the Everyone group has the Read share permission. This is a change from Windows 2000, which gave the Everyone group Full Control. Administrators can manage shared folders using Windows Administrative Tools, Windows Explorer, or the command-line tool net share.
Outcomes	After completing this project, you will know how to: ▲ review the default shared folders ▲ create a shared folder ▲ create a map to the share
What you'll need	To complete this project, you will need: ▲ a client computer ▲ a Windows Server 2003 computer connected to a local network
Completion time	45 minutes
Precautions	None

■ Part A: Review default shared folders

When you install Windows Server 2003, it creates default shared folders. You can view these folders on the local computer a number of different ways. You can use the Computer Management console, use Windows Explorer to select a specific shared folder's Properties dialog box, or run the File Server Management console.

1. Open the **Start** menu, point to **Administrative Tools**, and select **Computer Management** to open the **Computer Management** console. Expand the **Shared Folders** node and then select the **Shares** folder. The current folders that are shared will display in the right pane (Figure 9-36).

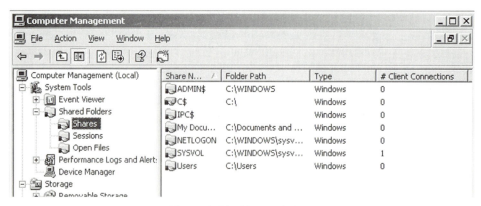

Figure 9-36: Shares folder

2. Notice that some of the shares have a dollar sign (**$**). These shares are called Administrative Shared Folders and are hidden from users. You will notice that the root of each volume and several other shares have the dollar sign appended to the share name. If you try to select these shares, you will receive an error message (Figure 9-37).

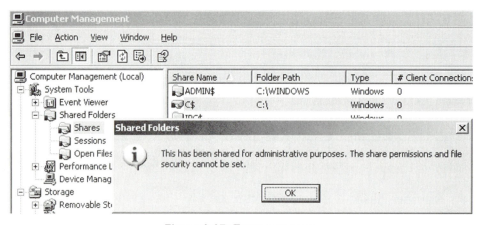

Figure 9-37: Error message

3. Open **Windows Explorer** and select the root volume. View the **C$** administrative share by highlighting **Local Disk (C:),** then selecting **Sharing and Security**. The **Local Disk (C:) Properties** dialog box displays showing the Default Share (Figure 9-38).

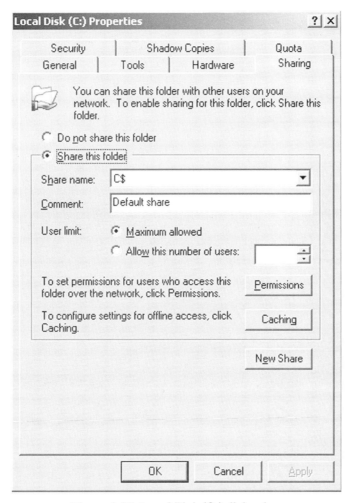

Figure 9-38: Local Disk (C:) dialog box

4. Select **Permissions** on this **C$** administrative share and you will receive an error message (Figure 9-39).

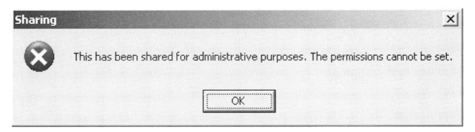

Figure 9-39: Error message

5. If you look at the **Users Properties** dialog box, you will see the sharing icon (Figure 9-40). This same icon is shown smaller in the **Windows Explorer** pane. Users browsing the network *do not* see the sharing icon, only the folder and folder name.

Figure 9-40: Sharing Icon

6. What keeps users from connecting to the root using the **C$** share name?

    _____

    _____

■ Part B: Review shared folder permissions

You can assign only one of three shared folder permissions to allow users to connect to the folder:

*   **Read** – allows viewing file names and subfolder names. It allows viewing data in files and running program files. Read is the default permission assigned to the Everyone group.
*   **Change** – allows all Read permissions, as well as the addition of files and subfolders. It allows data to be changed in files and the deletion of files and subfolders.
*   **Full Control** – allows all Read and Change permissions, plus Change permissions on NTFS files and folders only. Full Control is the default permission assigned to the Administrators group on the local computer.

1. Open **Windows Explorer**. Highlight a folder that has not been shared. You can also choose to create a new share by right-clicking the **Shares** folder in the **Computer Management** console and selecting **New Share** (Figure 9-41).

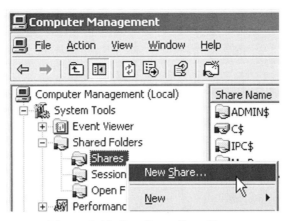

Figure 9-41: Creating a New Share

2. Right-click and select **Sharing and Security**. The **Sharing** dialog box displays asking you to enter the share name.

3. Select the **Permissions** button. The default permission on a new share on Windows 2003 are Everyone = Read (Figure 9-42).

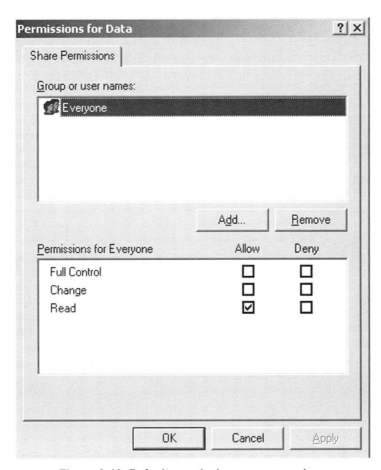

Figure 9-42: Default permissions on a new share

4. This example is a data folder that will be used by all employees. Because employees will need to make updates to folders and files in this folder, **Read** permission will be too restrictive. Assign the **Administrators** group **Full Control** and the **Domain Users** group **Change**. Remove the **Everyone** group. Click **Apply**, and then **OK**.

5. You should now be able to view this new share from your client computer. Test a regular user's access to this folder by attempting to add a file to this new share from your client computer. (You may need to **Refresh** your client's **Windows Explorer**.) Test the user's ability to change this share's permissions.

6. If a user receives an error while attempting to save a file to a network folder, what *two* types of permissions should be checked?

_____

_____

■ **Part C: Use the Share a Folder Wizard**

1. The **File Server Management** console does not automatically appear on the Administrative Tools list. Go to **Manage Your Server** from **Administrative Tools** (the File Server role must be activated) *or* you open the **Start** menu, select **Run**, and browse to the **filesrv.msc in the <systemroot>\Windows\system32\filesrv.msc** (Figure 9-43).

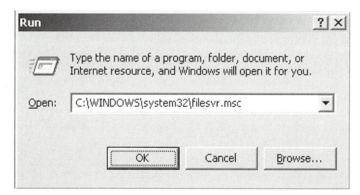

Figure 9-43: Accessing the File Server Management console

2. View shared folder names, descriptions, and their path, then select **Add a Shared Folder** (Figure 9-44).

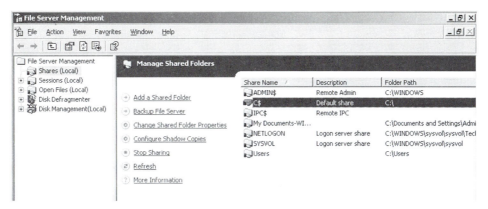

Figure 9-44: Adding a shared folder using the File Server Management console

3. The **Share a Folder Wizard** opens. Select **Next**

4. The **Folder Path** screen displays, allowing you browse to where you will place your new folder (Figure 9-45).

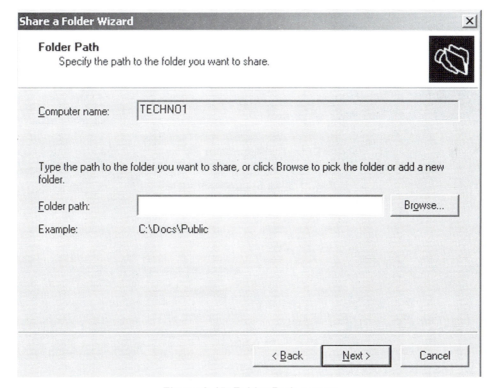

Figure 9-45: Folder Path screen

5. Enter a new name for your shared folder. Enter a short description that explains the shared folder's purpose to users. Record the name and description.

6. Enter the permissions you want on the share. Record your selections.

_____

7. Click the **Finish** button. The summary screen displays (Figure 9-46).

Figure 9-46: Summary screen

8. What is the default permission assigned to a new shared folder on Windows Server 2003? What is the default permission set on Windows Server 2000?

_____

_____

■ Part D: Map Network Drive

Users who regularly connect to a specific shared folder on a file server can map a drive letter on their computers.

1. Log on to your client and open **Windows Explorer**. Open the **Tools** menu and select **Map Network Drive**.

2. The **Map Network Drive** dialog box displays allowing you to select a drive letter and browse to the folder name (Figure 9-47). You can also request that the share reconnect at

logon. Notice the example shows the format **\\server\share**. This format is called the UNC (Universal Naming Convention) path.

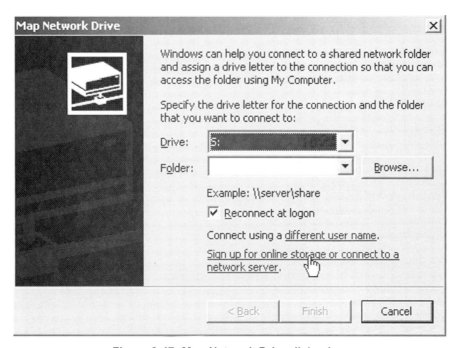

Figure 9-47: Map Network Drive dialog box

3. There are several different ways to gain access to a shared folder. Name two.

    _____

    _____

4. If a user has permission to access a file, but not the folder where the file is located, what can the user do?

    _____

    _____

■ Part E: Publish an Active Directory share

1. Open the **Active Directory Users and Computers** console. (You must have Domain Admins rights to publish a shared folder.)

2. Right-click the folder where you want to add the shared folder (i.e., the Marketing OU) and select **New**, and then select **Shared Folder** (Figure 9-48).

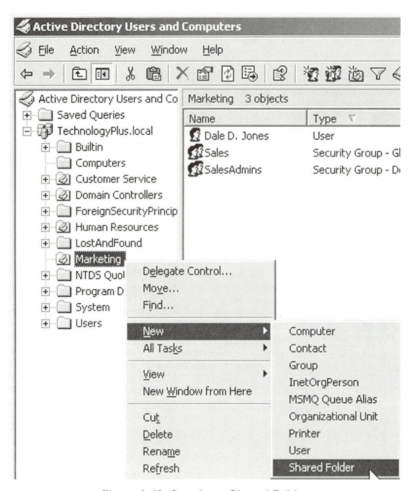

Figure 9-48: Creating a Shared Folder

3. The **New Object - Shared Folder** dialog box displays. This allows you to enter a name that users will be able to recognize and not the actual server name and folder name (Figure 9-49). Be aware that this is now an Active Directory object that *references* the real shared folder resource. It is not a new share. There is a difference between creating an Active Directory object and creating a shared folder.

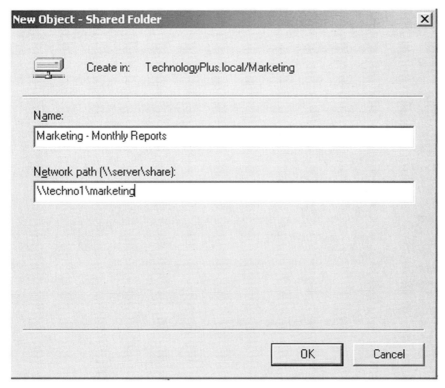

Figure 9-49: New Object – Shared Folder dialog box

4. View the new **Shared Folder** object in the OU. Highlight and right-click to view its **Properties** dialog box (Figure 9-50).

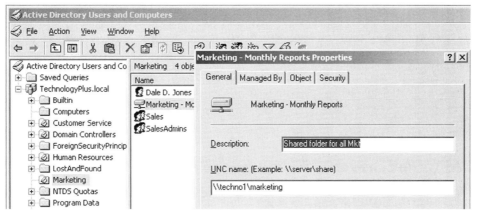

Figure 9-50: Properties dialog box for the Shared Folder object

5. Why would an administrator want to publish shared resources in Active Directory?

Project 9.6	Troubleshooting Permissions
Overview	It is not uncommon for users to have problems attempting to connect to network shared resources. Troubleshooting these problems requires careful examination of both shared folder permissions and NTFS permissions. Investigate problems by confirming the following: • Verify which groups the user belongs to and what permissions are assigned to those groups. • Verify the permissions assigned to the shared folders. • Verify the user's NTFS permissions on the Effective Permissions tab of the Advanced Security Setting dialog box. (Note: The Effective Permissions calculation *does not* include shared folder permissions.) • If the resource is on the local computer, shared folder permissions do not apply. • Check the resource to establish whether the permissions have changed due to copying and moving. If the user's permissions have changed recently, the user may need to log off and log back on to obtain updated credentials.
Outcomes	After completing this project, you will know how to: ▲ troubleshoot permission problems for NTFS ▲ troubleshoot permission problems for shared folders
What you'll need	To complete this project, you will need: ▲ a client computer ▲ a Windows Server 2003 computer connected to a local network
Completion time	20 minutes
Precautions	None

■ Part A: Troubleshoot NTFS permissions

1. Open **Windows Explorer** and select the folder the user cannot connect to.
2. Highlight the name and right-click. Select **Properties** to open the **Properties** dialog box for the folder and then select the **Security** tab.
3. Click the **Advanced** button to open the **Advanced Security Settings** dialog box. Select the **Effective Permissions** tab (Figure 9-51).

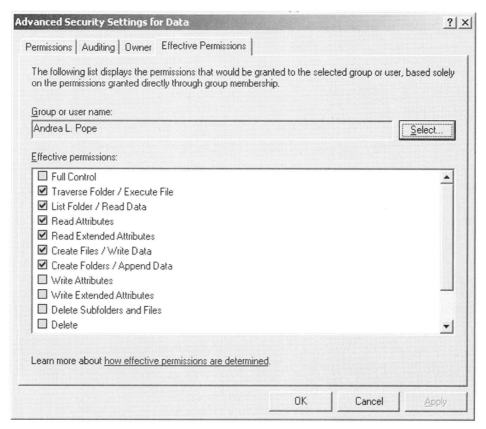

Figure 9-51: Effective Permissions tab

4. Click the **Select** button on the right.

5. Enter the user name in the box and click the **Check Names** button to verify the user name in Active Directory. Click **OK**. Review the user's permissions for the folder.

6. If a user is a member of several groups, each with different NTFS permissions to the resource, what is the guideline?

_____

_____

■ **Part B: Troubleshoot shared folder permissions**

1. Open the **Active Directory Users and Computers** console.

2. Select the OU where the user name is stored

3. Highlight the user's name and right-click. Select **Properties** to open the **Properties** dialog box, and then select the **Member Of** tab (Figure 9-52). Record the groups this user belongs to.

_____

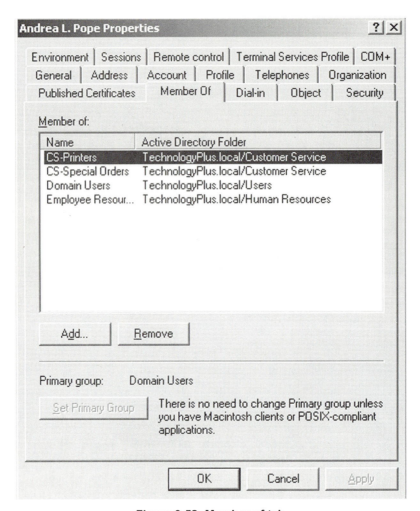

Figure 9-52: Member of tab

4. Open **Windows Explorer** and highlight the shared folder. Right-click and select **Properties**. Select the **Sharing** tab in the **Properties** dialog box, and then click the **Permissions** button to open the **Share Permissions** dialog box (Figure 9-53). Verify the users and groups that have share permissions for the shared folder.

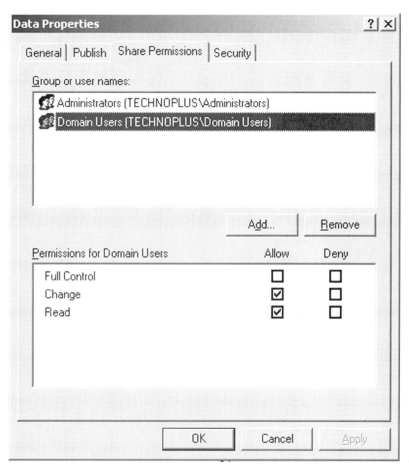

Figure 9-53: Share Permissions dialog box

5. If a user is a member of several groups, each with different shared folder permissions, what is the guideline?

    _____

    _____

6. What is the guideline if a user has *both* NTFS and shared folder permissions?

    _____

    _____

10

ADMINISTERING ROUTING AND REMOTE ACCESS

PROJECTS

Project 10.1	Understanding Routing and Remote Access on Windows Server 2003
Overview	Today's workers never seem to stay in one place. This constant mobility means resources that are available to users at their desks now need to be accessed from remote locations. Before wireless Internet connections became popular, the only way to access LAN resources from a remote location was by using a telephone line. Users with portable computers could dial a phone number via their modem and connect to another modem at the office. This functionality is still available to you on Windows Server 2003; however, as you will see, it also offers a number of other secure connections that use the Internet and private network links. To configure and manage these various connections, you use the Routing and Remote Access console and, while it is enabled as a single network service, you manage the connections individually. Once a connection is established, the protocols and services allow users to view Web pages, read e-mail, and send and receive files, although the speed of some remote access links can be a limitation. In the following activities, we review the way these various connections function.
Outcomes	After completing this project, you will know how to: ▲ explain Routing and Remote Access on Windows Server 2003 ▲ review RRAS functionality
What you'll need	To complete this project, you will need: ▲ a client computer ▲ a Windows Server 2003 computer connected to a local network
Completion time	45 minutes
Precautions	None

When you install Windows Server 2003, the Routing and Remote Access network service is installed but not enabled. This service provides a number of different kinds of connections, most of which are listed on the first screen of the Routing and Remote Access console:

- A secure connection between two private networks
- A virtual private network (VPN) gateway
- A dial-up remote access server
- Network address translation (NAT)
- LAN routing
- Basic Firewall

■ Part A: Explain the functionality of a secure connection between two private networks

1. Open the **Start menu**, point to **Administrative Tools**, and select **Routing and Remote Access**. The **Welcome to Routing and Remote Access** console will display (Figure 10-1).

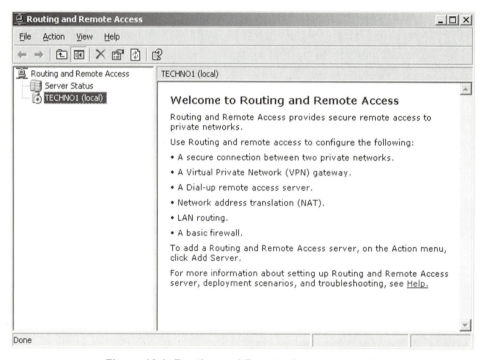

Figure 10-1: Routing and Remote Access console

2. Select the **Help** link on this screen. This brings up **Routing and Remote Access Help** (Figure 10-2). (**Note:** You can also bring up **Help** by selecting the icon with the yellow question mark.)

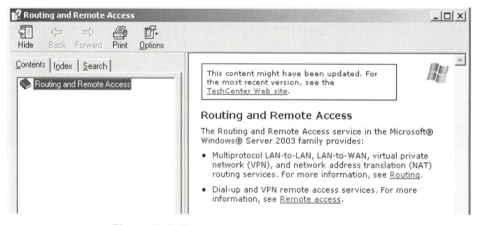

Figure 10-2: Routing and Remote Access Help

3. Select **Routing** and then **Concepts**. Select **Using Routing** under **Concepts** (Figure 10-3).

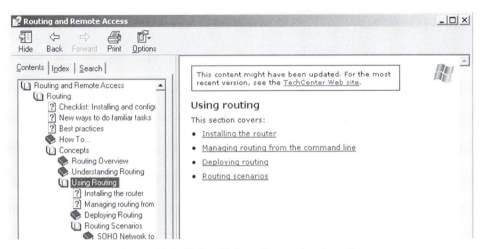

Figure 10-3: Using Help to learn about routing

4. Next, select **Routing Scenarios**. Select the **Dial-Up Branch Office Network** scenario (Figure 10-4).

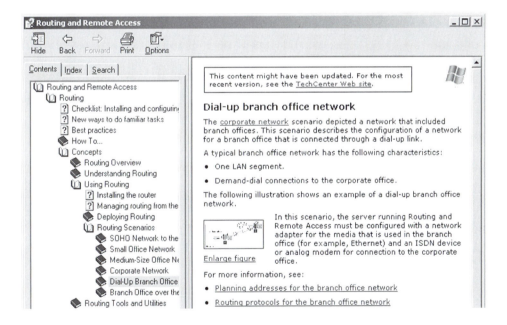

Figure 10-4: Using Help to learn about routing scenarios

5. Read about this example of a secure connection between two private networks. This section explains how to plan and configure a dial-up link to secure and manage data transmission. What kind of routes would be used for the connection between the branch office and the corporate office? What other services might be used at the branch office?

_____

_____

_____

■ Part B: Explain the functionality of a VPN gateway

A VPN enables traffic between two locations to be securely transmitted because the data are encapsulated using a tunneling protocol. Even though data may be traveling on a public network like the Internet, the VPN link between each point emulates a point-to-point connection. The data at both ends are encrypted for security and then encapsulated by the VPN tunneling protocol. Any interception along the public route would yield only encrypted data, making it unreadable.

1. Refer to part A of this project to access the **Help** console.
2. Select **Remote Access** and then **Concepts**. Select **Remote Access Overview**.
3. Select the link to **The remote access server as a virtual private networking server**. Review the information on this page, including the diagram. What must both the VPN client and the VPN server support to create a connection? How many point-to-point tunneling protocol (PPTP) ports can you create using Windows Server 2003? How many layer two tunneling protocol (L2TP) ports?

_____

_____

■ Part C: Explain the functionality of a dial-up remote access server

1. Refer to part A of this project to access the **Help** console.
2. Select **Remote Access**, and then **Concepts**. Select **Remote Access Overview**.
3. Select the link to **The remote access server as a dial-up networking server**.

4. Review this page, including the diagram. Select **Dial-up networking**. Name several of the functions a remote access server performs. From the diagram, what are the links between the remote access client and the remote access server? What are the stated components of dial-up networking?

_____

_____

_____

■ Part D: Explain the functionality of NAT

NAT enables an organization to use a limited number of public IP addresses by translating internal private IP addresses into public IP addresses. When RRAS is installed, the NAT protocol is installed as well; however, it must be configured to function properly.

1. Refer to part A of this project to access the **Help** console.
2. Select **Routing** and then **Concepts**. Select **Routing Overview** under **Concepts**.
3. Select **Internet Connection Sharing and network address translation**. Review this page. Notice the table showing the difference between Internet connection sharing and NAT. What is the difference between a translated connection using Internet connection sharing and NAT provided by RRAS?

_____

_____

_____

■ Part E: Explain the functionality of LAN routing

A RRAS server with two network interface cards can be configured to route traffic between two network segments. This is called LAN-to-LAN routing or, if TCP/IP is used, IP routing. Another name for a server that has two NIC cards is a multihomed computer. A server running RRAS can route IP and Appletalk traffic.

1. Refer to part A of this project to access the **Help** console.
2. Select **Routing** and then **Concepts**. Select **Understanding Routing** under **Concepts**.

3. Select **Understanding unicast routing** and **Routing Configurations**. Review this page, including the simple routing scenario. What routing protocols can be used on a server running RRAS? What happens at each hop between the source and destination in a routed network? What routing protocols are used in the simple routing scenario?

_____

_____

_____

■ Part F: Explain the functionality of Basic Firewall

RRAS includes Basic Firewall, which allows you to filter traffic from a public network. When an interface is protected by Basic Firewall, it will route only traffic that is sent in response to a request from the server.

1. Refer to part A of this project to access the **Help** console.
2. Select **Routing** and then **Concepts**. Select **Routing Overview** under **Concepts**.
3. Select **Basic Firewall**. Review this page. How does Basic Firewall filter unsolicited network traffic?

_____

_____

Project 10.2	Configuring a Remote Access Server and Dial-up Networking Client
Overview	In this project, you will learn how to configure both sides of dial-up networking. Although at one time dial-up networking was the most common form of remote access, now there are faster, more secure, and less expensive methods of giving users access to network resources. That being said, learning the basics of dial-up networking will give you a first-hand look at RRAS. Successfully connecting a client computer to your server using telephone lines takes a number of fairly complex steps. First, a modem (or modem pool) is required for your server along with individual phone lines for each modem connection needed. Next, you enable your server, which is a member of a domain with RRAS, and configure it to accept an inbound connection to a specific port. A *port* is a communications channel capable of supporting a single PPP connection. Then, the dial-up networking client uses a computer equipped with a modem and a phone line to make an outbound connection to your server's modem. The client must also have software installed on the computer that is configured to make the PPP connection. Finally, the server negotiates authentication following the RRAS configuration settings and verifies the user's credentials, which have been entered in Active Directory.
Outcomes	After completing this project, you will know how to: ▲ set up dial-up networking on the server ▲ set up dial-up networking on the client
What you'll need	To complete this project, you will need: ▲ a client computer ▲ a Windows Server 2003 computer connected to a local network ▲ two separate telephone lines and two modems to test the remote access server and dial-up networking
Completion time	30 minutes
Precautions	None

■ Part A: Set up the Remote Access service for dial-up networking on Windows Server 2003

1. Open the **Start** menu, point to **Administrative Tools**, and select **Routing and Remote Access**.

2. The **Routing and Remote Access** console opens showing **Server Status**, and under that, the local server name in the left pane (Figure 10-5). There will be a red arrow facing down in a circle on the server name. This indicates that RRAS is *not* enabled. RRAS is disabled by default when Windows Server 2003 is installed.

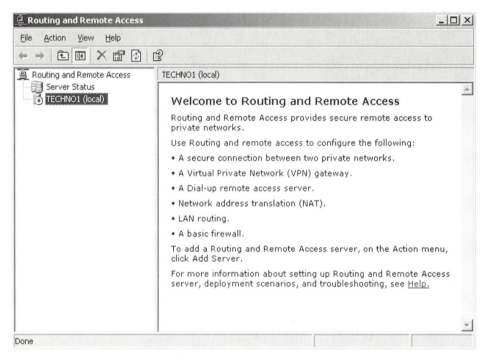

Figure 10-5: Routing and Remote Access console

3. Highlight the server name and right-click to open the pop-up menu (or open the **Action** menu on the menu bar). Select **Configure and Enable Routing and Remote Access**. This starts the **Routing and Remote Access Server Setup Wizard** (Figure 10-6).

Figure 10-6: Routing and Remote Access Server Setup Wizard

4. Click **Next**. The **Configuration** screen appears (Figure 10-7). Select the radio button for **Remote access (dial-up or VPN)**, which allows remote computers to dial in using a modem *or* to connect to the network using the Internet.

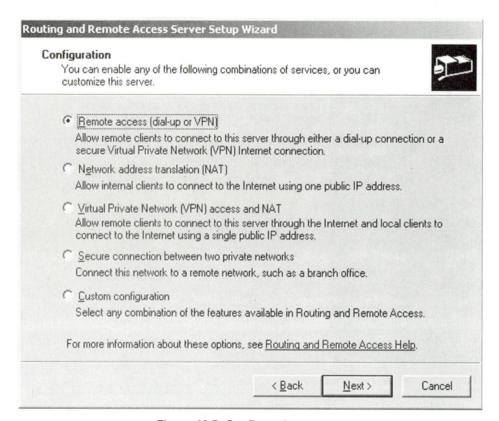

Figure 10-7: Configuration screen

5. Click **Next**. The **Remote Access** screen appears. Enter a checkmark in the **Dial-up** check box (Figure 10-8).

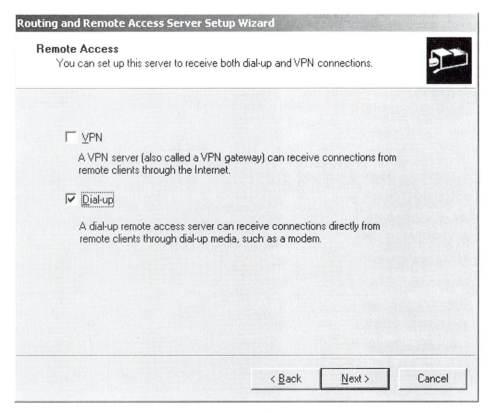

Figure 10-8: Remote Access screen

6. Click **Next**. The **IP Address Assignment** screen appears (Figure 10-9). If you will be using DHCP to assign addresses to remote clients, select **Automatically**. If you are not using DHCP, then you can give remote clients IP addresses from a preselected range. Select **From a specified range of addresses**.

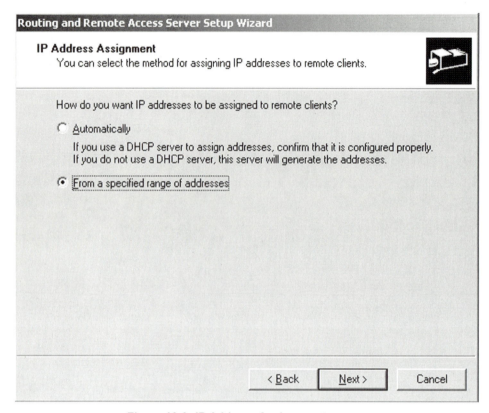

Figure 10-9: IP Address Assignment screen

7. Click **Next**. Selecting a specified range of addresses opens the **Address Range Assignment** screen. Click **New** (Figure 10-10).

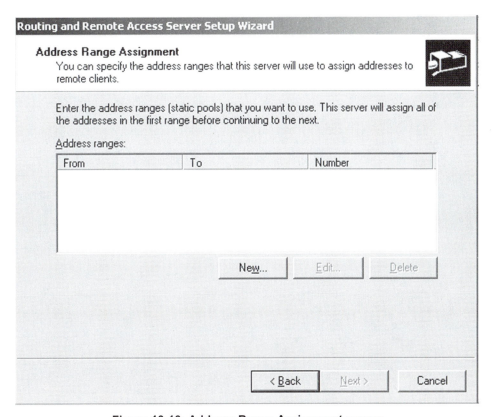

Figure 10-10: Address Range Assignment screen

8. Enter the range of IP addresses available and click **OK**. The **Address ranges From** and **To** and the number of addresses in the range will be shown on the **Address Range Assignment** screen (Figure 10-11).

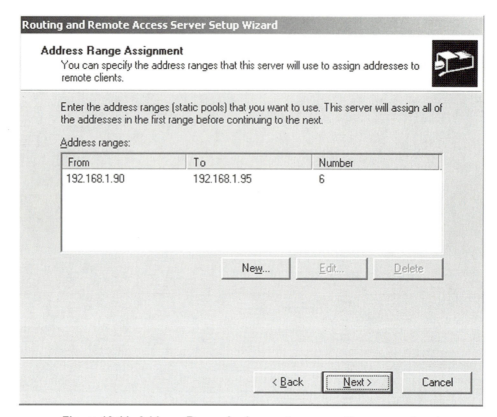

Figure 10-11: Address Range Assignment screen with range entered

9. Click **Next**. If you select DHCP, then you will see a message reminding you to configure a relay agent (Figure 10-12). Once RRAS is enabled, you will see DHCP Relay Agent under IP Routing.

Figure 10-12: DHCP warning message box

10. The **Managing Multiple Remote Access Servers** screen displays asking if RADIUS will be used. Select **No** (Figure 10-13).

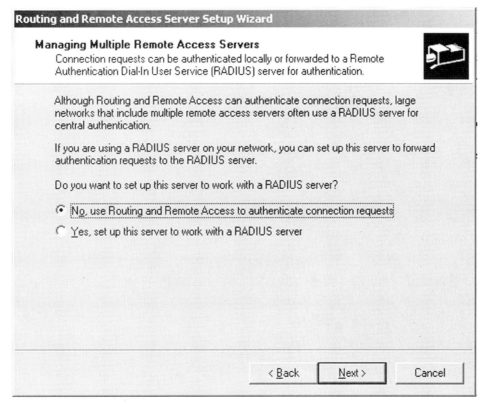

Figure 10-13: Managing Multiple Remote Access Servers screen

11. The summary screen displays (Figure 10-14). Select **Finish**.

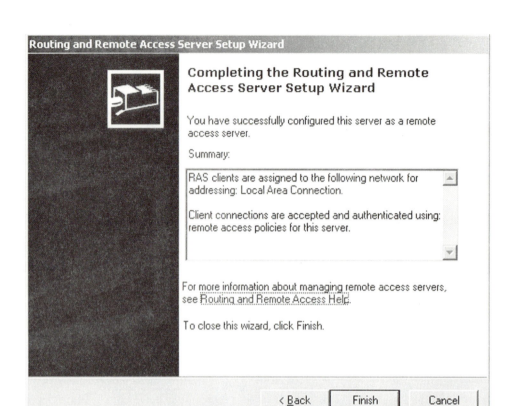

Figure 10-14: Summary screen

12. The RRAS service starts, showing the configuration you entered and other selections (Figure 10-15).

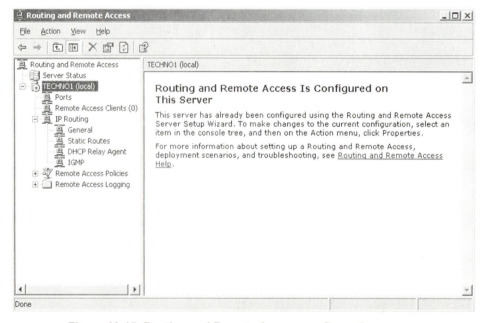

Figure 10-15: Routing and Remote Access configured on server

13. Under **Remote Access Concepts** in **Help**, the **"Common server configurations for remote access servers"** section explains how you can configure additional options once the wizard is finished. What are two of these additional options?

_____

_____

_____

14. It is suggested that you use the **Runas** command to open the **Routing and Remote Access** console reducing the risk of using administrative credentials. What is the file name of the RRAS console? Where is this file located?

_____

_____

15. What user account credentials do you need to enable and configure RRAS?

_____

_____

■ Part B: Configure a dial-up connection from a client computer

To allow a client computer to make an outbound call and connect to your Remote Access server, the client will need a modem (internal or external) and communication software. The client's modem will be connected to a phone line, allowing it to call the phone number of the server.

1. On the client computer, open the **Control Panel** and select **Network Connections**.
2. Open the **File** menu and select **New Connection**.
3. The **New Connection Wizard** displays (Figure 10-16). Click **Next**.

Figure 10-16: New Connection Wizard

4. On the **Network Connection Type** screen, select **Connect to the network at my workplace** to create the dial-up connection (Figure 10-17), and then click **Next**.

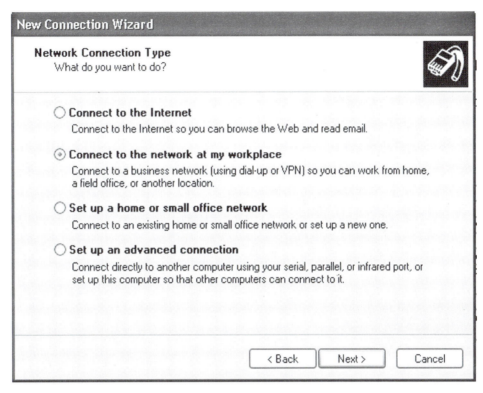

Figure 10-17: Network Connection Type screen

5. On the **Network Connection** screen, select **Dial-up connection** (Figure 10-18) and click **Next**.

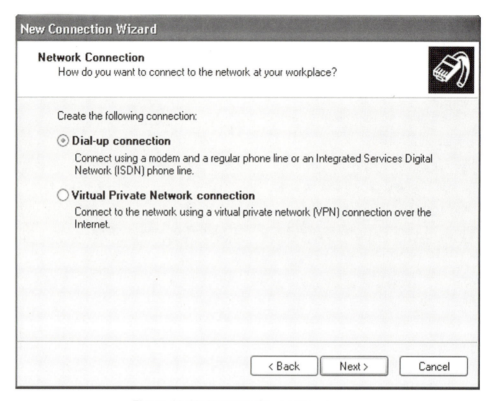

Figure 10-18: Network Connection screen

6. On the **Connection Name** screen, enter a name for the connection (Figure 10-19) and click **Next**.

Figure 10-19: Connection Name screen

7. On the **Phone Number to Dial** screen, enter the phone number of the Remote Access server (Figure 10-20) and click **Next**.

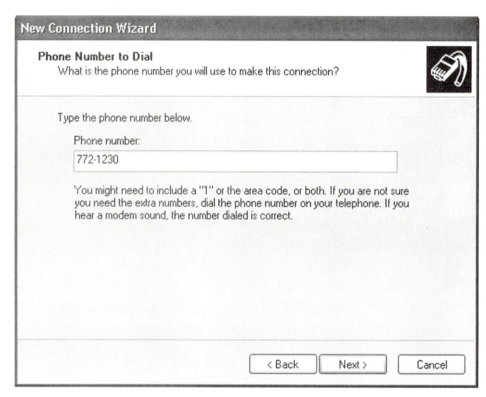

Figure 10-20: Phone Number to Dial screen

8. The **Summary** screen will display showing the new connection (Figure 10-21). Click **Finish**.

Figure 10-21: Summary screen

9. What is the most common remote access protocol used for dial-up connections?

_____

_____

10. When you use the **New Connection Wizard** on the client computer to create the dial-up connection, does this wizard also install the software for the modem?

_____

_____

Project 10.3	Understanding VPNs
Overview	Microsoft defines a VPN as "the extension of a private network that encompasses links across shared or public networks like the Internet". What this definition leaves out is the vulnerability of sending sensitive data over public networks. An organization's data should not travel on shared or public networks without being encrypted, and that is just what you get when you implement a VPN using Windows Server 2003 RRAS.
	The RRAS VPN emulates a point-to-point link. Instead of just sending data as is, the VPN protocols encrypt the data and then encapsulate it inside a header that provides the routing information. Both ends must implement the exact same protocol, which is why it is called a tunnel. The protocol tunnels its way through the Internet from one end to the other.
	You can configure RRAS for two types of VPNs: remote access and site-to-site. With remote access, the encrypted communication is between a remote access VPN client and the remote access VPN gateway. The VPN gateway (server) authenticates the client and then provides the client with access to resources on the network like e-mail and shared folders. For site-to-site VPNs (also known as router-to-router VPNs), the encrypted tunnel connects two routers (VPN gateways) that are in separate sites. On one side is the VPN client or the calling router, and on the other is the answering router, the VPN server. The VPN client (calling router) is configured for a demand-dial interface, in other words, the IP address of the VPN answering server, a PPTP or L2TP port, the user account credentials for the domain, and for a L2TP/IPSec connection, a valid certificate. The VPN server (answering router) must have a demand-dial interface with the same account configured to recognize the incoming connection. In most cases, users in each site who connect to this demand-dial router-to-router VPN may not even be aware that their data are being carried over an encrypted link.
	RRAS administrators can choose between two remote access VPN protocols: PPTP or L2TP with IPSec.
	• Point-to-point tunneling protocol (PPTP) uses point-to-point protocol (PPP) authentication methods and Microsoft point-to-point encryption (MPPE).
	• Layer two tunneling protocol with Internet protocol security (L2TP/IPSec) uses PPP authentication methods and IPSec for computer-level authentication using certificates and data encryption.
	There are several advantages to implementing a VPN; an organization can reduce long-distance phone or leased line costs without a lot of increased administration or risk to their data.

Project 10.3	Understanding VPNs
Outcomes	After completing this project, you will know how to: ▲ explain how the two VPN protocols function ▲ describe encapsulation ▲ select between VPN protocols
What you'll need	To complete this project, you will need: ▲ a client computer ▲ a Windows Server 2003 computer connected to a local network
Completion time	20 minutes
Precautions	None

To understand VPNs, we need to take a closer look at tunneling technology. RRAS offers two choices: PPTP and L2TP with IPSec. Let's look first at PPTP.

As you have learned, PPP enables two devices to establish a TCP/IP connection. The PPP negotiation includes link control protocol to establish communication, and a number of other protocols that provide negotiated authentication, compression, and size parameters. Once the negotiation is complete, IP packets can be exchanged. Although PPP works well, it does not provide a secure transport for an organization's data. That is what PPTP does by encrypting and encapsulating the PPP payload. (You can also look at RFC 2637, which outlines PPTP at **http://www.ietf.org/rfc/rfc2637.txt?number=2637**.)

PPTP provides a good level of security for most organizations, especially those who do not want to issue computer certificates, and user's credentials can be verified either on the server or in Active Directory. PPTP can also be configured with extensible authentication protocol (EAP) for smart cards. PPTP can be used through most NATs, with no modifications required for either the client or server.

1. Access **Routing and Remote Access Help**.

2. Select **VPN Tunneling Protocols**, and then **Point-to-Point Tunneling Protocol**. Review the information. What is added by PPTP to the PPP frame? Where are the source and destination IP addresses of the VPN client and VPN server? When the PPP frame is encrypted with MPPE, what are the three types of encryption keys used?

_____

_____

_____

3. Now let's review L2TP. One advantage of using L2TP with IPSec over PPTP is that it can be used on frame relay, X.25, and ATM networks, not just IP. Both Cisco and Microsoft contributed to the design of L2TP, and it is the protocol used in a number of firewall products. L2TP does require the use of certificates, and both users and computers can be authenticated. Other advantages include data integrity (data may not be modified en route) and replay (credentials cannot be used again by a hacker). Finally, in Windows Server 2003, IPSec-protected packets are encapsulated as UDP messages, which allows L2TP/IPSec connections to be created for client and server computers located behind one or multiple NATs.

4. Select **VPN Tunneling Protocols** in **Help**, and then **Layer Two Tunneling Protocol**. (You can also review the L2TP RFCs: RFC 2661, 3193, 3931.)

5. Review the illustration of L2TP and IPSec (Figure 10-22).

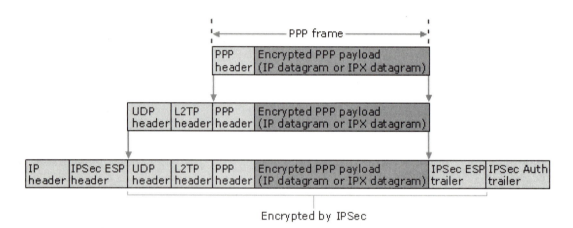

Figure 10-22: L2TP and IPSec

6. What else besides the PPP frame is encrypted by IPSec? How does a Windows XP client negotiate an L2TP connection? Where are the source and destination IP addresses of the VPN client and VPN server?

_____

_____

_____

Project 10.4	VPN Configuration
Overview	There are a number of VPN configuration options, but for this project you will configure your Windows Server 2003 to accept incoming VPN client connections. You will need two network interface cards installed in your server, one that connects to the Internet and one that connects to your private network. Normally, the Internet connection is dedicated with sufficient bandwidth to let VPN users connect to your private network and vice versa. Dedicated connections are private or leased lines, rather than public lines.

As mentioned previously, there are two types of VPN scenarios – remote access and site-to-site access. In this project, we configure the VPN as a remote access server (VPN gateway) that allows remote access clients to connect.

The client configuration is easy as long as you have the IP address of the remote access server and the right user credentials. Use the same New Connection Wizard as in the dial-up networking example to create a new VPN connection. |
| Outcomes | After completing this project, you will know how to:

▲ configure a VPN server |
| What you'll need | To complete this project, you will need:

▲ a client computer

▲ a Windows Server 2003 computer connected to a local network |
| Completion time | 45 minutes |
| Precautions | None |

■ Part A: Configure a Windows Server 2003 remote access VPN

This configuration allows a remote access VPN client who can establish a connection to the Internet either by dial-up or by using a DSL or cable connection to authenticate and then transmit encrypted packets to the remote access VPN server.

1. Once you have installed both network interface cards, open the **Network Connections** window (Figure 10-23). Check to see that both network connections are functioning properly.

Figure 10-23: Network Connections window

2. Open the **Routing and Remote Access** console. If RRAS is not enabled, select the server name and right-click. Select **Configure and Enable Routing and Remote Access**. This starts the **Routing and Remote Access Server Setup Wizard**. Click **Next**.

3. The **Configuration** screen appears. Select the radio button for **Remote access (dial-up or VPN)**, which allows remote computers to dial in using a modem *or* to connect to the network using the Internet (Figure 10-24). Click **Next**.

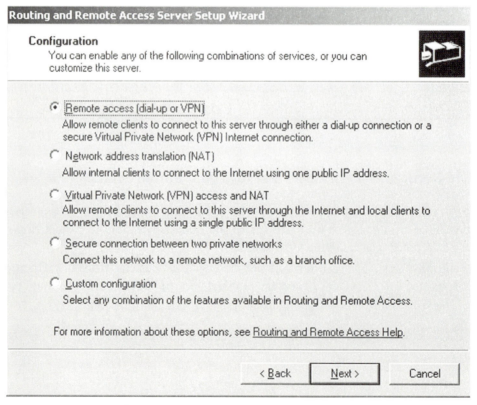

Figure 10-24: Configuration screen – VPN

4. The **Remote Access** screen appears. Select the checkbox in front of **VPN** (Figure 10-25). Click **Next**.

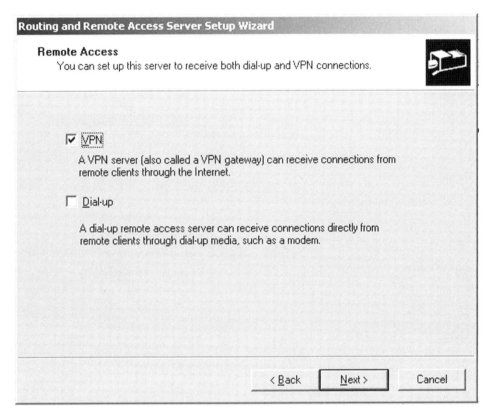

Figure 10-25: Remote Access screen – VPN

5. The **VPN Connection** screen appears. Highlight the interface that is connected to the Internet (Figure 10-26). Click **Next**.

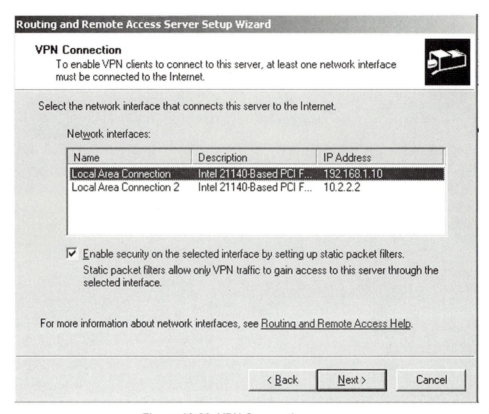

Figure 10-26: VPN Connection screen

6. The **IP Address Assignment** screen opens. Determine how you want to assign IP addresses to remote clients – either use DHCP or assign a range of IP addresses.

7. If you decide to assign a range of IP addresses, the **Address Range Assignment** screen will open. To enter the address range(s), select **New**.

8. The **New Address Range** dialog box will open. Enter the **Start IP address** and the **Number of addresses,** and the **End IP address** will fill in automatically (Figure 10-27). Click **OK**, and then click **Next**.

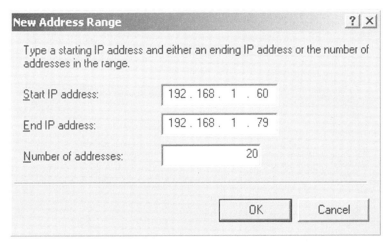

Figure 10-27: New Address Range dialog box

9. The next screen asks if you are using RADIUS for authentication. Choose **No**, and then click **Next**.

10. The last screen is a summary of your settings (Figure 10-28). Check the settings and select **Finish**.

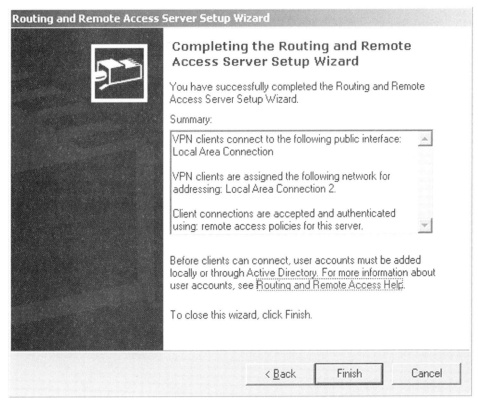

Figure 10-28: Summary screen

11. You may receive a message regarding the DHCP Relay Agent.

12. The RRAS service starts. The red down arrow will change to a green up arrow on the RRAS server. Now take a look at the new entries in the RRAS console. Highlight **Network Interfaces** to see the LAN and demand dial interfaces in the right pane (Figure 10-29).

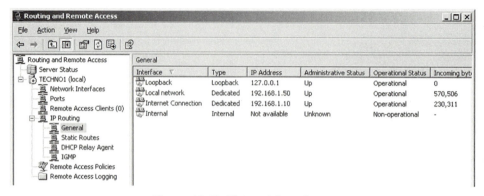

Figure 10-29: Network Interfaces

13. Highlight **Ports**, and you will see the PPTP and L2TP ports display in the right pane (Figure 10-30). You can modify the default number of ports in the **Port Properties** dialog box.

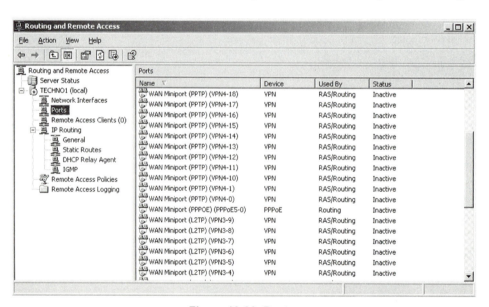

Figure 10-30: Ports

14. If you select the check box to **Enable security on the selected interface by setting up static packet filters**, where can you view static IP filters after you have created the VPN connection?

_____

_____

_____

15. How many default VPN ports are enabled when you configure RRAS for VPN? How do you modify the number of ports?

_____

_____

_____

Project 9.5	Routing and Remote Access Policy Configurations
	Not that long ago, the only remote access policy was either Allow or Deny. Now, network administrators can define a set of rules to determine exactly what is allowed or denied. They can define conditions, profile settings, and remote access permission settings.
	When a connection is authorized, the remote access policy profile designates a set of connection restrictions. The dial-in properties of the user account also provide restrictions, and, if different, user account connection restrictions override the remote access policy profile restrictions.
	Remote access policies can be set for remote access permission, group membership, the type of connection, time of day, authentication methods, and other conditions.
	Once the connection is authorized, other options can be set such as idle timeout, maximum session time, encryption strength, and IP packet filters.
Outcomes	After completing this project, you will know how to: ▲ explain remote access policy ▲ configure a new remote access policy
What you'll need	To complete this project, you will need: ▲ a client computer ▲ a Windows Server 2003 computer connected to a local network
Completion time	30 minutes
Precautions	Creating and setting a restrictive remote access policy may limit your Internet access.

■ Part A: Review dial-in policy for domain users

1. Open the **Active Directory Users and Computers** console. Highlight a domain user and right-click. Select **Properties** and select the **Dial-in** tab. Review the user's **Remote Access Permission (Dial-in or VPN)**.

■ Part B: Create a new Remote Access Policy

1. Highlight **Remote Access Policies** in the left pane of the RRAS console. Right-click and select **New Remote Access Policy**.

2. The **New Remote Access Policy Wizard** displays (Figure 10-31). Click **Next**.

Figure 10-31: New Remote Access Policy Wizard

3. The **Policy Configuration Method** screen displays, asking if you want a typical or custom policy configuration and what you want to name the new policy. Choose to use the wizard to set up a typical policy and enter a name for the new policy (Figure 10-32).

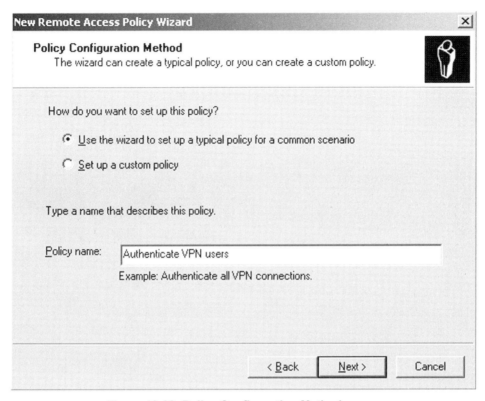

Figure 10-32: Policy Configuration Method screen

4. The **Access Methods** screen appears. Choose **VPN** (Figure 10-33). Click **Next**.

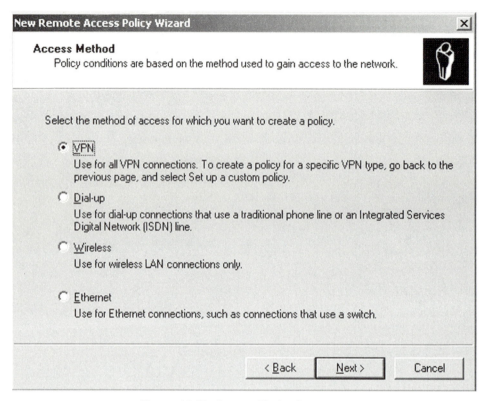

Figure 10-33: Access Methods screen

5. The **User or Group Access** screen appears. For **Group**, select **Add**. The **Select Groups** dialog box displays, allowing you to enter a group name (Figure 10-34). Click the **Advanced** button. Then, select **Find Now** to show the available groups.

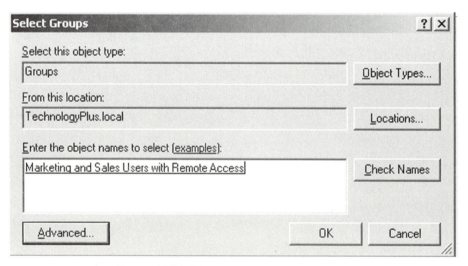

Figure 10-34: User or group access screen

6. Click **Next**. On the **Authentication Methods** screen, the **Microsoft Encrypted Authentication version 2 (MS-CHAPv2)** authentication protocol is selected by default (Figure 10-35).

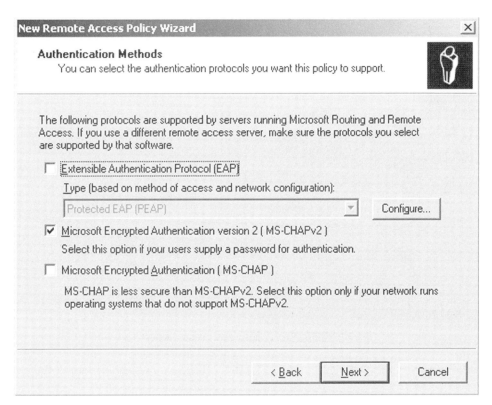

Figure 10-35: Authentication Methods screen

7. Click **Next**. On the **Policy Encryption Level** screen, clear the **Basic encryption** check box and leave the **Strong encryption** and **Strongest encryption** check boxes selected (Figure 10-36).

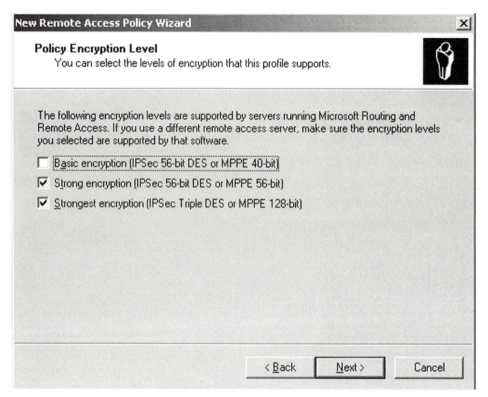

Figure 10-36: Policy Encryption Level screen

8. The final screen is the summary showing you the settings you created (Figure 10-37).

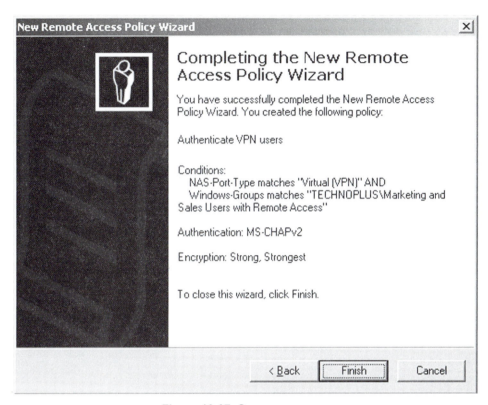

Figure 10-37: Summary screen

9. Once the policy is created, you can view the setting by highlighting the policy in the right pane and selecting **Properties**.

10. When you set the strongest encryption, what are you selecting? What is the default authentication policy if users must supply a password?

    _____

    _____

    _____

11. What is the default Remote Access Permission for a user? When a user's Properties dialog box for Remote Access Permission (Dial-in or VPN) is set to Control access through Remote Access Policy, what does that mean?

    _____

    _____

    _____

11
MONITORING AND TROUBLESHOOTING RRAS

PROJECTS

Project 11.1	Managing and Monitoring RRAS
Overview	Once your users discover that they can access the network remotely, there will be constant demand. In larger organizations, manually managing the hundreds of remote access connections is too labor intensive, especially if there are a number of servers providing different types of connections. In this situation, you can set up a centralized method of managing and monitoring remote access servers to make the process more efficient.
	How exactly do you implement a centralized system? The short answer is to configure Internet Authentication Service (IAS) on a Windows Server 2003 system. IAS is Microsoft's implementation of the Remote Authentication Dial-In User Service (RADIUS) protocol. As a RADIUS server, IAS performs centralized connection authentication, authorization, and accounting (AAA) for remote access connections. With IAS, you can configure an unlimited number of RADIUS clients and remote RADIUS server groups. Plus, IAS integrates with Active Directory, allowing you to take advantage of the user and computer accounts you already maintain.
	An IAS server can be configured to authenticate the connection requests it receives or to forward requests to another IAS server for authentication. It can authenticate different types of connections such as dial-up line or VPN, or site-to-site access.
	If Active Directory is used, the RRAS service must be run in the security context of a computer account that is a member of the RAS and IAS servers security group.
Outcomes	After completing this project, you will know how to:
	▲ explain the function of Internet Authentication Service (IAS)
	▲ review the implementation of IAS (RADIUS)
	▲ configure RADIUS in RRAS
What you'll need	To complete this project, you will need:
	▲ a Windows Server 2003 computer connected to a local network
Completion time	30 minutes
Precautions	None

■ Part A: Explain the function of RADIUS and configure RRAS for use with IAS

In a small organization, the RRAS server can authenticate and authorize remote users based on local policies and then log user activities. When there are hundreds or thousands of remote users, Windows Server 2003 domain controllers can be configured with IAS to provide centralized authentication and logging. This enables multiple RRAS servers to act as clients to IAS. Figure 11-1 from the Help mmc shows you a diagram of how the RADIUS (IAS) server connects to RRAS servers.

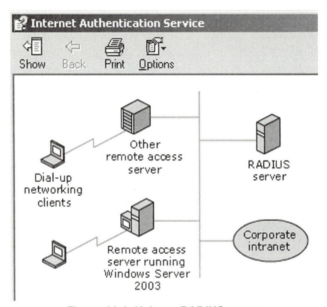

Figure 11-1: Using a RADIUS server

Figure 11-2 shows you how to install IAS as a separate service on an Active Directory domain controller to provide authentication and authorization of user and computer accounts.

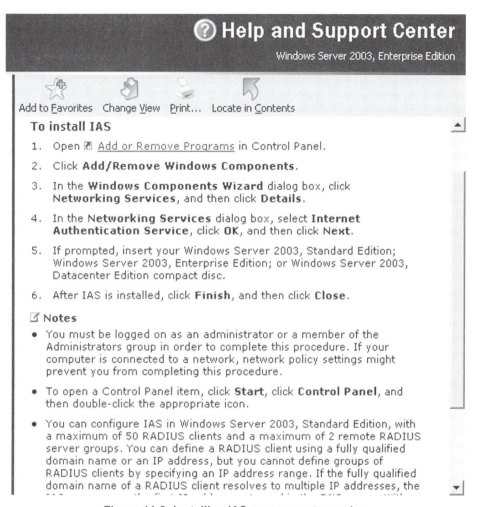

Help and Support Center

Windows Server 2003, Enterprise Edition

Add to Favorites   Change View   Print...   Locate in Contents

To install IAS

1. Open ⊠ Add or Remove Programs in Control Panel.

2. Click **Add/Remove Windows Components**.

3. In the **Windows Components Wizard** dialog box, click **Networking Services**, and then click **Details**.

4. In the **Networking Services** dialog box, select **Internet Authentication Service**, click **OK**, and then click **Next**.

5. If prompted, insert your Windows Server 2003, Standard Edition; Windows Server 2003, Enterprise Edition; or Windows Server 2003, Datacenter Edition compact disc.

6. After IAS is installed, click **Finish**, and then click **Close**.

✎ **Notes**

- You must be logged on as an administrator or a member of the Administrators group in order to complete this procedure. If your computer is connected to a network, network policy settings might prevent you from completing this procedure.

- To open a Control Panel item, click **Start**, click **Control Panel**, and then double-click the appropriate icon.

- You can configure IAS in Windows Server 2003, Standard Edition, with a maximum of 50 RADIUS clients and a maximum of 2 remote RADIUS server groups. You can define a RADIUS client using a fully qualified domain name or an IP address, but you cannot define groups of RADIUS clients by specifying an IP address range. If the fully qualified domain name of a RADIUS client resolves to multiple IP addresses, the

Figure 11-2: Installing IAS as a separate service

From Chapter 10, the RRAS service should be configured to authenticate users based on local policies. Now you will configure your RRAS server to use IAS authentication, making your RRAS server into an IAS client.

1. Open the **Routing and Remote Access** console. Highlight the server name and right-click. Select **Properties**.

2. Select the **Security** tab. Select the arrow on the **Authentication provider** drop-down list box (Figure 11-3).

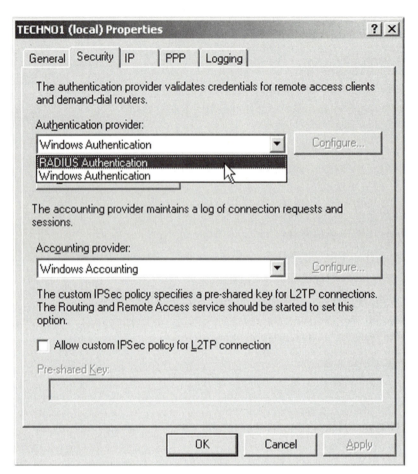

Figure 11-3: Selecting RADIUS Authentication

3. Select **RADIUS Authentication** and the **Configure** button will become available. Select **Configure**.

4. The next dialog box shows the RADIUS servers that are available. Notice that if there are a number of RADIUS servers, you can configure which one this RRAS client will contact first. Select **Add**.

5. The **Add RADIUS Server** dialog box displays (Figure 11-4). You will add the IAS **Server name** and then select **Change** to add an entry to **Secret**. Secret is used on both the RRAS and the IAS servers to verify their association.

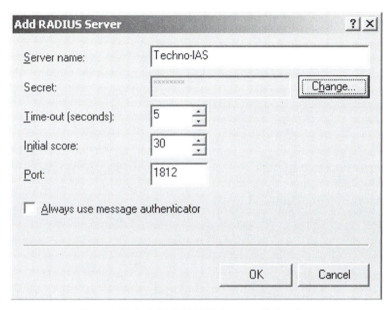

Figure 11-4: Add RADIUS Server dialog box

6. Select the **Time-out** in seconds, the **Initial Score**, and the **Port** – default port is 1812. (**Note:** If you configure RADIUS using the RRAS wizard, the primary RADIUS server has an initial score of 30 and the alternate RADIUS server has a score of 29.)

7. Select the check box on message authenticator if you have the **Request must contain the Message Authenticator attribute** option set. The **Message-Authenticator RADIUS** attribute includes information encrypted with the shared secret to provide verification to the receiving RADIUS server that a configured RADIUS client sent the message.

8. Once you have completed the configuration, you will need to stop and restart RRAS (Figure 11-5).

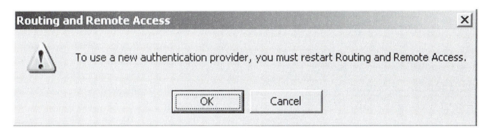

Figure 11-5: Restart RRAS

9. If there are several RADIUS (IAS) servers available, they receive requests from RRAS servers in order from highest on the list to lowest. Explain why you would want several IAS servers.

_____

_____

_____

■ Part B: Configure RRAS to use IAS accounting

This is *very similar* to the activity you just completed; however, there are some differences. An IAS server can be configured to store audit and usage information in a log file. Although your RRAS server also creates logs, IAS logs provide central administration and can support a log file format that can be imported into a database.

1. Open the **Routing and Remote Access** console. Highlight the server name and right-click. Select **Properties**.

2. Select the **Security** tab. Select the arrow on the **Accounting provider** box (Figure 11-6).

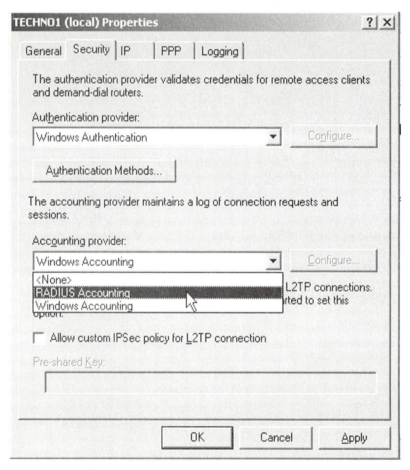

Figure 11-6: Selecting RADIUS Accounting

3. Select **RADIUS Accounting**. The **Configure** button will become available.

4. The next dialog box shows the RADIUS servers that are available. Select **Add**.

5. The **Add RADIUS Server** dialog box displays (it looks *almost* like the previous activity) (Figure 11-7). You will add the IAS **Server name** and then select **Change** to add an entry to **Secret**. Secret is used on both the RRAS and the IAS servers to verify their association. Select the **Time-out** in seconds, the **Initial Score**, and the **Port** – default port is 1813.

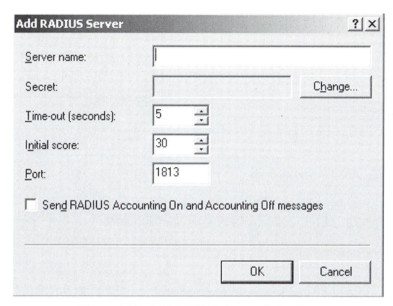

Figure 11-7: Add RADIUS Server dialog box

6. Select the check box for **Send RADIUS Accounting On and Accounting Off messages**. This tells the IAS server that the RRAS service has started and stopped, and allows it to store information regarding restarts.

7. What does the accounting provider do? What are two advantages of using RADIUS for accounting?

_____

_____

_____

■ **Part C: Configure Authentication Methods**

1. Select the **Security** tab on the **Properties** dialog box. Select the **Authentication Methods** button (Figure 11-8).

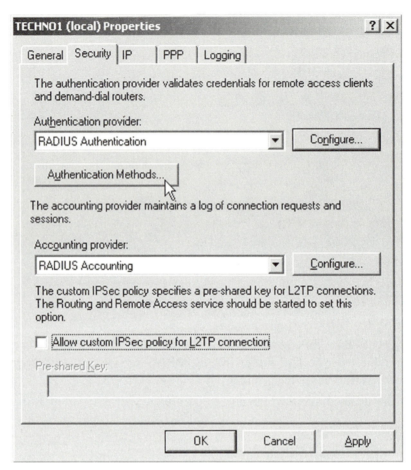

Figure 11-8: Authentication Methods button

2. The **Authentication Methods** dialog box opens, showing the selections for authentication. They are listed in the order shown. The first on this dialog box is a check box for **Extensible authentication protocol (EAP)** and a button with **EAP Methods** (Figure 11-9).

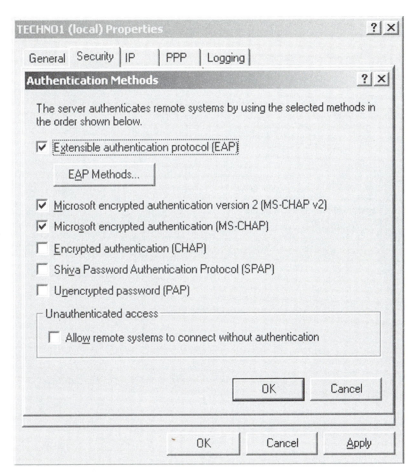

Figure 11-9: Authentication Methods dialog box

3. Select the **EAP Methods** button. There are several default EAP methods installed with RRAS including EAP-TLS (EAP-Transport Level Security) and MD5-Challenge. Others can be added. Both the remote access client and the authenticator must support the same EAP type. EAP can be used to support authentication schemes such as Generic Token Card, One Time Password (OTP), MD5-Challenge, and Transport Level Security (TLS) for smart card and certificate support, and can adapt to future authentication technologies (Figure 11-10).

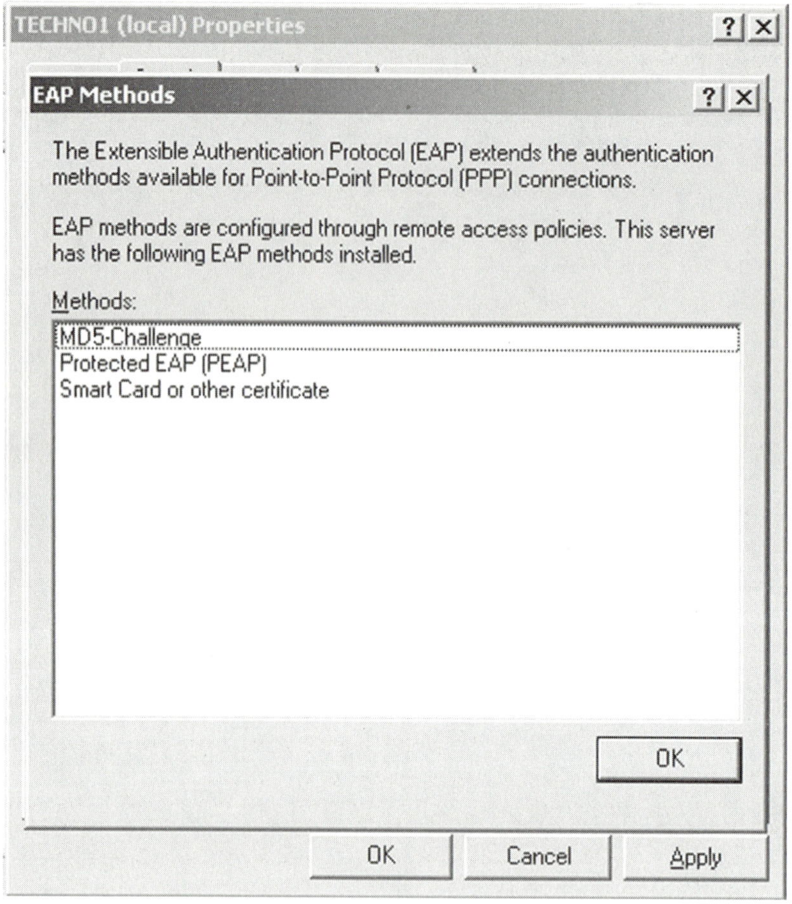

Figure 11-10: EAP Methods dialog box

4. Review the EAP-TLS section in RRAS Help. What is the basis for EAP-TLS? How is EAP-TLS configured?

_____

_____

Project 11.2	**Reviewing and Configuring RRAS Logs**
Overview	As a network administrator, you determine who can use the RRAS service and the kind of access the users will be given. Once set, your next responsibility is to monitor RRAS access and troubleshoot RRAS problems. You may also have requirements in your organization where you must document user activity and connection status to bill other departments for their usage.
	RRAS itself includes a number of local configurations to log user access. If you use RADIUS, then the IAS service will provide most of the AAA logging. Either way, knowing how to log and monitor remote access activity is a valuable skill.
Outcomes	After completing this project, you will know how to:
	▲ set up dial-up networking on the server
	▲ set up dial-up networking on the client
What you'll need	To complete this project, you will need:
	▲ a client computer
	▲ a Windows Server 2003 computer connected to a local network
	▲ two separate telephone lines and two modems to test the remote access server and dial-up networking
Completion time	30 minutes
Precautions	None

■ Part A: Set up the RRAS for dial-up networking on Windows Server 2003

When the RRAS service is installed, certain monitoring functions are enabled by default including those in Event Viewer.

1. On the system where RRAS is installed, select **Administrative Tools**.
2. Select **Event Viewer**. Highlight the **System** folder in the left pane.
3. Right-click for the pop-up menu and then select **Properties**.
4. Select the **Filter** tab and use the arrow on the **Event source** box to find **Remote Access** in the drop-down list (Figure 11-11). This will filter for just Remote Access events.

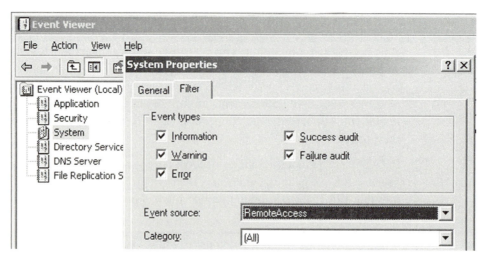

Figure 11-11: Filter tab in the System Properties dialog box

5. Take a look at the example in Figure 11-12. This event shows an *error* indicating there are no RADIUS servers found on the network. A quick look at this error would enable you to troubleshoot user connection problems

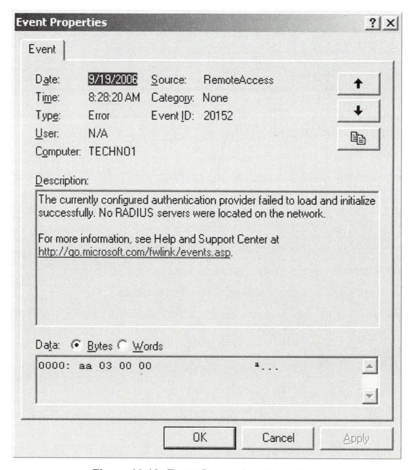

Figure 11-12: Event Properties dialog box

6. Review your **System** folder in **Event Viewer** for Remote Access events. What events were shown as **Errors**? Which were shown as **Warnings**?

_____

_____

■ Part B: Change the default settings for Event Viewer and the PPP.log

1. Open the **Routing and Remote Access** console. Highlight the server name and right-click. Select **Properties**.

2. Select the **Logging** tab (Figure 11-13). The default is **Log errors and warnings**. Select **Log all events**. (**Note:** This selection would create too many events under normal operations but will allow you to review events during this activity. As soon as you finish reviewing the events, reset this entry back to the default – **Log errors and warnings**.)

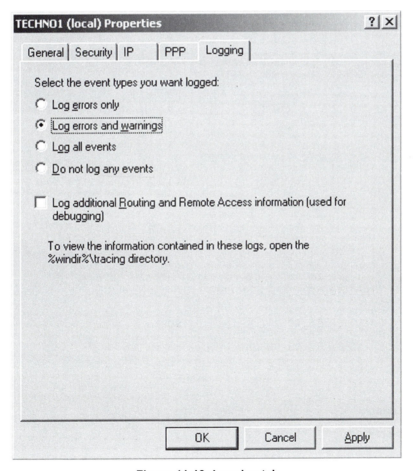

Figure 11-13: Logging tab

3. Also, notice the check box for **Log additional Routing and Remote Access information**. This configures logging for PPP connections. This log is stored in **<systemroot>\Windows\tracing**. The name of this log is the **PPP.log**.

4. Enter a check in this check box. Next, select **Apply** and **OK**.

5. Allow some time to pass for users to create RRAS connections and then review the **Event Viewer** to see the additional entries.

6. Open **Windows Explorer** and navigate to the **<systemroot>\Windows\tracing** folder. Double-click on the **PPP.log** (it will display using Notepad) and review this log (Figure 11-14).

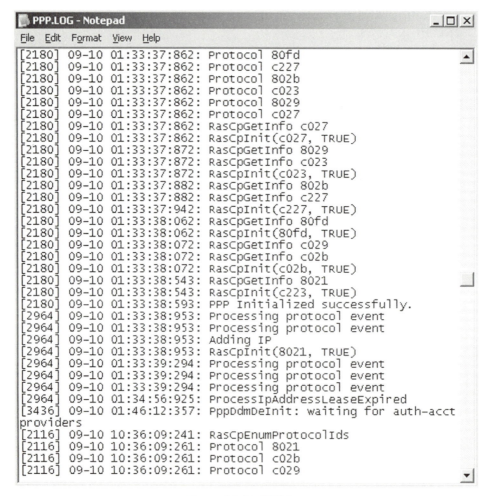

Figure 11-14: PPP.log

7. What additional events were shown in **Event Viewer**? What did the **PPP.log** file show?

_____

_____

Project 11.3	Remote Access Logging
Overview	A Windows Server 2003 system configured as a remote access server supports local logging of authentication and accounting information that is separate from the events recorded in the Event Viewer under the System folder.
	You can use the local logged information to track remote access usage and authentication attempts for users who connect to this specific server. Authentication and accounting logging is especially helpful for troubleshooting because it can reveal remote access policy issues. Any authentication attempt is recorded and displays the name of the remote access policy that either accepted or rejected the connection.
	If the remote access server is configured for RADIUS authentication and accounting and the RADIUS server is a Windows 2000 computer running IAS, the authentication and accounting logs are stored in the <systemroot>\System32\LogFiles folder on the IAS server computer.
Outcomes	After completing this project, you will know how to: ▲ configure remote access logging
What you'll need	To complete this project, you will need: ▲ a client computer ▲ a Windows Server 2003 computer connected to a local network
Completion time	20 minutes
Precautions	None

■ Part A: Configure remote access logging

You can configure the authentication or accounting activity to be logged and configure log file settings in the Remote Access Logging folder.

1. Open the **Routing and Remote Access** console. Select the plus sign (**+**) to the left of the server name in the left pane. The folders under the server name will display showing the **Remote Access Logging** folder at the bottom of the list.

2. Highlight **Remote Access Logging**. The **Local File** will display in the right pane.

3. Highlight **Local File** and right-click. Select **Properties**.

4. There are three check boxes on the **Settings** tab (Figure 11-15):
   - Accounting requests (e.g., accounting start or stop)
   - Authentication requests (e.g., access-accept or access-reject)
   - Periodic status (e.g., interim accounting requests)

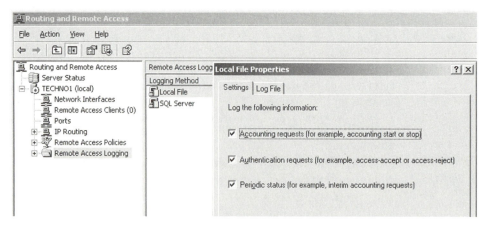

Figure 11-15: Settings tab

5. On the **Log File** tab, you can choose the file format (either IAS or database compatible), when the log file will be created (daily, weekly, etc.), and a path to the log file directory.
   Note: The *Name* of the file changes at the top of that dialog box when you change the creation time. In Figure 11-16, the **Daily** setting creates a log file with a name of **INyymmdd.log**. This enables you to immediately determine the time frame the log file covers.

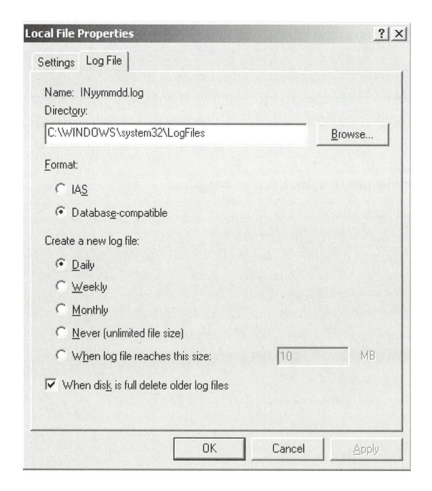

Figure 11-16: Log File tab

6. Once you have enabled daily logging, open **Windows Explorer** and navigate to the **<systemroot>\Windows\system32\LogFiles** folder and take a look at the new log (Figure 11-17). (You may need to start and stop the RRAS service.)

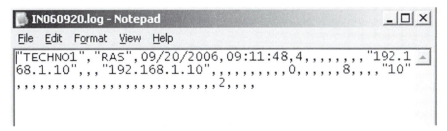

Figure 11-17: Log file

7. If you select the radio button for **Monthly** on the **Create a new log file**, what does the log file name change to? Give one advantage and one disadvantage of choosing the **When disk is full delete older log files** check box.

_____

_____

Project 11.4	Logging, Tracing, or Monitoring?
	Let's review how logging, tracing, and monitoring differ.
	Logging can take a number of different forms such as recording anomalies in the function of a service, or recording the start up or shut down of a service. In many cases, logging is enabled by default when the component or service is installed. You have seen events logged in Event Viewer that provide various notifications such as warnings or errors. Logging can also be enabled to record activities such as when a user authenticates or when a user is denied access. Logs are invaluable for troubleshooting because they provide a record of system activity.
	Tracing records a sequence of programming functions called by a component and then stores the data in a log or trace file. If you are having connection problems, you can enable tracing, try to connect, and then review the logs to troubleshoot the problem. Tracing is disabled by default and because it often uses significant system resources, it should be disabled when you are finished troubleshooting. You can use the netsh command to enable and disable tracing for specific components or for all components.
	Monitoring is often indistinguishable from logging; however, Network Monitor is an example of how you capture network traffic and use that data to troubleshoot remote access problems. Network Monitor can capture remote access dial-up or VPN traffic.
Outcomes	After completing this project, you will know how to: ▲ explain how logging, tracing, and monitoring differ ▲ capture remote access traffic with Network Monitor ▲ review modem diagnostics
What you'll need	To complete this project, you will need: ▲ a client computer connected via VPN to a Windows Server 2003 computer configured as an RRAS server
Completion time	30 minutes
Precautions	Creating and setting a restrictive remote access policy may limit your Internet access.

■ Part A: Use Network Monitor to capture remote access traffic

You can capture and analyze information to diagnose network problems, including dial-up or VPN connections. Capture and view the traffic sent between the remote access server and a remote access client during the connection process or during data transfer. Of course, if the transmissions are encrypted, you can only review the connection traffic.

1. Select **Start**, open the **Administrative Tools** window, and select **Network Monitor**. Select **Capture** on the menu bar and then select **Networks** (Figure 11-18).

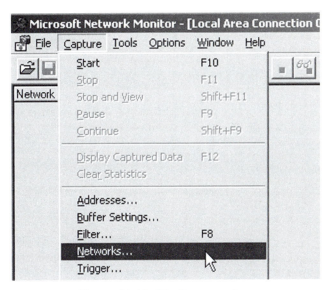

Figure 11-18: Starting a capture

2. Select the plus sign (**+**) in front of **Local Computer** and then **Dial-up Connection or VPN** (Figure 11-19).

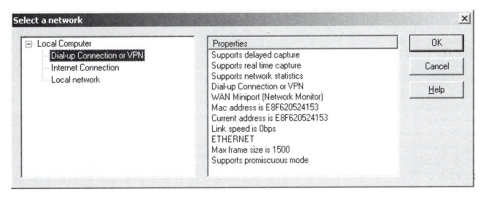

Figure 11-19: Selecting a network

3. Select **OK**. Select **Start** to begin a capture.
4. If client computers are accessing your RRAS server, the capture will record the activity.
5. Explain how the Network Monitor capture of a remote dial-up connection could provide troubleshooting information even if it was encrypted?

_____

_____

■ Part B: Use remote access diagnostics to review logs

1. Select the **Phone and Modem Options** icon in the **Control Panel**. Select the **Modems** tab, highlight a modem and click the **Properties** button. Select the **Diagnostics** tab (Figure 11-20).

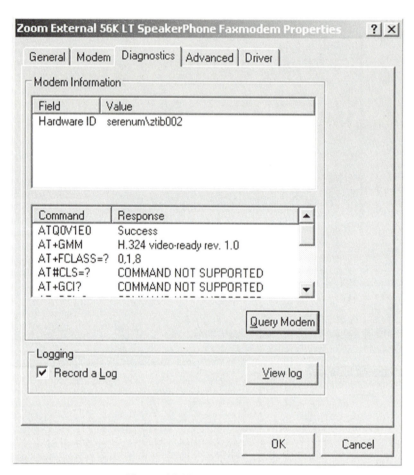

Figure 11-20: Diagnostics tab

2. **Logging** is at the bottom of the tab. If logging is enabled, there will be a checkmark in the box and you can use the **View log** button to review the log (Figure 11-21).

Figure 11-21: Viewing the Log file

3. You can also run specific diagnostics by using the **netsh ras diagnostics** utility in **Command Prompt** (Figure 11-22).

```
C:\>netsh ras diagnostics

The following commands are available:

Commands in this context:
?              - Displays a list of commands.
dump           - Displays a configuration script.
help           - Displays a list of commands.
set            - Sets configuration information.
show           - Displays information.

To view help for a command, type the command, followed by a space, and then
type ?.

C:\>
```

Figure 11-22: Using the netsh ras diagnostics utility

4. Can you identify any information in the modem log that might be helpful for troubleshooting?

_____

_____

Project 11.5	Using IAS Parse
Overview	IAS parse is a tool that is available on the Windows Server 2003 CD (in the Support.cap folder) that converts log file data into either IAS or database format and then produces a summary. Review the RRAS Help file to see the full list of fields that can be logged for user activity and accounting. IAS format is used if you need to record more detailed information; however, the database format lets you track a specific set of attributes. You can use this format to import data into a database.
	The actual log files can be confusing; however, Iasparse.exe takes the log file information and presents it in user-friendly way. It is a command-line tool that simplifies administration and provides troubleshooting data when a user fails to authenticate. It can also provide billing and diagnostic information such as finding out the RADIUS attributes received and sent.
Outcomes	After completing this project, you will know how to: ▲ explore the IAS parse.exe command-line tool
What you'll need	To complete this project, you will need: ▲ a client computer ▲ a Windows Server 2003 computer connected to a local network ▲ AS installed on a domain controller, if you are going to test the IAS parse tool
Completion time	20 minutes
Precautions	None

■ Part A: Review entries to interpret IAS logging

1. Open the **RRAS** console and select **Help**.
2. Navigate to **Interpreting IAS-formatted log files**.
3. Review the information logged under **Entries recorded in IAS-formatted log files**.
4. Navigate to **Interpreting database-import log files**.
5. Review the information logged under **Entries recorded in database-import log files**.

■ Part B: Review IAS parse tool

IAS collects the authentication and accounting information it receives in a log file. Log files can be collected in two formats: IAS-formatted logs and database-import logs (also called ODBC files). IAS uses the information in the dnary.mdb file to find out the ODBC log sequence and to determine if a particular attribute has been logged.

1. Insert the **Windows Server 2003 CD-ROM** into CD-ROM drive. Cancel if it attempts to install. Use **Windows Explorer** to review the contents. Select the **Support** folder, the **Tools** folder, and then the **SUPPORT.cap** file. Highlight and right-click to see the contents. You will see the **iasparse.exe** and **iasparse.doc** files.

2. If you have installed IAS on a domain controller, you can use the IAS Parse tool. By default **iasparse.exe** uses the file **<systemroot>\WINDOWS\system32\logfiles\iaslog**.

3. Figure 11-23 shows an example of properties table in IAS database using Microsoft Access.

Bag	Name	Type	StrVal
2	Description	VT_BSTR	IAS
4	Component Prog Id	VT_BSTR	IAS.RadiusProtocol
4	Accounting Port	VT_BSTR	1813,1646
4	Authentication Port	VT_BSTR	1812,1645
4	Component Id	VT_I4	262144
5	msNPAction	VT_BSTR	Use Windows authentication for all users
5	msNPSequence	VT_I4	1
5	msNPConstraint	VT_BSTR	TIMEOFDAY("0 00:00-24:00; 1 00:00-24:00; 2 00:00-24:
6	msAuthProviderType	VT_I4	1
10	msRADIUSFramedProtocol	VT_I4	1
10	msRADIUSServiceType	VT_I4	2
10	msNPAuthenticationType2	VT_I4	3
10	msNPAuthenticationType2	VT_I4	4
10	msNPAuthenticationType2	VT_I4	9
10	msNPAuthenticationType2	VT_I4	10
10	msNPAllowDialin	VT_BOOL	0
14	Component Prog Id	VT_BSTR	IAS.IasHelper
14	Component Id	VT_I4	262145
20	msNPAction	VT_BSTR	Connections to other access servers
20	msNPConstraint	VT_BSTR	TIMEOFDAY("0 00:00-24:00; 1 00:00-24:00; 2 00:00-24:

Record: ◄◄ ◄ 1 ► ►◄ ►✱ of 427

Figure 11-23: Properties table in an IAS database

4. If your company wants you to calculate how much remote access time users in the Accounting Department spend connected to the network, what steps would you take?

_____

_____

Project 11.6	Troubleshooting RRAS Connectivity
	RRAS connectivity problems fall into a number of areas, including routing problems, dial-up problems, and VPN problems. They can be related to software, hardware, or a combination of both.
	As in most troubleshooting scenarios, you begin by establishing the scope of the problem. You first determine where the problem started. Has a user contacted the support center to say they cannot connect or was there a system alert?
	Next, begin asking a basic list of questions. Is it only one user who cannot connect? Does the user have RRAS permissions? Does the user have an incorrect configuration? Is a specific RRAS server unreachable, or is the RRAS service not running?
	The RRAS console provides status information on a variety of connections from network interfaces to port status and IGMP states. Each of these provides a different view of the RRAS service. Also, as you have seen in the previous activities, the logs, traces, and monitors offer detailed data for troubleshooting. Finally, you can use the command-line tools and utilities from other chapters to troubleshoot TCP/IP connectivity.
Outcomes	After completing this project, you will know how to: ▲ review the status of RRAS connections
What you'll need	To complete this project, you will need: ▲ a client computer ▲ a Windows Server 2003 computer connected to a local network
Completion time	30 minutes
Precautions	None

■ **Part A: Review the status of RRAS connections**

1. Open the **RRAS** console. Select the plus sign (**+**) in front of the server name. Highlight **Network Interfaces** in the left pane. Review the **LAN and Demand-Dial Interfaces** including the **Status** and **Connection State** in the right pane (Figure 11-24).

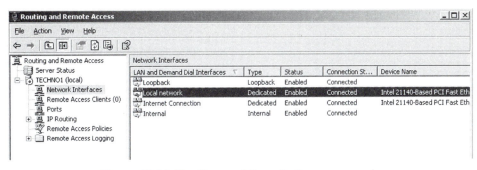

Figure 11-24: Routing and Remote Access console

2. Highlight the **Remote Access Clients** and review the **User name** and **Duration**.

3. Select the **Ports** and review the **Status**.

4. Select the plus sign (**+**) in front of **IP Routing**. Select **General** in the left pane. Review the **Administrative Status** and the **Operational Status**. Also review the **Incoming** and **Outgoing bytes** to get an idea of the amount of traffic being transferred. Highlight **General** (Figure 11-25) and right-click. Select **Show TCP/IP Information**.

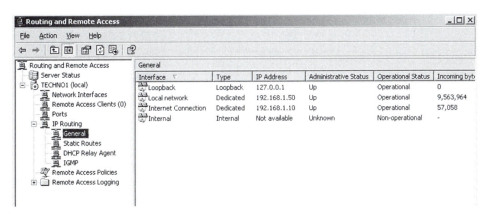

Figure 11-25: IP Routing

5. Highlight the **Internet Connection** in the right pane and right-click. Select **Show IP Routing Table**. The current IP routes in memory display (Figure 11-26).

TECHNO1 - IP Routing Table					⊠
Destination	Network mask	Gateway	Interface	Metric	Protocol
0.0.0.0	0.0.0.0	192.168.1.1	Local network	20	Network r
127.0.0.0	255.0.0.0	127.0.0.1	Loopback	1	Local
127.0.0.1	255.255.255.255	127.0.0.1	Loopback	1	Local
192.168.1.0	255.255.255.0	192.168.1.50	Local network	20	Local
192.168.1.0	255.255.255.0	192.168.1.10	Internet Con...	20	Local
192.168.1.10	255.255.255.255	127.0.0.1	Loopback	20	Local
192.168.1.50	255.255.255.255	127.0.0.1	Loopback	20	Local
192.168.1.255	255.255.255.255	192.168.1.50	Local network	20	Local
192.168.1.255	255.255.255.255	192.168.1.10	Internet Con...	20	Local
224.0.0.0	240.0.0.0	192.168.1.50	Local network	20	Local
224.0.0.0	240.0.0.0	192.168.1.10	Internet Con...	20	Local
255.255.255.255	255.255.255.255	192.168.1.50	Local network	1	Local
255.255.255.255	255.255.255.255	192.168.1.10	Internet Con...	1	Local

Figure 11-26: IP Routing Table

6. Select the **Static Routes** and review the entries.

7. Finally, review the status of the **DHCP Relay Agent** and the entries for **IGMP** protocol.

8. When you troubleshoot a single user's connectivity problems, what two things can you rule out if other users are connecting without problems?

    _____

    _____

9. If a quick review of the Remote Access Clients list in RRAS does not show the user's name, does it mean the user is not connected?

    _____

    _____

12
CONFIGURING AND TROUBLESHOOTING IPSEC

PROJECTS

Project 12.1	Understanding IP Security
Overview	Billions of TCP/IP packets traverse Internet connections each day, and it is estimated that only about 6% to 7% of this Internet traffic is encrypted. This is up from about 1% several years ago because Web browsers now include support for secure sockets layer (SSL). As you can imagine, that means a substantial amount of confidential information is being sent over insecure links. In many cases, it is possible for an attacker to eavesdrop on a communication between a user's browser and a Web server, or between a remote location and a corporate server.
	Why doesn't TCP/IP provide internal safety features to indicate a malicious attack has occurred? Although the original design does include a very basic integrity check, it is not enough. This process runs a checksum or data addition computation for portions of the IP packet that let the receiving computer know if a packet has been corrupted. However, IP protocol can be compromised, enabling packets to be intercepted, modified, and recomputed.
	To reduce this threat, in 1998 the IETF (Internet Engineering Task Force) (refer to RFC 2401) designed a security architecture that provides both encryption of packet contents and verification of packet source. IPSec uses dynamic cryptographic key technology to protect IP packets during transmission.
	When you employ IPSec, you make it possible to transfer sensitive information without fear that unauthorized people will be able to capture it and read it in transit, or modify it and resend it.
	You can use IPSec to authenticate and/or encrypt connections between two computers. This is called end-to-end mode (or transport mode) because network traffic is protected *before* it leaves the sending computer, and it remains secured until the receiving computer gets it and decrypts it. You use transport mode when you require packet filtering. There is also a second process that uses IPSec to secure traffic being sent over public links called tunnel mode, so named because encrypted traffic is tunneled from site-to-site.
	Because IPSec is implemented at such a low level on the TCP/IP protocol stack – the Network Layer – it is transparent to users and does not require changes to your applications. That's not to say that network administrators do not find it challenging to learn and complex to manage.
	Because IPSec provides two separate services, authentication and encryption, there are several ways it can be configured. For authentication, the IPSec process provides a way for two computers to agree on a secret key before sending any data. The two computers use the Internet key exchange (IKE) protocol to create an IPSec security association (SA). The authentication header (AH) protocol digitally signs the entire contents of each packet. This signature provides three separate benefits:

Project 12.1	Understanding IP Security

- *Protection against replay attacks*: If an attacker can capture packets, save them until a later time, and send them again, then they can impersonate a current network computer. This is called a replay attack. IPSec's authentication mechanism prevents replay attacks by including the sender's signature on all packets.

- *Protection against tampering*: IPSec's signatures provide data integrity, meaning that an interloper cannot selectively change parts of packets to alter their meaning.

- *Protection against spoofing*: IPSec authentication headers provide authentication at each end of a connection to verify the other end's identity.

IPSec also provides encryption. Although authentication protects your data against tampering, it does nothing to keep people from seeing what is being sent. It is encryption that obscures the payload of each packet to thwart any attacker who attempts to read the data as it goes by. To encrypt data, IPSec provides encapsulating security payload (ESP). ESP is used to encrypt the entire payload of an IPSec packet, rendering it undecipherable by anyone other than the intended recipient. ESP only provides confidentiality, but it can be combined with AH.

IPSec appears to be a single unified protocol, but it is a combination of different protocols plus a number of Windows Server 2003 drivers and services.

The Internet security agreement/key management protocol (ISAKMP) provides a way for two computers to agree on security settings and exchange a security key. An SA provides all the information needed for the two computers to communicate securely. The SA contains a policy agreement to control which algorithms and key lengths the two computers will use plus the security keys to securely exchange information.

Once the ISAKMP SA is in place, the two computers use the Oakley protocol to securely agree on a shared master key. This key, called the ISAKMP master key, is created with the Diffie-Hellman key exchange algorithm and is negotiated in the ISAKMP SA to establish a secure connection. After the secure connection is created, the two computers start another round of negotiations. These negotiations cover the following topics:

- Will the AH protocol be use?

- Will the ESP protocol be use?

- Will the encryption algorithm be used for the ESP protocol?

- Will the authentication protocol be used for the AH protocol?

Once these negotiations are finished, each computer has two IPSec SAs:

Project 12.1	Understanding IP Security
	one for inbound traffic and the other for outbound traffic. At this point, Oakley is used again to generate a new set of session keys. The master ISAKMP key is used when new SAs are negotiated. Although this all sounds pretty complex (and it is!), implementing IPSec has been simplified because it is enabled on Windows Server 2003 using policies. The IPSec Policy Agent is a service on each Windows Server 2003 or Windows XP computer and can also be centrally configured and stored in Active Directory. Plus, there are several new tools in Windows Server 2003 that help improve management.
Outcomes	After completing this project, you will know how to: ▲ explore IPSEC Services ▲ examine default IPSec policies
What you'll need	To complete this project, you will need: ▲ a Windows Server 2003 computer connected to a local network
Completion time	30 minutes
Precautions	Selecting Assign from the pop-up menu or from the Action menu in the Policy Settings console will enable the policy and may cause network traffic to be filtered and blocked.

■ Part A: Explore the function of IPSec

IPSec is enabled as a service on newly installed Windows Server 2003 and Windows XP systems.

1. Open the **Start** menu, point to **Administrative Tools**, and select **Services**.
2. Select **IPSEC Services** from the list and review the **Description** (Figure 12-1). Notice that this service is between clients and servers. This may be confusing because the computers at either end of the IPSec connection act as either a client or a server, depending on whether they are sending or receiving. The IPSec service starts automatically by default.

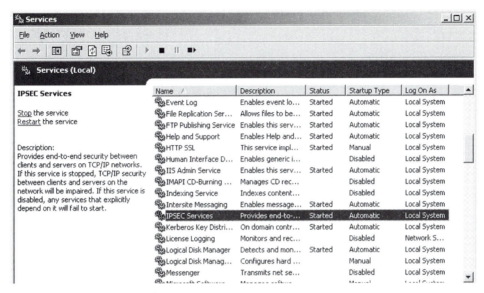

Figure 12-1: IPSEC Services

3. Highlight **IPSEC Services** and right-click. Select **Properties**. Notice on the **General** tab that the Service name is **PolicyAgent** (Figure 12-2).

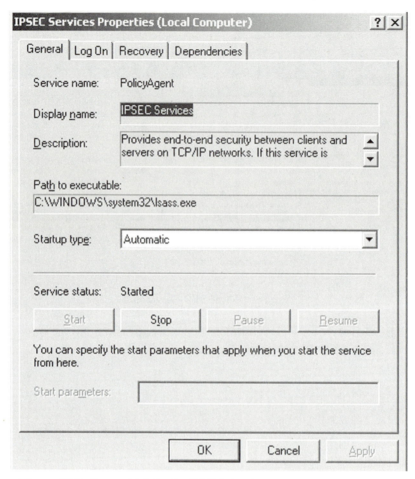

Figure 12-2: General tab in the IPSEC Services Properties dialog box

4. Select the **Dependencies** tab (Figure 12-3). Wait a few seconds to view the system components.

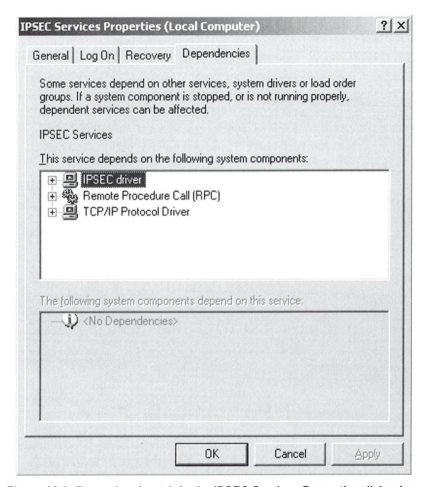

Figure 12-3: Dependencies tab in the IPSEC Services Properties dialog box

5. What is the name and path of the executable of IPSEC Services?

_____

_____

_____

6. Which system components are required for IPSEC Services to function?

_____

_____

■ Part B: Examine the default IPSec policies

When Windows Server 2003 is installed as a domain controller, both the Default Domain Controller Security Policy console and the Default Security Settings console show the folder IP Security Policies on Active Directory. You can also view these default security policies on the Local Security Settings console. Security policies are a set of rules and filters that define the security level, the signature and encryption algorithms, and other settings that apply to the packets transferred between the two end computers if the policy is assigned. In this snap-in, you can view three predesigned policies to learn how to create your own.

1. Open the **Start** menu, select **Run**, and then enter **secpol.msc** to start the **IP Security Policy Management** snap-in. (You can also enter **mmc** and add the **IP Security Policy Management** snap-in to a custom console.)

2. Highlight **IP Security Policies on Local Computer** (Figure 12-4).

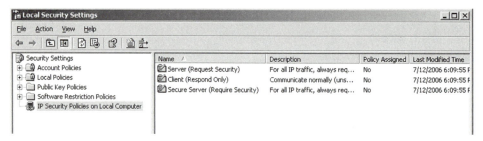

Figure 12-4: IP Security Policies on Local Computer

3. In the right pane, you will see three default security policies: **Client (Respond Only)**, **Server (Request Security)**, and **Secure Server (Require Security)**.

4. Highlight the **Server (Request Security)** policy and select **Properties**.

5. The **Rules** tab shows the IP Security rules, including **Filter List**, **Filter Action**, and **Authentication** (Figure 12-5).

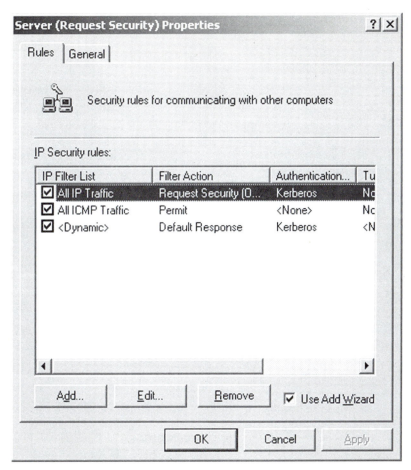

Figure 12-5: Rules tab in the Server (Request Security) Properties dialog box

6. The **General** tab includes the policy name and the description (Figure 12-6).

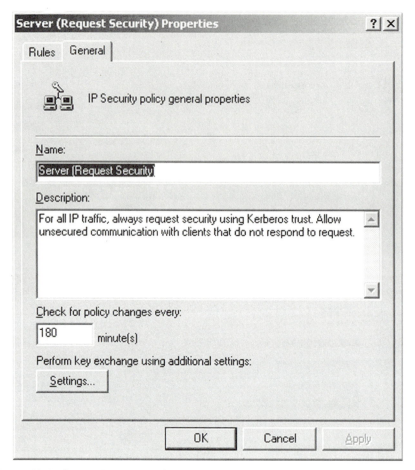

Figure 12-6: General tab in the Server (Request Security) Properties dialog box

7. Click the **Settings** button on the **General** tab and the **Key Exchange Settings** dialog box opens (Figure 12-7).

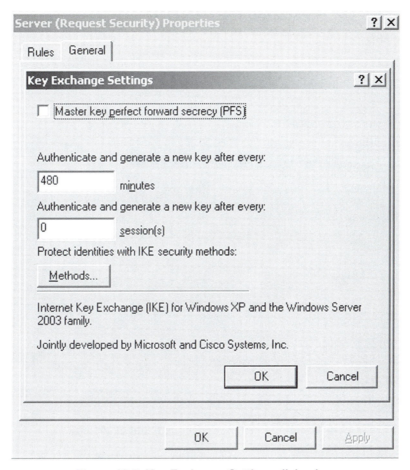

Figure 12-7: Key Exchange Settings dialog box

8. Click the **Methods** button in the **Key Exchange Settings** dialog box and you will see the preference list of security methods (Figure 12-8).

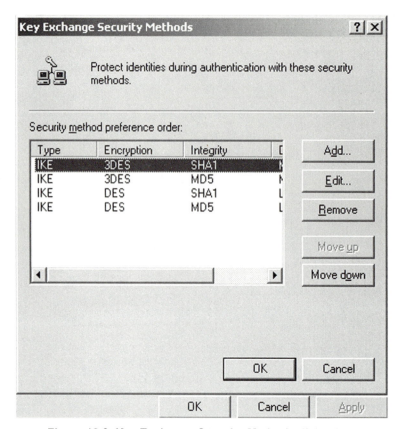

Figure 12-8: Key Exchange Security Methods dialog box

9. From the description on the **General** tab of the **Secure Server (Require Security) Properties** dialog box, what does this policy require? What is the description for **Client (Respond Only)**?

_____

_____

_____

_____

_____

_____

Project 12.2	Exploring IPSec Components
Overview	In the previous project, we explored IPSec on a domain controller or a local system. Now let's review the IPSec components as implemented in the Windows operating system. When you install Windows Server 2003 or Windows XP, there are three specific IPSec components that are automatically installed: • IPSec Policy Agent service • IKE • IPSec driver The purpose of the IPSec Policy Agent is to retrieve policy information and pass it to other IPSec components that require this information. You have seen it shown in IPSec services (see Project 12.1). It retrieves the appropriate IPSec policy from Active Directory if the computer is a domain member or from the local registry if the computer is a stand-alone. Once retrieved, this assigned IPSec policy information is sent to the IPSec driver. The IKE centralizes security association management and generates shared, secret keys used to secure information. Its purpose is to define the SA, which holds the mutually agreed settings. There are two types of SAs: one used to protect the security negotiation (used first) called the main mode, and one for protection of the data called quick mode. For each computer, SAs are negotiated for both outbound and inbound traffic. That means there are four used during a computer-to-computer communication. The last component is the IPSec driver. This driver receives the security policy information, and then attempts to match the inbound and outbound packets against the filter list in the policy. When a packet matches the filter, then the filter action is applied. In other words, if the filter matches and the filter action says to block, then the packet is discarded. If the filter matches and the filter action says negotiate security, then either the main mode or quick mode SA is used to negotiate the authentication method and/or the encryption used for the transmission.
Outcomes	After completing this project, you will know how to: ▲ explain how IPSec components function
What you'll need	To complete this project, you will need: ▲ a Windows Server 2003 computer connected to a local network
Completion time	30 minutes
Precautions	Selecting Assign from the pop-up menu or from the Action menu in the Policy Settings console will enable the policy and may cause network traffic to be filtered and blocked.

1. Highlight **IP Security Policies on Local Computer** and right-click. Select **Help**.

2. Highlight **Internet Protocol Security (IPSec)**. Select **Concepts**, select **Understanding Internet Protocol Security**, and then select **IPSec components**.

3. Review the three components: **IPSec Policy Agent service, Internet Key Exchange (IKE)**, and **IPSec driver**

4. Examine the diagrams showing these components. These illustrate the negotiation process between the two computers and can help you understand how IPSec is integrated into the Windows operating system.

5. Is it a requirement that the Policy Agent connect to and receive policy information from Active Directory? When does the Policy Agent start?

_____

_____

_____

6. In the IKE main mode negotiation, what four mandatory parameters are negotiated?

_____

_____

7. Where does the IPSec driver store current quick mode SAs?

_____

_____

_____

Project 12.3	Configuring IPSec Authentication
Overview	IPSec supports three separate authentication methods: Kerberos, certificates, and preshared keys. If you are setting up IPSec on computers that are part of an Active Directory domain, then the easiest authentication method is the default, Kerberos V5. However, according to Microsoft's recommendations, you may want to carefully investigate using certificates instead. There are several reasons for this, such as: • If you have computers running Windows XP Home Edition. These do not support Kerberos V5. • If you have computers connected to the Internet. The concern here is that each IPSec peer sends its computer identity in unencrypted format to the other peer. The computer identity is unencrypted until encryption of the entire identity payload takes place during the authentication phase of the main mode negotiation. An attacker can send an IKE packet that causes the responding IPSec peer to expose its computer identity and domain membership. Certificate authentication, which is based on public/private key technology, is certainly the most secure authentication method and has the advantage of interoperability with external systems. However, it requires the installation and management of certificate services and can take significant administrative resources. Finally, Microsoft does not recommend the use of preshared key authentication (although it is offered in the configuration) because it is a relatively weak authentication method and preshared keys storage is insecure. Preshared key authentication is provided for interoperability purposes and to adhere to IPSec standards. **Note:** If you are using IPSec to secure Kerberos traffic, IPSec only negotiates security associations if the authentication method is *not* using Kerberos.
Outcomes	After completing this project, you will know how to: ▲ explore IPSec authentication methods ▲ create a Kerberos authentication policy
What you'll need	To complete this project, you will need: ▲ a Windows Server 2003 computer connected to a local network
Completion time	30 minutes
Precautions	Selecting Assign from the pop-up menu or from the Action menu in the Policy Settings console will enable the policy and may cause network traffic to be filtered and blocked.

■ Part A: Examine default IPSec authentication methods

1. Highlight **IP Security Policies on Local Computer** in the **Local Security Settings** console.
2. In the right pane, highlight **Server (Request Security)** and right-click. Select **Properties**.
3. Select the **General** tab (Figure 12-9).

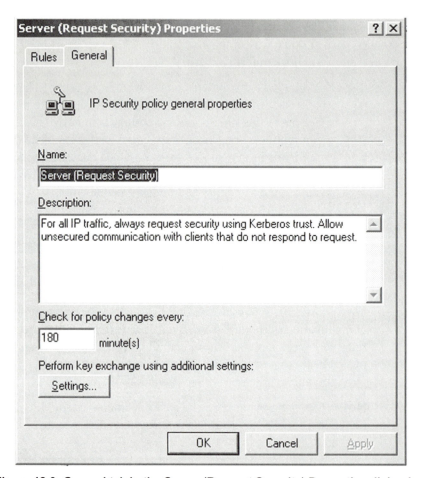

Figure 12-9: General tab in the Server (Request Security) Properties dialog box

4. Click the **Settings** button. Notice the check box for the **Master key perfect forward secrecy (PFS)** (Figure 12-10). Selecting this check box requires the system to generate new master keys for each new session.

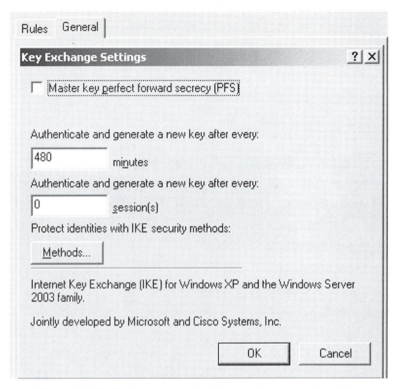

Figure 12-10: Master key perfect forward secrecy check box

5. Click the **Methods** button. The Security method preference order displays showing the list of security methods and the precedence order with the highest on the list used first.

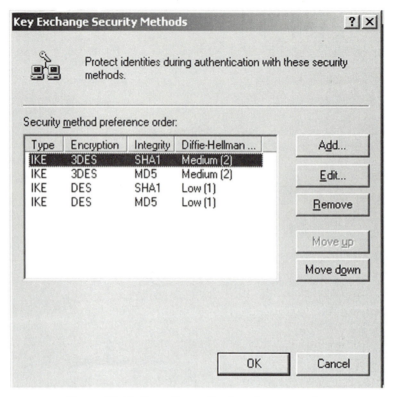

Figure 12-11: Security method preference order

6. Highlight one of the methods and click **Edit**. In Figure 12-12, the strongest Diffie-Helman Group for the 2,048 bit key is shown.

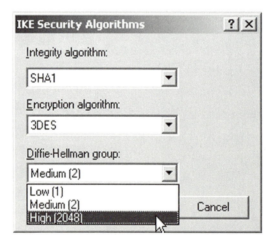

Figure 12-12: IKE Security Algorithms dialog box

7. By default, how often will a new authentication key be generated?

    _____

    _____

    _____

8. What are the three settings for the IKE Security Algorithms?

    _____

    _____

    _____

■ Part B: Create an IP Security Policy with Kerberos Authentication

1. Open the **Local Security Settings** console and highlight **IP Security Policies on Local Computer**.
2. Right-click and select **Create IP Security Policy**.
3. The **IP Security Policy Wizard** will display. Select **Next**.
4. Name the new policy and give it a short description (Figure 12-13).

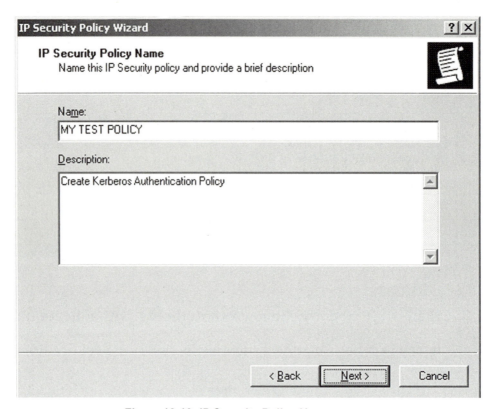

Figure 12-13: IP Security Policy Name screen

5. The **Request for Secure Communication** screen displays. The default is to **Activate the default response rule** (Figure 12-14).

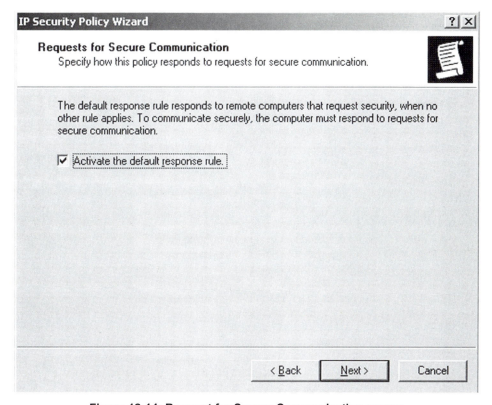

Figure 12-14: Request for Secure Communication screen

6. The **Default Response Rule Authentication Method** screen displays showing **Active Directory default (Kerberos V5 protocol)** (Figure 12-15).

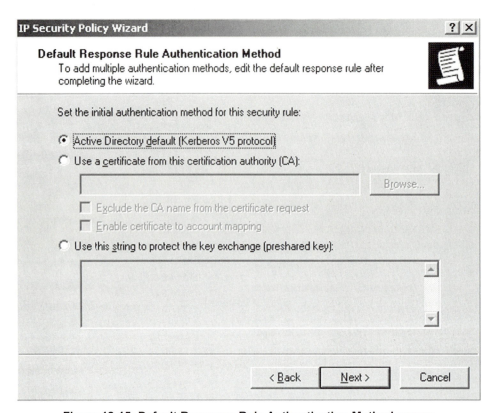

Figure 12-15: Default Response Rule Authentication Method screen

7. The last screen displays showing a check box that lets you edit your policy once you have selected **Finish** (Figure 12-16). You have now created a new policy with Kerberos V5 as the authentication method. You will see your new policy in the right pane.

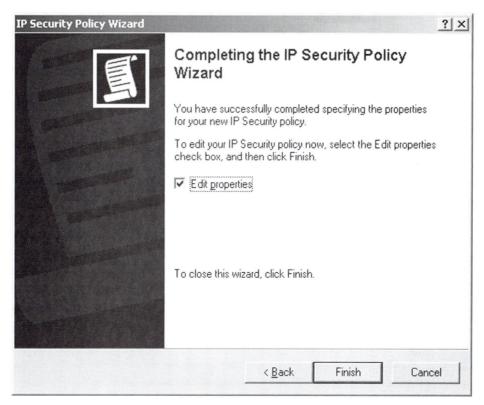

Figure 12-16: Completing the IP Security Policy Wizard screen

8. The **Properties** dialog box for the new policy displays showing a **Rules** tab and a **General** tab (Figure 12-17).

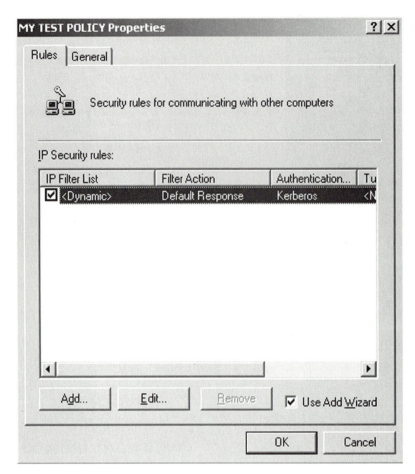

Figure 12-17: Properties dialog box for the new policy

9. On the **Rules** tab, highlight the IP Security rule and select **Edit**. Select the **Authentication Methods** tab (Figure 12-18).

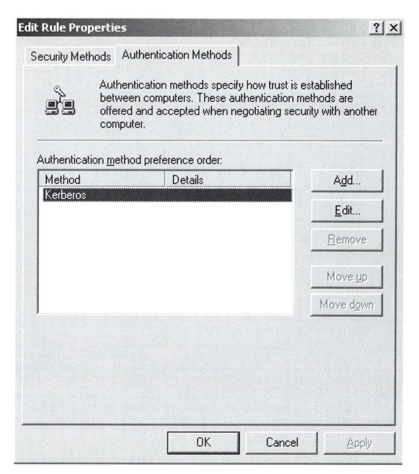

Figure 12-18: Authentication Methods tab in the Edit Rule Properties dialog box

10. According to the information in **Help**, how are preshared keys stored?

_____

_____

_____

Project 12.4	Managing IP Filter Lists and Filter Actions
Overview	You can manage filter lists and filter actions using the Rules tab, but that obscures the fact that these items are available to any policy. Instead, you can use the Manage IP filter lists and filter actions command from the pop-up menu. This displays the two tabs: Manage IP Filter Lists and Manage Filter Actions. There are two default IP filters available: one for all IP traffic, and one for all Internet Control Message Protocol (ICMP) traffic.
	Filters specify a source and destination, but they also must specify what action should take place when there is a match with the criteria specified in the filter. The following five actions can be selected: Permit unsecured IP packets to pass through, Accept unsecured communication, Allow unsecured communication with non–IPSec-aware computers, Use these security setting, and Block IP packets.
Outcomes	After completing this project, you will know how to:
	▲ explore IP filters and IP filter actions
What you'll need	To complete this project, you will need:
	▲ a Windows Server 2003 computer connected to a local network
Completion time	30 minutes
Precautions	Selecting Assign from the pop-up menu or from the Action menu in the Policy Settings console will enable the policy and may cause network traffic to be filtered and blocked.

■ Part A: Explore default IP filters

1. Open the **Local Security Settings** console and highlight **IP Security Policies on Local Computer**.
2. Right-click and select **Manage IP filter lists and filter actions**.
3. Highlight **All IP Traffic** in the **IP Filter Lists** box on the **Manage IP Filter Lists** tab (Figure 12-19). Click the **Edit** button.

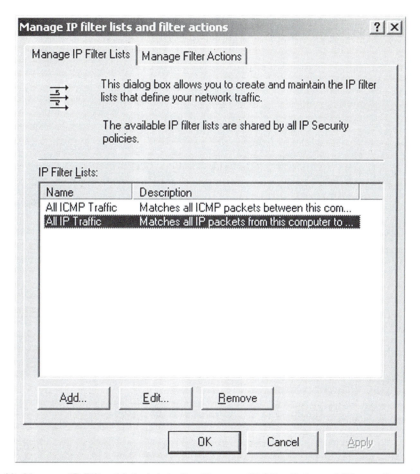

Figure 12-19: Manage IP Filter Lists tab in the Manage IP filter lists and filter actions dialog box

4. The **IP Filter List** dialog box displays showing the default IP filters. The default description shows the exceptions, including the ISAKMP (IKE) traffic (Figure 12-20).

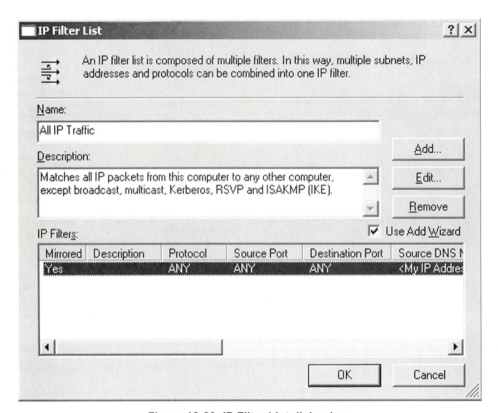

Figure 12-20: IP Filter List dialog box

5.   Click **Edit**. The **IP Filter Properties** dialog box displays showing three tabs. On the **Addresses** tab, you can select the **Source address** and the **Destination address**. Select **A specific IP Address** from the drop-down list. You will be able to enter an IP address. Select **A specific IP Subnet** and you can add the IP Network address and Subnet mask.

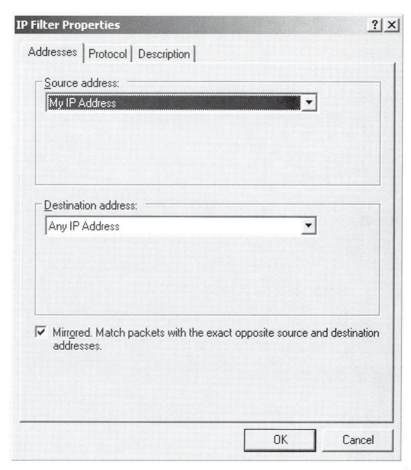

Figure 12-21: IP Filter Properties dialog box

6. Select the **Protocol** tab and view the various protocols that can be filtered. Select **UDP** from the drop-down list (Figure 12-22). You can select the UDP port numbers for filtering traffic.

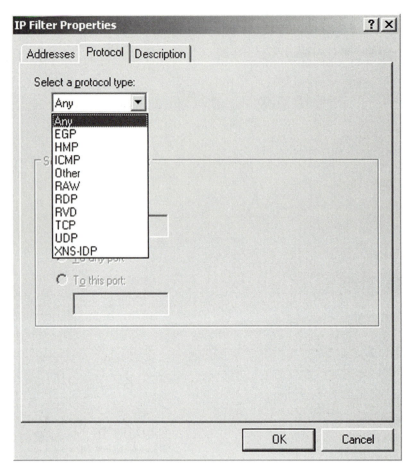

Figure 12-22: Protocol tab in the IP Filter Properties dialog box

7. Select the **Description** tab (Figure 12-23). You can enter a name and description for the filter.

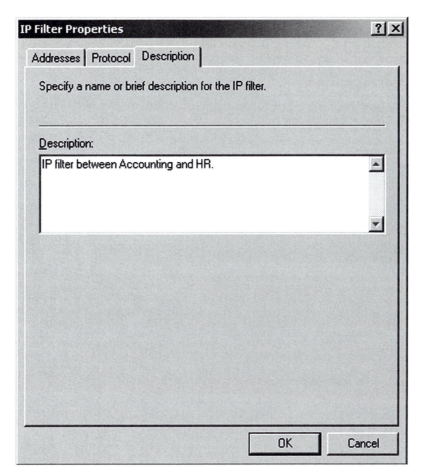

Figure 12-23: Description tab in the IP Filter Properties dialog box

8. What are the names of the two default filters? When you want to add a new filter, what are two of the entries you need to make?

_____

_____

_____

■ Part B: Explore default IP filter actions

1. Select the **Manage Filter Actions** tab in the **Manage IP filter lists and filter actions** dialog box. Highlight **Request Security (Optional)** in the **IP Filter Actions** box. Click the **Edit** button.

2. A dialog box displays showing two tabs: **Security Methods** and **General** (Figure 12-24).

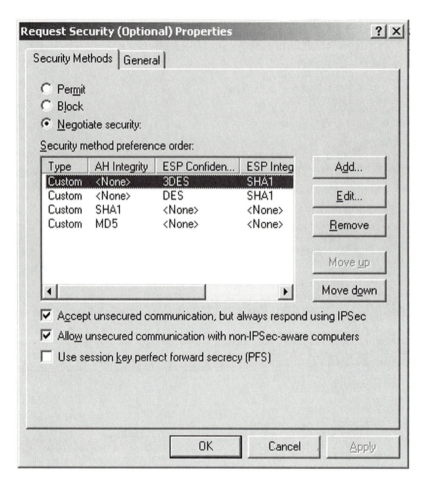

Figure 12-24: Request Security (Optional) Properties dialog box

3. Review the actions for **Request Security** by highlighting the **Filter Action** and click **Edit**. Cancel and review **Permit** filter action and **Require Security**.

4. Notice the check box for **Use session key perfect forward secrecy (PFS)**. Enabling **session key perfect forward secrecy (PFS)** ensures that master key keying material cannot be used to derive more than one session key.

5. Can you combine more than one filter (rule) into an IPSec policy?

_____

_____

_____

Project 12.5	Using IP Security Monitor
	The Windows 2000 version of the IP Security Monitor was an executable program (IPSecmon.exe). Now, the IP Security Monitor for Windows Server 2003 and Windows XP is a Microsoft Management Console (mmc).
	You can use this console to monitor IPSec information for your local computer and for other computers. It lets you view details of all IPSec policies, view generic and specific filters, view statistics, view security associations, customize the display, and search for specific filters by IP address. It shows the Main Mode and Quick Mode folders with filters, statistics, and SAs.
Outcomes	After completing this project, you will know how to: ▲ create an IP Security console ▲ explore the functionality of the IP Security Monitor
What you'll need	To complete this project, you will need: ▲ a Windows Server 2003 computer connected to a local network
Completion time	30 minutes
Precautions	None

By default when you add the IPSec Security Monitor snap-in, you monitor IPSec information on the local computer.

1. Open the **Start** menu, select **Run**, and enter **mmc**.
2. **Console1** with **Console Root** displays.
3. Open the **File** menu and select **Add/Remove Snap-in**.
4. When the **Add/Remove Snap-in** dialog box opens, click **Add**.
5. Select **IP Security Monitor** and then click **Add**. Click **Close** and then **OK**. Figure 12-25 shows the IP Security Monitor snap-in added as an mmc console.

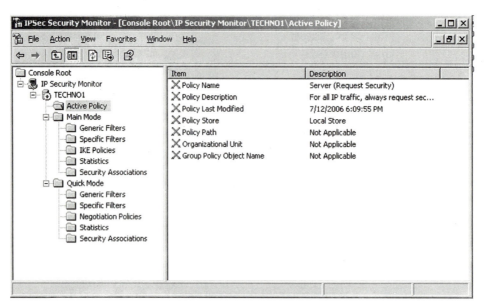

Figure 12-25: IPSec Security Monitor console

6. If you want to save your console setting, open the **File** menu, select **Save**, and name your console. The example shown is named **IPSec Security Monitor.msc**.

7. Once you have saved your console, you can open it again by entering the path to the **.msc** file in the **Run** dialog box.

8. For easy administration, you can add other computers to the **IP Security Monitor** console by selecting **Add Computer** from the pop-up menu (Figure 12-26). If you are in a domain, you must have administrative privileges for the domain to add remote computers.

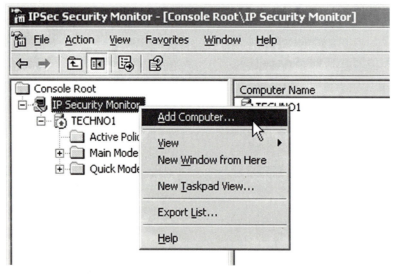

Figure 12-26: Adding other computers to the IPSec Security Monitor console

9. If you were having problems with IPSec, what would you do to investigate?

_____

_____